God Save The Kinks

God Save The Kinks

A Biography

Rob Jovanovic

Aurum
Press

First published in Great Britain
2013 by Aurum Press Ltd
74-77 White Lion Street
Islington
London N1 9PF
www.aurumpress.co.uk

This paperback edition first published in 2013 by Aurum Press Ltd.

A catalogue record for this book is available from the British Library.

ISBN 978-1-78131-591-0

Typeset in Specrum MT by SX Composing DTP, Rayleigh, Essex

Printed in Denmark by Nørhaven

Contents

When I first heard *Village Green Preservation Society* in 1971, I got this picture in my head of small-town English life: village greens, draught beer. But when R.E.M. went to England in 1985, I drove through Muswell Hill – and it certainly wasn't romantic looking. From 'Waterloo Sunset', I had this picture of a gorgeous vista – when it's really a grimy train station area. I realised these songs were all acts of imagination, that Ray was commemorating an England that was slipping away. There is a great air of sadness in those songs.

Peter Buck, R.E.M.

Introduction

After half a century of performing, Ray Davies was preparing for the biggest event of his life. He was backstage at a stadium in London as 20 million UK viewers and an estimated worldwide audience of 750 million tuned in to watch the closing ceremony of the biggest sporting event in the world, the London 2012 Olympic Games. Titled *A Symphony of British Music*, the £20 million production utilised more than 4,000 people and a host of high-profile performers. Ray Davies' segment was to be at the centre of the show and he was to sing his most famous song live. But things weren't going to plan and, as his appearance on stage grew closer, he was still unhappy about the set up. '[The earpiece] wasn't working when I was cued to go on,' he recalled. 'I said, "I'm not going on."' He was told he had no choice. 'This isn't fucking well working,' he replied. 'I could just hear this crackling in my ear,' he remembered. 'And I said, "Excuse me, it's still not working," and they slammed the door in my face! I didn't know till I opened my mouth whether anything would come out.'

The Kinks have been around for a long time. Their first attempts at making music date back fifty years and their story encompasses distinct phases and metamorphoses: early Merseybeat imitators, British Invasion leaders, late-sixties innovators, concept album champions, new-wave godfathers and, now, revered elder states-men. The Kinks may have 'split up' in 1996, but they have never really left us. In fact, the past few years have seen their influence grow and grow. Box sets, movies, stage shows, documentaries, deluxe album re-issues and, of course, books have all continued the task of securing their place in rock and roll history, alongside The Beatles and The Rolling Stones, as one of the founding acts of modern pop.

My own first recollection of The Kinks dates from the mid-1970s, when I used to play with my mum's collection of 45 rpm singles. Just about old enough to operate her ancient portable record player, I scratched the discs to pieces in the process, but, at the age of six, it was a great education to get my hands on the songs of The Beatles, The Hollies and The Kinks, whose characters struck a fairy-tale chord at a time when my friends were listening to novelty offerings from The Wombles. I didn't know who had created this wonderful music, and The Kinks didn't stand out, but evidently the songs lodged somewhere in my memory.

Fast-forwarding to 1983, by which time I was at secondary school, I heard a song called 'Come Dancing'. It wasn't the hippest record I heard that year, but it was incredibly catchy, and it was almost impossible to disobey the instruction in the song's title: it made me want to move my feet. I had no idea this was the same band that had written 'You Really Got Me', 'Waterloo Sunset' and 'Sunny Afternoon' two decades earlier – songs I'd played to destruction on my mum's old record player.

A few years later, when I was in the sixth form, The Kinks briefly became fashionable again, at least in my immediate social circle of mainly U2 and R.E.M. fans. I went out and picked up a *Greatest Hits* LP and discovered the extent of their genius. At that moment, I became a fully-fledged enthusiast; a worshipper, in fact.

As I ventured beyond the *Greatest Hits*, buying the albums and learning more about the band who made them, I discovered The Kinks sprang from a particular time and place, and that their story is that of a culture now fading from memory. They stand for individualism and for the best of what it means to be English; they made a career out of the act of observing, recording and remembering things that were both ordinary and important. They were a product of bomb-scarred post-war north London and that, more than anything else, has defined who they are. Theirs is a tale in which a group of young, ambitious and often angry working-class men take on the music establishment – not always successfully – as they battle along their own eccentric path to stardom.

Brothers Ray and Dave Davies, as principal songwriters and vocalists, have always been at the heart of this story, and at the centre of attention, especially when they engage in their characteristic feuding through the press. But the supporting cast of Pete Quaife, Mick Avory, John Dalton, John Gosling and many others, were essential to making The Kinks what they were: an extremely talented, sometimes infuriating band with killer tunes and a clever turn of phrase.

More than The Beatles, the Stones or The Who, The Kinks were an English band. Their music defied easy categorisation. After early dabbling with Merseybeat and American-influenced R&B, they ceased to follow trends, choosing instead to pursue what sometimes seemed like wilfully weird avenues, but often leaving new genres in their wake.

Ray Davies is a songwriter who has often seemed to have too much on his mind, but there is humour in the songs, albeit black. 'Life is hard' comes the message, and The Kinks' certainly missed plenty of opportunities and had a knack of finding a way to lose when a win looked inevitable. They spearheaded the British invasion of the United States, then got themselves banned at the very point when they looked poised to take America by storm. But their enforced dedication to the English scene gave Ray the chance to write some of the band's best albums and, after some potentially calamitous personal crises in the early seventies, the group went down the road of theatrical rock opera productions before a new burst of enthusiasm from the US made them unlikely stadium stars in the eighties.

The songs that have stood the test of time and lingered in the popular memory are often sharply focused character studies – portrayals of mundane English life made significant by Ray Davies' natural ability to focus on details that others would have missed.

They are tales of class conflict, of envy and struggle. Stories of the streets, of family, of home. Working-class suburbia never sounded so good. Though they weren't the only musicians from London – The Who, The Small Faces, Sandie Shaw and The Dave Clark Five were among their contemporaries – The Kinks, more than any other band, made their home city the very subject of some of their most memorable songs, and thus kept it on the pop music map.

Today, The Kinks are the most likely of all the great 1960s bands to be cited as an influence by the hippest of the younger generations of musicians, seen as a more discerning choice, perhaps, than the ubiquitous Beatles. In the past two decades, Oasis, Blur, The Kooks, The Pixies, and The Killers, to name but a few, have all highlighted The Kinks' lasting importance. They've also cropped up on the soundtracks of quirky, cool films like *Rushmore* and *Juno*.

For all that, of all the sixties giants, they are perhaps the least known – recognised by most people only for their hit singles, despite an endless list of musically magnificent non-hits, B-sides and album tracks. They've sold more than 50 million albums worldwide, and were ranked at number five on *Rolling Stone* magazine's list of top ten rock bands of the twentieth century, and yet The Kinks remained relatively under-appreciated for a surprisingly long time. In fact, being under-appreciated is almost part of their 'brand': even when they were producing memorable albums such as *The Kinks are the Village Green Preservation Society* and *Arthur*, long-running US publication *Teenbeat* magazine led a 1969 article with, ACHIEVEMENTS OF THE KINKS NOT FULLY RECOGNISED.

Perhaps such under-appreciation is a curse of longevity. They did, after all, endure for more than three decades before ignobly fizzling out. Even the indomitable Rolling Stones and the restlessly creative David Bowie have discovered that long careers suffer the vagaries of fashion, as well as pop's constitutional aversion to the inevitability of ageing. Then again, maybe The Kinks simply weren't pretty enough, with their shaggy hair and bad teeth. Or perhaps they didn't play the media game sufficiently astutely.

Personally, I don't understand why they aren't better loved and more widely known. In my opinion, if you were to line up the best twenty Beatles songs, the best twenty by The Kinks would more than hold their own. Though the Beatles might edge the competition based on the quality of their production, the strength of The Kinks' musicianship, the craft of their songwriting, the acute observational style of Ray Davies' lyrics, and their sheer originality, mean The Kinks tick every box, in a way The Rolling Stones, for instance, never could.

When they're reminded of The Kinks' existence, people do love them. In the summer of 2011, BBC Four hosted a Kinks night, and Twitter came alive with thousands of people commenting, with apparent surprise, at how strong a band they were; on the brilliance of Ray Davies' lyrics; and that they'd forgotten just how many great songs The Kinks had created.

Other musical giants of the sixties have been chronicled in exhaustive detail, with countless books devoted to anatomising both their lives and their music. Indeed, the greatest of The Kinks' peers have been deemed worthy of academic study: keen students of sixties pop can now take a master's degree in 'Beatles-ology'. The Kinks, however, have not enjoyed an equivalent level of scrutiny and their legacy remains fragile. They deserve to be remembered and talked about.

Their little known tale can now be told, in the words of those who were there. The list of contributors to this book includes band members from their first three decades, producers, photographers, tour personnel and engineers, friends and family members. Life with The Kinks – in the studio, on the road and in private – is ready to be exposed.

It didn't take long for me to realise that The Kinks' story was a biographer's dream. It is built around an intense family background, brotherly rivalry, feuding bandmates, chart success (and failure), managerial conflicts, beautiful songwriting, commercial mistakes, a ban from America, a journey to the very heart of Englishness, obscure self-indulgent tangents, a surprise critical and commercial re-birth and a lasting legacy of some of the twentieth century's best pop music.

So where did the title *God Save The Kinks* come from? It's more than just a pun, it was the motivation behind the US publicity drive of the mid-1970s that helped take the band from being a cult act to filling arenas across North America. It was a phrase coined by the band's US publicist at the time, John Mendelssohn, and became the password for fans spreading word of The Kinks' brilliance. I now use it as a call to arms.

While still fretting over and playing with his faulty earpiece, Ray Davies heard a knock at the dressing room door. 'Mr Davies, your taxi is here,' called the voice from the corridor. Not sure whether this was about to be a disaster, Davies opened the door and walked to the cab, ready to be watched by more people than he could imagine. This was a long way from a wet summer night in 1973 when his career, and much more, seemed to be over.

Part 1

He came down from Highgate thro' Hackney & Holloway
towards London
Till he came to old Stratford, & thence to Stepney & the Isle
Of Leutha's Dogs, thence thro' the narrows of the River's side,
And saw every minute particular, the jewels of Albion . . .

Leutha, William Blake

The Beginning and the End

I t had been a strange day all around. The previous weeks of stress and pressure, emotional turmoil and helplessness had come to a head. A morning of regret and uncertainty had given way to a miserable afternoon spent drinking under a greying summer sky. The scene had captured his mood perfectly. As far as he was concerned, it was no good: this would be the end. He was fed up with the grind of writing and touring, and even today, when he tried to tell everyone that he had had enough, no one had listened. The most important words of his life had been met with indifference. Maybe no one could take him seriously because, in make-up and a bow tie, he looked like a clown. At least he had been able to down a whole bottle of pills to numb the pain and push the problems into the distance. He thought that the end was in sight, but some deep-seated will to continue must have been tugging away at him. That was why, for the second time in just a few weeks, he could see the hospital ahead of him. He just had to keep going a little longer.

In many ways, 1973 was a grim year. The UK had joined the EEC but was being crippled by unrest at home and the troubles in Northern Ireland. In May, more than 1.5 million people went on strike in protest at pay and rising prices. Oil shortages, a three-day week and inflation over 8 per cent were just some of the problems facing Edward Heath's Conservative government. Trawler wars were breaking out in the North Sea. In the USA, the headlines were filled with the unsatisfactory end of the Vietnam War and the Watergate scandal. Around the world planes were falling out of the sky, hijacked, shot down or crashed.

To escape the daily drudgery, people flocked to see *The Exorcist* and *Enter the Dragon* at the cinema, while Roger Moore was making his James Bond debut in *Live and Let Die*. Musically it was the year of Pink Floyd and Mike Oldfield: the former's *Dark Side of the Moon* would go on to top charts internationally, and the latter's *Tubular Bells*, the first album released on Richard Branson's fledgling Virgin label, would sell more than 16 million copies. It was also the year when glam rock reached its apogee: Slade had two number one singles and then sold out London's Earl's Court; and, on 3 July, David Bowie retired Ziggy Stardust. Ten days later, the Everly Brothers, a key inspiration behind the British beat boom of the 1960s, split up.

The Kinks had been busy throughout the early part of 1973. Long gone were the chart-topping three-minute singles of the previous decade, and Ray Davies was now taking the band down an altogether more theatrical road. The world had been given the first glimpse of this in January with a show at London's Theatre Royal on Drury Lane, in a performance which featured an ensemble cast and multimedia presentation. A BBC TV special followed, then ten UK dates and throughout the band were nipping back into the studio to work on the forthcoming *Preservation* album. Twelve North American dates were shoehorned into a fortnight which saw them travel coast to coast. The Kinks were also in the midst of setting up their own studio in north London.

This hectic schedule was taking its toll on Ray Davies' brittle state of mind, family life and health. Dave Davies later admitted that he and Ray were drifting further apart than ever and that his own heart was not really in it anymore.

On 20 June, Ray's wife Rasa moved out, taking young daughters

Victoria and Louisa with her, and heading to her parents in Bradford. Ray was devastated. The following day, on his twenty-ninth birthday, he called Dave and told him what had happened. Dave swiftly travelled to Yorkshire with sister Joyce and attempted to get Rasa to reconsider, but to no avail. Ray was left alone in his East Finchley house listening over and again to Mahler's second symphony, *The Resurrection*. It is a piece that addresses funeral rites – a march of the dead – and expresses the desire to be set free from miserable, meaningless life.

Ten days later, Ray made his first trip to hospital after overdosing on Valium and alcohol. He was kept in for observation and then discharged. After returning home, he refused to leave his house.

A new Kinks single, 'Sitting in the Midday Sun', was issued on 2 July but, despite harking back to *The Kinks are the Village Green Preservation Society* era and rekindling memories of 'Sunny Afternoon', it failed to chart on either side of the Atlantic. The apathy seemed to be spreading.

In spite of his problems, Ray agreed to play at the upcoming Great Western Express Festival at the White City Stadium in west London. The venue was strangely in tune with his state of mind in the summer of 1973. It had originally been constructed for the 1908 Olympic Games and was a wide open space with the infield pitch surrounded by tracks for running and cycling. But, by the early 1970s, just like The Kinks in the eyes of many, it was past its best and, a little more than a decade later, would be demolished. That year it was used in the film *Steptoe and Son Ride Again*, which featured the father and son rag-and-bone men tethered together, as ever, in an unhealthily dependent, rather bleak relationship – a fitting mirror to the road-weary Kinks staggering into view.

The day of the festival was grey and overcast, the stadium damp and draughty. The band were due to play alongside such acts as the Edgar Winter Group, Lindisfarne, Canned Heat and Barclay James Harvest, with headliners Sly & the Family Stone, an American funk act, relegating The Kinks, a group with sixteen majestic hit singles, to the role of also-rans. It was a good time to be depressed.

Right up until show time, The Kinks were preparing to perform without Ray Davies. Even if he did show up, no one could be sure if he would be in a fit state to go on stage. Dave Davies had been given the task of taking on vocal duties if his brother did not make an appearance, but, in the end, Ray arrived without too much time to spare. He looked awful – matted hair, gaunt cheeks, hiding behind shades in the mid-afternoon gloom. He was wearing white linen trousers and an ugly white shirt with a red design splashed across it and the eccentric ensemble was finished off with a blue bow tie.

He had been prescribed 'uppers' and before the show he was popping them down his throat like they were going out of fashion. He was also drinking again. 'Ray never drinks,' said press secretary Marion Rainford at the time. 'When he does it's not a very good sign.' His behaviour was certainly erratic: laughing one minute and crying the next. 'The doctor had given me pills,' explained Ray. 'He said, "Take one of these when you feel a bit down, it'll make you feel better." I was doing what I thought was my last show and I felt down every ten seconds, so I just kept taking them.'

Roy Hollingsworth was backstage before the show reporting for *Melody Maker*. Marion was outside Ray's dressing room and he heard her saying, 'He's in a dreadful state, Christ, he's in a dreadful state.'

'He was very subdued backstage,' recalled drummer Mick Avory. 'The road manager had to sort of coax him on stage.'

They opened with 'Victoria' and 'Brainwashed', before a rush through the expected singles: 'Dedicated Follower of Fashion', 'Lola', 'Waterloo Sunset' and a somewhat sarcastic rendition of 'Sunny Afternoon'. In Ray's mind, this was the gig at which he was going to end it all. In his confused state, he believed that if he shut down the band – gave up the touring and the recording sessions – it would be enough to bring Rasa back to him. Another more destructive impulse counselled that if he drank enough and downed enough pills, he could end his pain.

Like many twists in The Kinks' story, things did not follow the expected course, or at least not the narrative Ray Davies had in mind. On what was supposed to be a glorious summer's day, the crowd at White City was subdued by a drizzling rain. At the end of the set, Ray stepped forward to make his big announcement.

The final chords of 'All Day and All of the Night' drifted away across the rooftops of London, he opened his mouth to speak . . . and then a between-bands backing music tape began to play at volume, in an effort by the organisers to maintain the party atmosphere. Ray was all but drowned out. Balancing a can of beer on his head he proclaimed, 'I'm fucking sick of the whole thing. I'm sick up to here with it!' He declared it their final show and said he was retiring from music, but to many in the crowd his words were inaudible.

'There wasn't even a stunned silence, because most of the audience didn't even hear him,' remembered Roy Carr, who was at the show for the *New Musical Express* (*NME*). 'I don't think the band really knew what was going on.'

'We didn't know what to expect from Ray at that point,' added Dave Davies. 'He'd been very depressed in the preceding few weeks, partly because he was working too hard, which he always did, but mostly because [of] Rasa. I had extra musicians standing by in case we had to go ahead and perform without him.' The rest of the band, Mick Avory, John Gosling and John Dalton, did not know what to make of it. Was Ray being serious? He was known for his melodramatic behaviour. Dave was so angry with his brother that he went home as soon as he left the stage.

'I should have died,' said Ray. 'And a part of me did die that day on stage. I realised a lot of the mistakes I made. I should never have got married, but then I wouldn't have had those two wonderful kids. It was just a learning curve. Unfortunately, my encounter with myself took place in front of 15,000 people.'

Roy Hollingworth's report in the *Melody Maker* on 21 July was heartfelt and to the point. 'The Kinks are dead, Long live the Kinks!' he wrote. 'Ray Davies should never have been at London's White City Stadium on Sunday. Physically, and more important, mentally, Davies was in no fit condition to play.'

There was no happy ending to the story. Ray survived but Rasa filed for a separation and they eventually divorced. The *Preservation Act I* album was released to an apathetic public. It failed to chart at all in the UK and scraped to number 177 in the USA.

When Ray Davies wrote his autobiography, *X-Ray*, in the 1990s, he ended it in 1973, despite having a further two decades of tales with which to regale his readers. 'I finished it then for a good reason,' he explained. 'I felt writing about the development was very important, the genesis of the band and all that, and then I realised that first curve, that bunch of songs I wrote, was about that first time finding myself. I thought it was an ideal time to end at the White City concert where I nearly died afterwards.'

The impressive-looking Jenner Building at the Whittington Hospital in Islington, London, had been in operation for 125 years when a weird-looking man stumbled through its doors and into the reception on the night of 15 July 1973. He approached the desk unsteadily and announced calmly, 'Hello, my name is Ray Davies. I am the lead singer of The Kinks. I am dying.'

Still dressed in his garish stage outfit, not far from being a clown's costume, he cut a strange figure. The nurse looked at the peculiar sight in front of her sceptically. 'Oh, we believe you,' she said. Then, while filling out a form declaring his next of kin, he collapsed into a heap. He was immediately ghosted to an emergency room where his stomach was pumped, removing the detritus of an afternoon's drug and beer binge. When he came around enough to be asked who the staff should call on his behalf, he had to take a moment to think. His wife had recently walked out on him, taking the children with her, so that left him with only one option.

Across London, the telephone rang. Upon answering, Dave Davies was informed that his brother had tried to kill himself and was in the Whittington Hospital – could he come to see him as soon as possible?

'When I got there he looked lost, he looked like shit,' said Dave. 'I felt heartbroken for him. We were known for having very public arguments, but there was always a deep bond between us. With all the success we'd had, we kind of always believed we were invincible but, in that moment, I suddenly realised how fragile we all are.'

After having his stomach pumped, Ray was told he could go

home but, as he said to Dave, he could not face returning to an empty house. He had nowhere to go. 'The only thing to do was to take him back to my place,' said Dave. 'Me and my wife looked after him for a couple of weeks. It was a terrible time for us, but in a way it led to Ray and me reconnecting and it made us stronger.'

CHAPTER 2: 1878 TO 1957

Not Like Everybody Else

Dave Davies was 7 years old before he had a bedroom to himself, even if only for a short time, while his brother Ray was in hospital for a minor operation. That night, Dave lay alone and awake, thinking. He could hear noise from the pub across the road, not twenty yards from his front door: the familiar sounds of loud chatter, the occasional burst of a song and glasses clinking. It felt strange. He was used to having to share not only the room but also his bed, in that overcrowded three-bedroomed end-of-terrace house. After what seemed an age, he drifted off into a restless sleep.

Then, at 3 a.m., startled, Dave awoke from a dream. He was drenched in sweat and gasping for breath. In fact, he was almost suffocating. Bleary eyed, he stumbled into his parents' room, gasping and motioning to his throat. His mother, Annie, got out of bed and comforted her son, fetching him a glass of water as he slowly began to breathe more easily. When he was calm she took him back to his room and tucked him in.

The next morning, Annie set off to visit Ray at St Thomas' Hospital. When Annie returned, she reported that Ray had almost died the previous night, saved only by an emergency tracheotomy which made it possible for him to breathe. The operation had been carried out at the exact moment Dave had awoken from his dream in terror.

Ray and Dave's maternal grandmother, Kathleen Bowden, was born in Islington in 1878, but her Hansom cab-driving father abandoned her with his spinster aunt who raised her alone. In the 1890s, she met one Albert E. Wilmore. He was three years her senior and the son of a wealthy French polisher, a well-respected trade in the nineteenth century. Albert was an only child and when his parents learned that he was about to marry an 'orphan', he was immediately disowned and cut off from the family inheritance. Albert and Kathleen had their first child, Catherine, in 1899; Albert E. junior arrived in 1902; and then Annie Florence in 1906. According to Dave Davies in later interviews, Kathleen and Albert produced twenty-one children, but the 1911 census shows that they had a total of five (the twins, Rose and Lilly had been born in 1910), while a further three had died. By this time, Kathleen was 33 years old, and while she may well have given birth again, another sixteen offspring seem unlikely.

Ray and Dave's father, Frederick George Davies, came from a Welsh and Irish background. His mother, Amy Kelly, would be known as 'Little Granny' (Kathleen Bowden being 'Big Granny') and came from a large family in Ireland. Fred's father was Harry Davies, an ex-miner and slaughterman from the Rhondda Valley.

Annie and Fred Davies married while Annie was still in her teens. She had the first of her eight children, a daughter called Rose, in 1924, when she was 18. Living in King's Cross, London, the couple had five further daughters: Irene in 1926, Dolly in 1928, Joyce in 1930, Kathleen (known to everyone as 'Peg') in 1932 and, finally, Gwen in 1938. Like his father, Fred Davies worked as a slaughterman, but the 1930s was a hungry decade and he and Annie struggled to feed their growing brood.

In September 1939, with Gwen only a year old, the Second World War broke out and many children were evacuated from the capital. Annie could not bear the thought of sending her six daughters away and, instead, decided to move the family from the obvious German bombing target of the railway lines at King's Cross to the relative suburbia of Huntingdon Road in East Finchley, north London. This would only be a short-term move, however, as the Davies family were the only ones on their street with children, which did not sit well with their new neighbours – and their numbers had been further swollen with the addition of Little Granny and Fred's sister, Rose. In January 1940, they moved again, this time just along the road to Muswell Hill, and the end house in a short terraced row on a street called Fortis Green, directly across from the Clissold Arms pub.

Within living memory, Fortis Green had been rural and wild, and, for centuries, the area had lain undeveloped as common and wasteland. It was first referred to as 'Fortessegreene' in the seventeenth century. Not until the Enclosure Acts more than two hundred years later did anyone think to do anything with the area, and it would be the 1890s before the council produced plans to lay out Fortis Green as a tree-lined road and build houses along it.

King's Cross is only about five miles from Muswell Hill, but the difference in environment made their new surroundings seem a world apart. Fortis Green was a leafy lane and nothing like the grimy, close-quartered hub they had left behind. The new house was, however, too small for the number of people living there. It had three upstairs bedrooms, a parlour in the front room, a dining room and a kitchen, into which were crammed a family of eight.

Fred Davies found work as a butcher and then as a gardener, when he was employed at all. He enjoyed a drink too many and could be harsh to his wife. Annie held the family together. It was she who made sure everyone had enough to eat, had clothes to wear and got to work or school on time. Her resourcefulness was stretched even further, though, when she had a seventh child, this time a boy.

Raymond Douglas Davies was born on 21 June 1944 and, with six older sisters to coo over him, was instantly the star of the show. The girls used to take turns walking around with him to try and get him to sleep, and would play the gramophone to help him settle. But his position as baby of the family did not last long.

Shortly after the end of the war, Annie was pregnant again, and

Ray's brother, David Russell Gordon Davies, arrived on 3 February 1947. 'Ray's probably resented me since he was three years old,' said Dave. 'I fucked it up for him. He was the baby of the family, the centre of attention for three years. Then I came along and stole his thunder.'

The winter months of early 1947 were tough for everyone. Bread had started to be rationed and London's bomb damage was only slowly being repaired, when heavy snow brought the country to a halt. Coal stocks at the pits froze solid and power stations ran out of fuel. February was the coldest for three hundred years and almost three million people had to stop work.

The Davies family house had been too small, even before Dave came along, though the age gaps between the eight children was beginning to alleviate the overcrowding: sister Rene met and married a Canadian serviceman and the couple left for Canada; and Rosie had married in 1943, moving to south London. She took Little Granny with her. Even so, the house was full to capacity. The three upstairs rooms were shared by Dolly and her husband Joe; Joyce and husband Ken Palmer; and remaining sisters Peggy and Gwen. Annie and Fred had a downstairs room. Ray and Dave had to share the parlour until others moved out, though Ray was sent to live for a while with Rosie, her husband Arthur and young son Terry. In all, there were often ten people living in a three-bed, six-room house. They must all have given a sigh of relief when Joyce and Ken had a daughter, Irene, and moved into the vacant house next door.

The 1950s were a time of change. Wartime austerity and rationing were slowly left behind, and the country began to rebuild itself. The NHS had been launched in the summer of 1948 and Britain was becoming a country of suburbs, with estates of semi-detached houses spreading out from the edge of the cities, replacing pre-war terraces and slums. It was also maintaining its position as Europe's most urbanised country – and London was Britain's most urbanised city. It was estimated that 60 per cent of England was still working class, but that would change. The population became mobile, no longer being born, going to school, working and dying within a radius of a few miles. And, as the decade came to an end, people had money to spend like never before on radios, gramophones and even televisions, all of which filled parlours, while fridges, toasters and electric kettles arrived in kitchens. In 1957, Harold Macmillan famously summed up this decade of prosperity, declaring that Britons had 'never had it so good'.

British culture was changing, too. The growth of cinema helped destroy the music halls – why pay to watch a tired old act when you could go and see Elvis Presley or James Dean on the big screen? Rock and Roll was born and 'teenager' became the byword for rebellion and youth. It was in this shifting popular culture and its increasing targeting of youth that the Davies brothers grew up.

Real life was, of course, harsher than the glitz of the cinema screen or the glamour of the pop charts. 'From an early age, eight or nine, I saw how unequal the world was and that's kept me the way I am,' said Ray. 'I saw relatives unemployed and was always around adults talking about the way the world really was. Maybe that shocked me.' He grew up distrusting the world.

With an almost suffocating home life, he also soon realised that he needed to get out, to find his own space. Even at the age of five, he had tried to get away, packing a case and walking to Highgate where one of his sisters lived, before being ushered back home. When he was old enough, he would go on lots of long walks and ride buses for hours. He loved the sound of the night trains in his bedroom because they were going somewhere and, while he felt love at home, he also felt destined for something else. The train spoke of adventure and excitement, and was the embodiment of striving for something better.

Ray's primary school education came at St. James', just along Fortis Green. He became the school conkers champion, playing on a playground that still had a large brick air-raid shelter at the side of it.

'I remember the fifties as sunny and bright,' he said. 'My dad was a market gardener, so we always had lots of veggies. I don't remember doing without. I always seemed to get what I wanted.'

Despite this, he had emotional problems while growing up. He would go through long periods when he refused to speak, and also suffered bouts of insomnia and sleep-walking. Such was his parents' concern over this behaviour that he was sent for some sessions with a child psychiatrist in Notting Hill. Looking back from the other side of the revolutionary sixties, many Britons would see the fifties as a time of emotional repression, when certain things were simply not spoken about or admitted. In this context the treatment given to Ray would certainly have been a source of shame. He has since described it as counselling, rather than clinical psychiatry, but with it came a taste of the serious stigma afflicting the thousands of people quietly hidden away and suffering in the nation's ageing 'lunatic asylums'.

Ray's father, while refusing to attend any sessions with his son, did try and help in his own way. Fred's love of the music hall rubbed off on Ray, and the humour in particular struck a chord with him. He especially liked Max Miller, an angry man with a political slant who did not care what he said. Fred also took Ray to the cinema and, later, to watch Arsenal play football at Highbury. In 1951, Fred and the 7-year-old Ray visited the Festival of Britain on London's South Bank. Ray thought it brilliantly futuristic, and knew that his younger brother Dave, always interested in the weird side of life, from science fiction to the occult, would have loved it.

Dave Davies was interested in the world but, like his older brother, had a mistrust of school and teachers. School was a problem for him from day one, at the age of five: after being half-dragged, kicking and crying, to St. James', he lasted half a day before walking out. He took himself home and told his mum that he had been to school and didn't like it. Annie had to calmly explain to her son that it was not a one-off deal – that he had to go every day. 'When we were children, Ray and I depended a lot on [sister] Rose,' said Dave.

> She was married before we had grown up, and her house was a continual haven in the storms of childhood. [One day] I was crying and banging on Rose's kitchen door. 'I won't go back to school!' I said through sobs.

'But you have only been in school for three days, love!'

'Well, there is a mistress there who shouts. She scares me. I threw some plasticine at her. Then I ran home.'

'What did you tell Mum?'

'That we had the rest of the day off. She tried to take me back to school. I ran away to you.'

The years that followed did little to change Dave's antipathy to education. One day, at primary school, the class was told that God had made everything, and Dave stuck up his hand and asked, 'If God made everything, who made God?' His question was brushed off and he was told to be quiet. He sat there feeling humiliated, but came to realise that it was important to question things and think for himself. His growing distrust of teachers was further cemented when a teacher laughed at one of his paintings, and Dave thereafter refused to attend art lessons.

In later life, he realised that his many sisters and relatives had nurtured in him more respect for family and love than for formal education. Though he preferred his own home to the classroom, he was often in trouble there as well, whether for throwing mud pies at the neighbour's washing line or other hi-jinks fuelled by his urgent desire to get as much fun out of life as he possibly could.

Dave also took an early interest in the fantastic. Sunday evenings were special for him because he listened to one of his favourite radio shows, *Journey into Space*, before he and Ray had their baths and went to bed. He was also fascinated by his mum reading tea leaves, and sometimes secretly watched through a crack in the door when she and his sisters held séances or used a Ouija board.

By 1955, Ray was attending the William Grimshaw Secondary Modern School, named after a local councillor, on Tetherdown. These days, it is known as Fortismere, but originally opened as Tollington School, a private establishment for boys, before converting to a grammar school, and then, finally, taking 'secondary modern' status following the public education reforms of 1944. Schools of this type were designed to accommodate the vast majority of pupils who had not scored highly in 'eleven plus' tests and who were not expected to go on to achieve great things.

Ray's uneven moods meant that he still had to attend sessions with a psychiatrist. 'During the time when Ray was eight to thirteen, he was very quiet, deep and lonely,' said Dave. 'He never shared anything – least of all his mind. And as a little boy I felt completely left out of his life. Rose was the one who really understood him. They had a sort of understanding between them that overcame everything, even silence.'

Ray could see the life that was being planned for him. Having failed his eleven plus exam and missed out on grammar school, the path to university for working class children, he knew he was being prepared for working life in a factory, or a clerical job at best. He could see how people of the older generation had been treated and how their lives had turned out as a result. Several of his teachers had been in the services during the Second World War, and one still wore his demobilisation suit to school, saying it was all he could afford on his wages. His father and uncles were often out of work, too. He was therefore primed to take an interest in tales of bleak futures and, when he was not allowed to watch Peter Cushing in a TV production of *1984* on TV, he read the book instead. It only confirmed his fears.

At home, there was always one time of the week when the family forgot their troubles: Saturday night, when the front room of 6 Denmark Terrace would play host to Fred Davies and his cronies from the pub. Along for a good time would be assorted aunts and uncles, cousins, nephews and nieces and, of course, Ray, Dave and the six sisters, who would all cram in for a sing-song around the piano, and a drinking session that went on into the early hours after the pubs had shut.

Fred would have a few drinks at the pub before coming home at closing time. There might be dozens of people somehow squeezed into the little house. A crate of beer would then materialise and the songs would start, first on the gramophone, with records by Fats Waller, Doris Day, Al Bowlly, Bing Crosby, Judy Garland, Hank

Williams and Buddy Holly, and then on the piano, with people taking turns to play and sing. Sometimes Fred would get his banjo out, or tap dance around the room balancing a pint on his head. If the mood took him, he might even bring the house down with his rendition of 'Minnie the Moocher'. It was a strange but exciting mix of people, music and chatter – a heady experience for two young boys to witness on a weekly basis.

Musically it was a source of lasting inspiration. From an early age, they were exposed to country and music hall, early rock and roll and Broadway show tunes. '[My sisters'] boyfriends always came to the house,' said Ray. 'I was very interested to meet them, to listen to their music. We used to watch them dancing in the front room – it was magical. I was a serious child, quite quiet, but I enjoyed picking up parts of their culture: big band music, romantic songs from during the war.' And, when Annie herself stepped forward to sing, the boys got a rare glimpse of real feeling at a time when the norm was emotional restraint and silence in the face of hardship.

In 1952, their sister Rene returned from Canada for a visit. From her letters home, it had been clear her marriage was not a happy one. Her husband was a big drinker and womaniser, and she had had enough. She bought her son Robert with her. The trip in 1952 was the first time she had seen Ray and Dave, then aged 8 and 5. They knew her only from the framed photograph on the front room mantelpiece, which showed her in white and her husband in his Canadian army uniform on their wedding day. She formed a special bond with Ray and, having been a teacher in Canada, applied those skills in patiently showing him how to play the piano. She also brought home some records which were yet to be released in England, furthering the boys' education in music.

Rene had suffered a heart condition since childhood, but she was not the only one of the sisters who struggled with ill health: Peggy had been hit by a stolen lorry in her younger years and had a damaged arm and hearing problems. Despite these setbacks, Peggy was good looking and had a choice of suitors always ready to take her dancing. Then she met 'Billy', a West African immigrant who was in Britain illegally, and got pregnant. He was deported to France and she was left to raise their daughter, Jackie, by herself. At the time, it was a minor scandal, and Jackie was the only black child in the area. The local children taunted the little girl, calling her 'Blackie Jackie'. In 2010 and 2011, filmmaker Julien Temple gained access to some Davies family home movies and used lots of the colour footage from the early 1960s in his documentaries *Imaginary Man* (on Ray) and *Kinkdom Come* (on Dave). These clips showed Dave dancing with Jackie in the front room at Denmark Terrace, surrounded by all the sisters, Annie and Fred, uncles and cousins, and both grandmothers.

With so much going on and so many people coming and going during their early lives, it is not surprising that, despite their undeniable bond, Ray and Dave were never that close as brothers while growing up. The clashes in later life have sometimes been blown out of proportion but they did fight as children, and there is one story that stands out: the two had had an argument and Ray ran outside, tripping and smashing his front teeth. It was this incident which left him with his famous gap-toothed smile.

The two brothers were completely different characters. Dave was outgoing and instinctively social, while Ray could be quiet and withdrawn. Dave was apt to dive headlong into a situation, while Ray was more considered and thoughtful. Nor did they actually spend that much time together, as Ray lived for a while with Rosie, and Dave sometimes stayed with sister Dolly, her husband Joe Warwick and their four children. Dolly's son Michael was more like a brother to Dave than Ray who, anyway, had his own surrogate sibling.

'I called Rosie 'Mum' until I was five years old,' said Ray. '[When] she said [that she was not] I couldn't believe it. Maybe that had a lot to do with the way my relationship with Dave was formed because I've never really had a brother relationship with him. I always thought that my nephew, Terry, he's only a year younger than I, felt like he was my brother.'

'The only time there was any closeness between Ray and me was when we were in trouble!' recalled Dave. 'We would face the storm of Mum's anger together. Ray would smile at me, shrug and say, "Don't worry, it'll blow over by tomorrow and if it doesn't there's always the next day."'

January 1957 had seen Prime Minister Anthony Eden resign due to poor health in the wake of the Suez Crisis, when Britain, in alliance with France and Israel, had failed to remove Gamal Nasser as the President of Egypt following his decision to nationalise the Suez Canal in defiance of British interests. Eden was replaced by Harold Macmillan who would guide the country through prosperous times, even though the remnants of Britain's former empire were evidently vanishing. School maps at the time still showed the countries that made up the Empire in pink and Empire Day continued to be celebrated until 1958. In the summer of 1957, two youngsters by the name of John Lennon and Paul McCartney met for the first time in Liverpool. Marilyn Monroe and Laurence Olivier were starring in *The Prince and the Showgirl*, while Elvis Presley and Lonnie Donegan topped the charts.

By now a disillusioned Ray was frequently skipping school, and his sleep-walking was still an issue. On one occasion, Dave had to follow Ray as he ran out of the house and down the garden before he was awakened. Dave for his part was, if not a naughty child, a restless and somewhat wild one. He was far happier watching *The Quatermass Experiment* on TV than he was reading a book. He was also repeating his older brother's truancy, avoiding lessons at St James', and was on his way to failing his eleven plus, just as Ray had done. Dave would get ready for school and set off at the correct time, but often never got there. He had a friend named George Harris whose father had died, and whose mother went to work, so they had an empty house in which to hide out. When his end of year report read that he had missed sixty days of school, he doctored it to read 'six' instead.

Ray was now taking an interest in music and had been asking for a guitar. On 21 June, his thirteenth birthday, Rene gave Annie some money to buy one for him. It was a Spanish acoustic model. Ray was overjoyed with the gift. That night, Rene showed her brother how to play a few simple tunes on the instrument, before getting ready to go dancing in the West End, against doctor's orders. She had had heart disease after going down with rheumatic fever as a child, but it had never stopped her before and it was not going to stop her now, despite the concern of Annie who waited at the gate to wave her off as she caught the bus.

Later that night, Dave awoke to the sounds of his mother wailing downstairs and heard his father's footsteps coming up the stairs. As Fred sat on the bed, Dave knew what he was going to say before he spoke. His father started crying and could only say, 'Rene is dead.' That night, at the Lyceum, she had collapsed on the dance floor and died in the arms of a stranger. She was just 31 years old. This chilling news had two effects on Dave's life from then on. First, seeing his dad break down, he decided that he had to be strong and grown up: at the age of ten, he matured very suddenly. Secondly, he started to think about life after death, something which has obsessed him ever since.

For Ray, Rene's death was a profound loss. The sister with whom he had the closest bond, who had patiently taught him piano, was gone. The guitar she had bought him and taught him to play would bring him fame and fortune, but all of that would forever be bound up in the memory of his sister's death. His birthday turned into a funeral.

Brothers in Arms

One of the Davies brothers' numerous uncles was Joe Warwick, who had married their sister Dolly. Joe had been an amateur boxer and, when Ray started to show an interest in sport, he gave his nephew impromptu lessons and lent him some old boxing gloves. Ray had some success as a boxer at secondary school and Dave was soon eager to enter the ring as well. One day, the pair were messing around, sparring in the front room at Denmark Terrace. It began to get a little heated, as these things can between brothers, until Dave hit Ray with an uppercut that caught the older brother flush under the chin. Ray stumbled backwards and fell, clipping his head on the piano as he went to ground. Dave froze: had he killed Ray? Dave rushed across the room and leaned over his brother who was on his back, his eyes shut. Suddenly Ray's eyes flipped open and his right hand flashed upwards, punching Dave right on the nose. 'I think that says a lot,' said Dave. 'About how he would wait for the right moment to hit back.'

Irene's funeral, in June 1957, was the Davies brothers' first encounter with death. The front room of 6 Denmark Terrace was the venue for a wake instead of the usual party, but, just as on most

Saturday nights, drinks were downed and the piano was played, while people gathered round to sing. Ray found it hard to understand why, at such a time of grief, the adults were singing. He failed to grasp that it was an outlet for their feelings, that they would rather sing than talk.

Ray was now living with Rosie, Arthur and Terry on Yeatman Road in Highgate, a mile and a half away. 'I came from quite a happy social environment, but I needed the space,' he explained. 'I suppose I was more introvert, more difficult to understand.' Then, almost overnight, after Rene's death, Ray decided he had had enough of being the quiet outsider, and that he would no longer just follow the line that everyone expected of him: school, office job, marriage and death. Instead of being a follower, he was going to be the leader – he would win every prize and be the best.

Initially, the best way he found of achieving this goal was through sport. Previously, he had gone along to the local park alone with his football and acted out a game, playing the parts of both teams. Now, he became a star of the school football team, one of the best track athletes and a local boxing champion. Things were going well. He was passed a note by a girl with a beehive hairdo saying that he had been voted 'Best Bum in the School' by the girls. He had discovered a new confidence. But it did not last long.

First, he injured his back in an athletics race and then exacerbated the injury when he fell onto the base of a football goalpost. His boxing career came to an abrupt end when he represented the school and was unfortunately paired against the British school's champion, Ronnie Brooks. Ray tried valiantly, but was well beaten and bruised. For a time, he continued running, despite his back problems. He usually started races from an upright position to save bending too much at the start but, on one occasion, decided to crouch down and start the same way as everyone else. As he rose, his back gave him a jolt of pain and, by the time he had regained his stride, he was well behind the field and could only recover to finish second. He gave up school sports altogether. He had tried to be like everyone else and the cost had been pain. It was a lesson that he would carry with him for the rest of his life.

*

As the 1950s drew to a close, two important acquisitions were made that would propel the Davies brothers' musical journey. In June 1959, Ray received his first amplifier for his fifteenth birthday and, the following December, Annie bought Dave an electric guitar on 'hire purchase' credit. Music was the thing that eventually brought the brothers together, now that they both had guitars, although they still had very different ideas about it. Ray was more artistic, and had improved his finger-picking style through practice and some instruction from Peg's husband, whereas Dave's approach was the polar opposite: he just wanted to make people dance. Dave would crank up the volume of the Harmony Meteor he had been given and hit what would become known as a power chord. He taught himself by listening to the hits of the day, among which Bert Weedon's 'Walk Don't Run' was a particular favourite.

Ray started to play a few solo shows at some local coffee houses, including the El Toro coffee bar on Muswell Hill Broadway. These shows usually comprised a few acoustic takes of popular songs of the day, with those by American country picker Chet Atkins always going down well.

Music provided Ray with a form of self-expression that allowed him to step out of his taciturn shell, but he still had a longing to be somewhere and someone else. When he was 14 he would sneak into local pubs and pretend he *was* someone else.

He and Dave began playing together when their dad arranged with a landlord to let them use a back room. 'I remember drinking beer before a show and thinking how wonderful it was to be grown up,' said Ray. 'We played Shadows and Cliff Richard hits, and early R&B like "Memphis Tennessee" and, for some reason, in north London "Ghost Riders in the Sky" was always being requested.'

'I started to improve around the age of eleven,' recalled Dave. 'I also started to play a guitar. Ray and I had one each and used to do duets. This was a big step forward. It meant my elder brother was beginning to accept me, and that mattered a lot . . . I had already started to dream of fame, though I don't think it occurred to Ray that we might one day be professionals.'

In April 1960, Peg's husband, Mike Picker, bought Dave a ticket to see American guitar legend Duane Eddy play live, and Dave just lapped up the energy coming from the stage.

After a few shows as an unnamed duo, the Davies' brothers started performing as The Kelly Brothers, using their grandmother's maiden name.

But Dave, despite his ability, was still only a child. He spent his spare time working on a giant papier-mâché mountain in his bedroom, into which he built car racetracks and train tracks, until it got too big to get out of the door. He was also impressionable, developing a fascination with other-worldliness. He had never been interested in the books he was told to read at school, but when he discovered the occult works of Londoner Dennis Wheatley, a whole new world opened up for him.

Having finished his fifth year of secondary school, Ray elected to sign up for a further two years of study, which would enable him to apply for art school. He entertained fellow pupils with his cartoon drawings and wanted to aim for something that might allow him to escape a mundane office job. He was still sent for an interview at the Youth Employment Office, which only reinforced his notion that he and his school friends were being groomed for a dull, grey life of hard work. He was sent for a stint at an architects' office, but did not relish the experience.

In the autumn of 1961, Ray Davies was back for his final year at William Grimshaw, to complete extra art coursework which would allow him entry to art school. He was also attending a music class run by a teacher called Bruce Wainwright. During one of the first lessons of the new term, Mr Wainwright asked if anyone could play a musical instrument. Ray was intrigued when a wiry-haired boy put up his hand and said: 'Yeah, I play guitar.'

Peter Alexander Greenlaw Quaife – Pete to his friends – was born on a foggy night in Tavistock, Devon, on 31 December 1943. In 1961, he lived with his parents, Stan and Joan, sister Ann and younger brother David at 59 Steeds Road, the middle of a short terrace of council houses on the Coldfall Estate, which spread to the north behind Fortis Green. The area had previously been the Coldfall Woods, but these were developed during the 1920s to provide more than four hundred new homes.

Stan Quaife owned a grocery shop on Park Road, Crouch End, though it still operated under the name of the previous owner, one H.F. Billman. Joan worked at the St Mary's Wing of the Whittington Hospital in Highgate. One of Pete's friends at the time was Jeff Bailey. 'I knew Pete from the age of about twelve when my family moved to Muswell Hill,' said Bailey. 'He lived in the next road to me, on the Coldfall Estate. We were always in and out of each other's houses.'

Pete spent his childhood hanging out with groups of friends on the estate, sometimes getting up to mischief. 'We found an old oxygen cylinder on a bomb site by my house,' he recalled. 'I suppose I was about 13, and it seemed like a good idea to the gang when we lit a fire under it and left it. The explosion blew out windows in the flats for miles around. I was about five miles away at the time, and shook like a leaf when I heard the bang. The neighbours thought it was an unexploded bomb.' As he got older his messing around with gangs got more serious. 'As a teenager I was part of a gang called the "Mussies",' he said. 'We had a feud with the Finchley boys which developed into a grand-scale punch-up one evening at their local dance hall. I was posted as lookout at the door, and when the law arrived I disappeared under a parked car. I was lucky, I got away. But many of the gang were sent to approved schools. That cured me of being a tearaway.'

'His parents were great and we used to go to gigs with them,' continued Bailey. 'When we were about 15 Pete went out with my girlfriend's best friend Nicola Start, and we all used to go to the cinema most Sundays, and frequented the local coffee bars.' It was at these coffee bars where Quaife saw the Davies brothers play and got to know Dave a little bit while walking home with him after a show.

Pete's musical grounding came after he cut his hand while playing on a local rubbish tip and a doctor suggested playing an instrument as good therapy for the injury. He started on the piano and then changed to guitar. Like Ray, Pete's plan was to go to art school, which is what led him to be sitting with the older Davies brother in Mr Wainwright's classroom, claiming to be a musician: 'I owned a big, horrible, Futurama [guitar], so half the story was true. Then Ray put his hand up. Cocky bastard. So the next week we brought our guitars and I played something by The Shadows.' Then Ray took his turn. On his Spanish acoustic he performed a perfect version of 'Malagueña', from Ernesto Lecuona's *Suite Andalucia*, which impressed Pete no end.

It was after a Kelly Brothers show that the Davies brothers first considered teaming up with Pete to form a band. He sat chatting with the brothers at their house and, once he had left, Ray and Dave discussed the idea further. Ray was in favour of it. If a drummer that Pete knew would join them too, they would have a full band. Dave was wary, but the next morning told Ray he was willing to give it a go.

Pete's drummer friend was John Start. Quaife introduced him to Ray and Dave, and suddenly the duo had become a four piece. They arranged to play at the William Grimshaw autumn dance, which was only a few weeks away. Pete's brother, David, remembered the Starts well. 'They were a Jewish family and had a jewellery shop in Wood Green,' he said. 'They lived on Ringwood Road and he was a really nice bloke but he was afflicted with a really bad stutter,' he recalled. Jeff Bailey also knew the family. 'John was always a little different to the others,' he said. 'He was always very smart, didn't wear jeans or more casual clothing. The family was quite well off.'

Initial rehearsals took place at John Start's house so he did not have to move his drum kit and, sometimes, the three guitarists would practise without him at Denmark Terrace. By the time of the autumn dance, they had a few instrumental cover versions worked up, including the material that The Kelly Brothers had been playing, 'Walk Don't Run', 'Apache' and 'Ghost Riders in the Sky'. They also shared vocals on the Everly Brothers' '(All I Have to do is) Dream', Chas McDevitt's 'Greenback Dollar', Cliff Richard's 'Living Doll' and Chuck Berry's 'Johnny B. Goode'. The show went as well as could be expected and they got a great reception from the pupils.

With some help from the Davies' extended family, they were soon playing regular gigs. Gwen's husband, Brian Longstaff, secured the boys a string of bookings at local clubs and, later, Mike Palmer got them at least one show. They appeared at weddings, youth clubs, and the Toc H, a hostel on Pages Lane in Muswell Hill. With time and practice, they were coming together as a tight, loud, fast, exciting band. Though it would not be unfair to say that the fledgling group were popular in part because they were local, they were also, by anybody's standards, very good. But a key issue in the line-up remained unresolved: they had so far taken it in turns to sing lead vocals because no one really wanted the job, but this could not go on, and so they began to look outside the quartet. In their search, the name of another William Grimshaw pupil kept coming up.

Younger than Pete and Ray, but older than Dave and John, Roderick David Stewart – better known as Rod – was the youngest of five children. He was born in Highgate and attended the Highgate Primary school before William Grimshaw. Like Ray, he was an Arsenal supporter, and a talented footballer, captaining his year; and, like Dave, he was an Eddie Cochran fan. He had already left school at the age of 15 and signed as an apprentice with Brentford Football Club in west London but, after pre-season training, decided that music, and not sport, would be his future.

Stewart practised with the as-yet-unnamed band a couple of times, but memories of him playing live are contradictory. No one can say exactly where and when, but it is likely he did go on stage with them at some point, most probably during a show at the Coldfall Estate Youth Club. He certainly rehearsed with them: sessions at John Start's house had to be moved out into the garage because John's mother could not stand the sound of Rod's now famous voice.

'He was on the football team, and he and Ray were both very competitive and hated each other,' said Pete Quaife.

'It makes me giggle,' said David Quaife when asked about Rod Stewart. 'He was briefly involved, but he wasn't singing, he had a harmonica, and once or twice was the most I saw of him. They did a little gig together, but everyone was like, "Oh bloody hell what's he doing here?"'

As the autumn of 1961 progressed, the band were introducing skiffle into their sound. Dave had got a new green Elipco amp from a local shop on Fortis Green and, through listening to Lonnie Donegan, had been introduced to Leadbelly and then Chuck Berry. Ray had watched an episode of the *John Grierson Show* on television which showed American blues legend Big Bill Broonzy playing in a club. Elvis Presley was another fan of Broonzy, a Mississippi man who sang country blues. He had played in Chicago with drums, bass and piano but, in England, the promoters just wanted to hear his raw acoustic guitar and voice, to feel his earthiness and pure straight-from-the-fields 'authenticity'. Ray loved everything about the performance, not just what he was playing, but how he was playing it and the way he held his guitar. The blues was the music of the downtrodden black man but it could be related to the working class in England.

While Rod Stewart was a good singer, he did not share the developing blues leanings of the others. He had already performed with a band called The Raiders and auditioned for legendary producer Joe Meek on Denmark Street, the epicentre of London's music business, and was already a well-known name in the area. Rod Stewart's involvement with the band ended, and other singers who were tried were soon discarded and the group continued to share vocal duties. 'The last time I met him was outside East Finchley Tube station with his harmonica playing on the pavement,' said David Quaife.

As the gigs kept coming, John Start's father paid for a set of matching black trousers, white shirts and blue cardigans. David Quaife recalled the rehearsal at his house and the Heath-Robinson approach the band took toward their equipment. 'They were down in the front room of number 59, tonking away on guitars,' he said. 'Dad was a bit of a technology expert and he'd built our first television set. I was only 6 years old at the time but I can remember it as clear as daytime when it was first switched on. He also built our family radiogram and then amplifiers. I remember Dave Davies turning up with a speaker from a local cinema which they were going to throw out and Dad built it into a cabinet. Perhaps that's what inspired Dave to start cutting up speakers. Dad did all his work in a little shed out in the back garden and late that night he quickly got this speaker working.' They then all piled into the back of Stan Quaife's car and drove the customised speaker to the venue where they were playing that night. It was hauled straight on stage just in time for the show, without any chance to try it out beforehand. Thankfully it worked fine and the show went on.

In late 1961, Dave Davies met Sue Sheehan. She was a year older than him and attended the Henrietta Barnett girls' school in Golders Green. She lived on Duke's Avenue in Muswell Hill with her parents, who strongly disapproved of Dave. When his partner in truancy, George Harris, was expelled from William Grimshaw in early 1962, Dave started to spend all his time with Sue, and any slight guilt he might have had about skipping school vanished completely. Dave was only fifteen but was deeply in love, and his affair with Sue became all-consuming.

One day in June, the couple set off for Kenwood House on Hampstead Heath. It was there, unseen in the high grass, that they most liked to make out, but, on that day, the grass had just been cut, and so they settled down near some trees. Unbeknown to the courting teenagers, they were being trailed by a couple of truant officers and, just as Dave got his trousers down, they were caught. When the report got back to the school Dave was called before the headmaster and caned, before being expelled, even though he had a year of schooling to go. He did not care – in fact, he felt liberated.

Sue was also expelled and the pair were banned from seeing each other, although they continued to meet secretly. She got a job in a department store but it was a different story for Dave: Annie Davies had her hands full trying to get him even to visit the Labour Exchange.

Then, in August, Sue announced that she was pregnant. Dave went out and bought an engagement ring, but his plans were soon shattered. Their parents got together and conspired to keep the young lovers apart. Sue was told that Dave did not love her anymore and did not want to see her, and he was told the same of her. Dave later found out that Sue had had a baby girl and called her Tracey. He would not meet his daughter for years to come. 'You carry that around with you as you grow up,' said Dave. 'I think it really messed me up a lot. It was motivating and perhaps I needed that anger to do what I was doing.'

Dave eventually got a job at Selmer's Music, the very shop on Charing Cross Road from which his first guitar had been bought. He worked in the warehouse where his tasks included cleaning any brass instruments that were brought in. One day, he had to polish Acker Bilk's clarinet, which he remembered being disgusting and grimy. Working alongside him was future television personality Derek Griffiths, of *Play School* and *Play Away* fame. Griffiths also played guitar and the pair would hold jam sessions during their dinner breaks.

Meanwhile, Ray and Pete were starting at the Hornsey College of Art, although Ray, at least, was not sure where it would lead him. In the early 1960s, British society was changing at a rapid pace. Social mobility was increasing and, whereas art schools had previously been the preserve of the upper and middle classes, they were now taking in working-class students, whose culture was making its mark in the theatre, films, literature and music.

Pete Quaife's tenure at Hornsey lasted less than a month. 'They said I was a Ted,' he recalled. Teds, or Teddy Boys, were, and are, a uniquely British rock and roll sub-culture, famous for their quiffs, Edwardian-style coats and, unfortunately, a tendency to violence. 'I said I wasn't. Well, after a couple of weeks of arguing, they said, very nicely, "I wonder, Mr Quaife, if you would care to leave this school?" So I did.' He got work as a commercial artist at men's fashion publication, *The Outfitter*, but sitting at a desk from nine to five did not seem to suit him either. The work itself was fine, but the environment was restrictive. 'I used to meet him at lunchtime,' said Dave Davies. 'We'd look around the shops and Pete and I got into fashion.'

Jeff Bailey was also involved in the scene. 'At the agency he worked for was Cathy McGowan who was one of the original comperes of *Ready Steady Go*,' he said. 'Pete and I became very, very close buddies. I was with him a lot. We confided in one another over many issues, not just about him, the band or music, but our home and private lives. He was wise, astute and had a business mind.' This interest in fashion would lead the band in all kinds of directions later on and even influence their choice of name.

On the night of 15 December 1962, the Hornsey Art School Christmas Dance took place, with blues guitarist Alexis Korner playing. During a break, Ray approached the father of British blues and asked him for any advice about how he could get a regular paying gig. Korner gave him the details of Giorgio Gomelsky at the Piccadilly Club in Soho and, within the week, Ray had auditions with the Dave Hunt Rhythm and Blues band. He was offered a regular club spot with them starting in the first week of the new year, and his life would never be the same again.

Two Well-Respected Gentlemen

For 16-year-old Dave Davies, this was heaven: a posh flat full of posh birds, more champagne than even he could drink, and license to do pretty much as he pleased. Dressed in thigh-high leather boots and with a sword – a real one – hanging from his belt, he approached one girl after another. The more outrageous he looked, the better, as far as he was concerned. This was his first time in Chelsea and first time drinking champagne. All he had to do during the evening was play a few songs to support the upper-class singer and then he was free to party the night away. This was living all right. And the parties just kept coming, although, eventually, he would stop taking the sword after he accidentally clipped someone's face with it, drawing blood.

It can be argued that the 1960s did not really begin until Beatlemania struck, bringing with it a tidal wave of teenage emotion, in the second half of 1963. That was the year in which the Profumo Affair shocked the world and threatened to bring down Harold Macmillan's government. US President Jack Kennedy made his famous declaration 'Ich bin ein Berliner' in June and was shot dead in November. The Great Train Robbery filled the headlines during August. In England, the whole year seemed to be underlined by growing social unrest: striking electricity workers caused black-outs in January, while 70,000 CND supporters marched through London in March. The BBC withdrew a ban on comedy about religion, sex, politics and royalty, opening up new horizons in television and radio, and falling into step with changing attitudes in the country. The stuffy post-war years were starting to give way to an exciting decade, soon to be positively swinging.

In music, Bob Dylan made his first UK appearance in December 1962, and the charts of early 1963 were dominated by The Shadows, with and without Cliff Richard: they scored six number one singles between January and April. Their smiling stage-faces and choreographed dance steps were soon to look stiff and chaste in comparison with Merseybeat and the pop genius of Brian Epstein. Epstein-managed acts accounted for eight of the twelve number one UK singles between April and December 1963, of which four were by The Beatles, three by Gerry and the Pacemakers, and one by Billy J. Kramer. Beat groups were what the public wanted and record labels were on the lookout for bands to fill that gap. Decca made sure they signed The Rolling Stones, having famously passed up the chance to nab The Beatles. As was usual at the time, the Stones dressed in matching outfits – tight black trousers, white shirts and leather waistcoats.

It was 1963 that was one of the fastest-moving, most turbulent years in the lives of members of the Ray Davies Quartet, as they were called at its outset. In the following twelve months, they would have four changes of name, three drummers, two new lead singers, and finally a trio of managers, a booking agent, a producer and a record label. In January, however, they were still a fledgling outfit, getting the odd gigs here and there, and sharing Ray with Dave Hunt's Rhythm & Blues Band.

Ray Davies was also throwing himself into his art school studies, but was increasingly drawn to the world of film. At Hornsey, he set up a film club with his friend Paul O'Dell and the pair worked on some projects together. Ray's sister, Joyce, worked at the Odeon down the street in Muswell Hill, and Ray would try and see a new movie every week, among them *Look Back in Anger*, *Saturday Night and Sunday Morning* and *The Loneliness of the Long Distance Runner*. All three were part of the 'British new wave', combining 'kitchen-sink drama' and the 'angry young man', and meshed perfectly with Ray's own background and grim view of the wider world. He was also prone to a fear that marked so much of Cold War culture. 'I was very aware of the Red Threat and totalitarianism, and it never felt very far away from me,' he said. 'I grew up with the fear of being crushed as an individual. I saw it where I grew up and went to school. I wanted to be an artist but the school system was teaching you to be factory fodder.'

For his art classes he would go out sketching in parks and at train stations. He was a skilled and sensitive observer, and transferred this sharp eye to good use in his filmmaking. He would later hone it to perfection in his songwriting.

On Saturday, 16 February, The Ray Davies Quartet played one of its biggest shows to date, as part of the Valentine's Day Ball at Hornsey Town Hall. It was the first time the band had their name up on a poster, even though they were erroneously billed as 'The Ray Davis Quartette', under the headlining Harry Pitch and his Band. In 2010, Ray returned to the derelict Hornsey Town Hall auditorium with presenter Alan Yentob and a BBC television crew to shoot a documentary. He claimed that this was always, at least subconsciously, the perfect venue for him, the place where he always envisaged his songs being performed.

Various friends came along to watch the 1963 show, as did the Davies' sisters. They were, in effect, there to fill in while the main act took a break, but were emblematic of the times: a bluesy skiffle band among the dying embers of the big band era.

Misspelled or otherwise, their name already looked out-dated. A new, dynamic, modern moniker was required, and they settled on The Ramrods later that spring. Ray was still a member of the band but, by now, Dave was the driving force, and Ray would join them only when he was not playing elsewhere.

When they did all get together, they were sufficiently confident to enter a recording studio. Their first two attempts came in February and mid-April, when the band paid for studio time to try out some instrumentals. These long-forgotten tracks were recorded on Great Portland Street, most likely at IBC Studios. The second attempt, at R.G. Jones Studio in Morden, took place just after a Rolling Stones session at the same venue. 'It was not often that a bunch of scruffy, half-arsed "musicians" had the chance to enter a recording studio to record their own music,' said Pete Quaife. 'Up until then we, along with every other group in Britain, had only tried to record their music on their Uncle's old tape recorder!' At this second session, on 16 April, a Dave Davies composition was recorded, but no one can remember its title, and no tapes survive.

By now, the Dave Hunt band had split up and Ray Davies had joined the newly formed Hamilton King band that rose from the ashes. That summer, Ray completed his first year at Hornsey Art School and made enquiries about switching from fine art to the film and theatre course instead. He was told that it would not be possible and if he wanted to change direction, he would have to do so elsewhere. He was too late to apply to the London School of Film but was accepted at the Croydon School of Art, starting in September.

John Start completed his five years at William Grimshaw that summer and then announced he was leaving the band. His parents wanted him to enter the family business and that put an end to his nascent music career. Start's departure came at a tricky moment for the band, as they had just been put in touch with a booking agent by the name of Danny Haggerty who had secured them a series of shows at US Air Force bases. They had to move quickly and settled on Mickey Willett as the new drummer. He came from Palmers Green and the others saw him as something of an elder statesman. He had played in various bands before and was a journeyman musician. For his part, Ray Davies thought Willett was too good for them.

With a new drummer on board, the group decided on another name change, this time to The Boll-Weevils. The name came from Dave Davies' love of the Eddie Cochran B-side 'Boll Weevil Song', the American rocker's take on an old blues standard, which dated back to the early days of the twentieth century. Their act was moving into more of an R&B vein as Ray Davies ended his involvement with the Hamilton King band and was now dedicating himself to his brother's quartet, which seemed to promise more of a future.

'When we first started out as The Boll-Weevils we played anywhere to get experience,' explained Ray Davies. 'One afternoon the vicar invited us to play for the old folks in Crouch End Church Hall, and afterwards this little old lady in a woolly hat waited for me by the door and said, "Ray this is wonderful music. It really got my feet tapping."'

In September, Mickey Willett made a crucial contact when he met 21-year-old Robert Wace in a pub, and the two started chatting about music. Wace was an imposing figure for the young musicians. He was well over 6ft tall, very well spoken and well educated – he had attended the prestigious Marlborough College in the 1950s. He was working for his father's block-making business but his life lacked excitement, namely a backing band to play while he sang at society parties for his upper-class friends. His father was not overly excited about his son's musical interests but nonetheless gave him £500 and told him to go and give it a try, no doubt expecting he would soon return to the fold when things did not work out.

Wace had a friend by the name of Grenville Collins, a man of a similar height and background. He was a dealer on the London Stock Exchange and had vague ambitions to get into the music business, about which neither he nor Wace knew anything. Willett arranged for Wace and Collins to come and see his new band play and decide if there was any chance of them working together. Wace was intrigued that all three guitars were plugged into one amp, and that Dave jumped up and down like a kangaroo. He saw enough and asked them to be his band. It was a strange juxtaposition, the very working-class band and the pseudo-aristocratic lead singer. 'Superficially they were upper-class twits, with these very plummy voices,' said Dave Davies. 'But there was more to them than that. Robert used to take the piss out of my accent. He'd copy the way we spoke and we'd copy them. But there was a lot of mutual respect.'

Grenville Collins paid for new outfits for the band, including pink shirts, and printed up some business cards:

A Raving Rhythm and Blues Session With:
'The Boll-Weevils'
3s 6d

At a typical show, The Boll-Weevils would play a selection from their bluesy repertoire, and then Wace would enter and sing four pop hits of the day, mainly to impress his social circle. His delivery was a crude mixture of Buddy Holly and Noel Coward. 'I was doing my four numbers at the end and they were having a good laugh,' said Wace. 'We were having a great time. I didn't have enough confidence to stay up there for half an hour.' The band, in turn, were enjoying their new, moneyed social scene. Dave Davies eagerly took to supping champagne and chatting up debutantes. How many shows Wace fronted remains unclear, but the band did play with him at the Guildhall and the Grocer's Hall, both in the City of London.

When they decided to branch out, it proved to be the end of Wace's singing career. In October, at Brady's Cub in the East End, Wace's vocal stylings did not go down well with the locals and he was booed off. Beyond the safety of his friends' parties, he realised he did not have what it took to lead a band and so retired from singing. Ray Davies suggested, however, that he stay on as their manager as he was obviously very enthusiastic about music, even if he had little experience of the business side of it. He and Collins took on the job together.

Before Wace's retirement from singing, he inadvertently helped the band make an important step forward: at one show, he managed to bash his own tooth with the microphone and had to rush from the stage, forcing Ray Davies to step forward and take over singing duties. He did it well and the band realised they might have a lead singer after all, even if he was a reluctant one.

At this point, before he was officially managing the band, Wace made a call to Brian Epstein, and actually got him to come and watch them play. Epstein turned him down and, although he expressed a vague interest in developing Ray as a solo act, nothing more came of it.

The band had been practising hard and decided to have another go in the studio. They headed to Regent Sound Studios at 4 Denmark Street to put down the Davies' brothers composition 'I Believed You', along with Jerry Lieber and Mike Stoller's 'I'm a Hog for You', which had caught Ray's attention when he had heard The Coasters' version in 1958. On the scratchy acetates that survive, both tracks, which clock in at less than two minutes each, sound like early Merseybeat, with Pete and Dave adding backing vocals to Ray's hurried delivery. They are decent tunes and fairly well performed, but neither is remarkable, and it is not surprising they failed to garner much interest when Wace and Collins started shopping them around.

With Wace out of the picture as far as performing was concerned, they decided to change the band's name yet again. On 23 November, they made their 'debut' as The Ravens, inspired by a recently released Vincent Price movie. 'The first gig as The Ravens, now that was good, a lot of people turned up, the place was packed,' said David Quaife. In the run up to Christmas, they also played a handful of parties for friends of Wace and Collins.

At that time so many new acts were bursting through to chart success that everyone concerned with The Ravens was determined they ought to make a serious bid for stardom themselves – and so contracts were drawn up. Robert Wace gave up his job at his father's business to dedicate himself to managing the band, and Grenville Collins, who continued to work the stock market, agreed to make 50 per cent of his annual profits available to the venture in return for a percentage of the group's earnings.

'We were still so young that our parents had to sign the contract for us and of course, they never read it,' said Ray Davies. Legally, no one under the age of 21 could enter into such an agreement; Mickey Willet was the only one old enough to sign the contract for himself. Ray was then 19 years old, Dave only 16, and Pete Quaife 20.

When the agreements were being signed, Pete made a shocking discovery: Stan Quaife, who he had grown up thinking was his father, was revealed to be his step-dad. 'It's one of those skeletons in the cupboard,' explained Pete's brother David Quaife. 'Pete's [biological] dad was an American soldier and in those days women would be sent away to have the baby and pop back a couple of months later . . . She was down south for three weeks. Pete didn't know about this until Grenville and Robert turned up to sign a contract. Because he wasn't 21 my dad stood up ready to sign and they said, "Oh no, you can't do that because you're not his father." I was only a kid but I can see Pete's face now – he was knocked right back.'

Once signed, the contracts gave Wace and Collins not only management of the band, and a share of all recording and concert profits, but also the right to assign any part of their management duties to a third party. This small print would later come to haunt The Ravens, but at the time their most pressing need was to produce a saleable acetate recording, so in December they returned to the studio for a second attempt. This time, they put down the fast-rocking instrumental 'Revenge' along with 'Ooladiooba'.

One of the first intimations of the new order in the band was not long in coming. A more experienced musician, Mickey Willett had never been too keen on taking orders from Wace or Collins, who he thought were dilettantes. Things came to a head, as they often do, over money. After a show in Lewisham, Willett took umbrage when his girlfriend found a receipt that appeared to show that the band had received over £60, from which the musicians had been paid just £5 apiece. Willett felt that his wage was unfairly small compared with the £20 each that Wace and Collins were taking home, without having played a note, so he spoke out. 'I told Ray and Dave about this and they were up in arms,' said Willett. 'That was the start of the rot.' By Christmas, however, he was gone. With his older style, both musically and in appearance, the drummer had always made an odd fit with the younger Ravens, and Wace and Collins requested that the band fire him. Willett recalled the events to *Mojo* magazine in September 2000: 'When I confronted Ray he got upset and said, "To be honest, Mike, I don't want you to go, but what can I do?"'

Ray himself was also moving on, his time at art school about to reach an end. 'He seemed to get on with the other students,' recalled tutor John Turney, 'but there was possibly a bit of friction because he was very independent.' In all Ray lasted three months at Croydon, which, after the year at Hornsey, gave him a good grounding in the subject at the start of an era in which the visual arts and pop would become ever more closely allied. Indeed, he was one of a batch of young musicians who left art school for musical fame in the early 1960s: Charlie Watts (Harrow), John Lennon (Liverpool), John Cale (Goldsmiths), Eric Clapton (Kingston), Ronnie Wood and Pete Townsend (both Ealing) are just a few among them. Ray did not, however, have any real desire to be an artist by this point – he thought the discipline required was beyond him – but playing in a band was something he believed he could handle.

One of the first people who Robert Wace approached about a publishing deal was Tony Hiller. 'I was General Professional Manager at Mills Music, an independent company,' says Tony Hiller. 'Robert Wace came to see me and told me about this band; he played some demos and I loved them. We spent a couple of hours together and we talked about all of the possibilities of what we could do together. We arranged a meeting for the next day, but I never saw him again! He obviously saw Larry Page, who is a very dear friend of mine, after me and that was that. I was very disappointed.' Hiller was right to be disappointed. He was also right about Wace's next stop.

Larry Page's real name was Leonard Davies. He was born just before the war in Hayes, Middlesex, and had a singing career in the 1950s. He had toured with Cliff Richard, appeared on television, and went by the moniker of Larry Page the Teenage Rage, while wearing over-sized glasses which became a kind of trademark. By the time he met Robert Wace, he had been an EMI Records packer, the general manager of Kassner Music and now ran his own business, Denmark Productions, named after the site of his office on Denmark Street, known to the business as 'Tin Pan Alley'.

Page agreed to go and see The Ravens rehearsing at a pub in Islington and, even though they were only playing covers, he could see some potential. 'I thought it was good that there were two brothers in the band,' recalled Page, 'but I didn't know then that it was brothers at war.'

Wace and Collins formed a company named Boscobel Productions, after Wace's home at 45 Boscobel Place, and signed it onto Denmark Productions, giving the latter 10 per cent of all the band's recordings and live income. Also significant was the integration of Page's firm into Kassner Music: it meant that any band signed to Denmark Productions would have their publishing rights automatically assigned to Kassner. The upshot was that Page had become a powerful player in the group's business affairs, getting a 10 per cent management commission plus the rights to place the publishing for a further fee.

'They were dandies,' said Larry Page of Wace and Collins. 'When you spoke to them they'd stand there in their £500 pinstripe suits, bouncing on the balls of their feet. They weren't managing, they were investing. I controlled the band.' However, Robert Wace's view of the structure was quite different. 'He [Page] was never the manager of the group,' he said. 'Although he might like to think of himself as one.'

Whatever his role in the band's management, Page wasted no time in advancing them to the next stage of their career. He immediately set about taking the demos around the record companies. 'I started by going for the biggest companies, with an international situation,' he said. 'I had a very good relationship with Dick Rowe at Decca, but he turned them down because he already had the Stones.' He had no better luck at Phillips. There, 'artists and repertoire' (A&R) man Jack Baverstock sat reading the paper, while Page played the tape, before answering with a firm, 'No.' Finally, Page went to see Louis Benjamin at Pye. Benjamin was moved enough to make an offer, but hardly a good one. The deal would give the band only 2 or 3 per cent, yet it was the only one on the table, so they took it.

The Ravens, by this time, had more back-up staff than they had band members. There were multiple managers, a publisher and a record label, and they were also in need of a booking agent. Robert Wace decided that Arthur Howes, who already handled The Beatles, would be the best man for the job. Wace arranged for The Ravens to play at Howes' favourite restaurant, the Lotus House, on Edgware Road, on New Year's Eve 1963, without Howes' knowledge.

Speaking to BBC TV in the early 1970s, Howes said: 'I was sitting down for my meal and saw all sorts of people coming in. Long-haired boys, amplifiers moving in and things we didn't usually see in a restaurant like that.' Howes was notorious for making decisions on the spot: one listen and you were either hot, or you were not. On that night, The Ravens impressed him, and he agreed to work with them. 'From then on I couldn't wait to get my hands on them.' As time ticked past midnight, the band had made the perfect start to 1964.

As he had proven with his own distinctive image and rhyming nickname, Larry Page knew how to work the media, such as it was in the early 1960s. He realised that to stand a chance, the band needed a new name and a new look. With this in mind, he made a call to a photographer he knew by the name of Bruce Fleming. 'I worked for the *Melody Maker*,' said Fleming. 'I loved jazz so I was at Ronnie Scott's four or five nights a week waiting for the stars to come in and I made money that way. I worked for a guy named Les Perrin, who was the top European PR man of all time. He was great, he looked after Sinatra and all the stars, including the Kray twins, would you believe. I worked for the Krays and did a few shots with them. Les also put me in touch with lots of bands that came to him for PR and I'd shoot them and go to work on them, it was a good living and fun, too. Larry Page had his own agency in Tin Pan Alley, and he called and said I've got this band, so I met them and we went to work.'

'They'd got some new clothes, suits and no collars, that sort of stuff,' said Fleming. 'I shot them from above and then Larry said he wanted something with "a bit more". They were a little bit introverted and strange and not the sunny Herman's Hermits type of guys, slightly more intense. I thought they were a bit crazy and so I dressed them up in long boots and leather jackets, with chains, it was all a bit hilarious. I got some bullwhips from a company that hired out armaments and a big sheet of plate glass, which I got behind and asked them to whip the glass in a rage. It was something I thought would get them noticed and it was, so much so that the

BBC and the MRM banned it as being brutal and not the kindly fun rock image that was usual.'

'I was having a chat with Larry after and looking through the shots, and Larry said, "I don't know what to call them",' Fleming recalled. 'So I said, "They're very kinky", so I think between me and him we named them, but I can't be sure of that.'

According to Page the band's new image and name were purloinings from the popular culture of the time: 'The image we settled on was all done because of *The Avengers* on TV,' he remembered. 'The word "kinky" was floating around. I came up with the name, Kinks. Ray didn't like it.' Neither did Dave, who, at the time, thought The Kinks was a 'silly' name, although he attributed it to Arthur Howes rather than Page or Fleming.

Regardless of the origins, Page was evidently set on the new moniker, so its adoption was all but assured. For Ray, in the midst of a potentially traumatic transition from unemployed art student to rock star, it represented another unsettling change and in time he would grow to hate it.

Part 2

That insane guitar started it all for me. But I have to be careful
about sharing my tastes in music because it comes back to haunt
you. I once said that I liked Van der Graaf Generator and was
accused of ripping them off.

John Lydon, talking about 'You Really Got Me'

Observer Music Monthly

You Really Got Me

Still without a permanent drummer, January 1964 saw Ray, Dave and Pete Quaife busy recording. Fed up with a never-ending stream of cover versions, Ray was also busy writing original material. Larry Page was nominally the producer for a session, probably at Regent Sound studios, at which 'You Still Want Me', 'You Do Something to Me' and 'I Don't Need You Anymore' were recorded, along with other undocumented songs which are rumoured to survive on a two-sided acetate. Highly derivative of the Merseybeat sound, distilled to the simplest boy-girl form of 'you' and 'me', nothing from the session stands out. The musicianship is tight but not spectacular and the Davies brothers often seem to be singing the main lyric together. It is easy to picture them, hands on headphones, singing into the same microphone like Lennon and McCartney in those classic images from the same era. The demos were fine, but Pye soon decided it was time to record a single with a professional producer, and their choice was an American who was new in town: Shel Talmy.

Born in Chicago in 1937, Talmy moved to Los Angeles as a child, where he got a place on the NBC TV show *Quiz Kids*, in which a panel of five children answered questions sent in by viewers. He did so well that he stayed on week after week. 'That was a life-changing experience for me,' he said. 'I was 12 years old and I thought "this is the business I wanted to be in". I was on for the last year of its existence, then Alka-Seltzer, who was the sponsor, dropped them, and they went off the air for about thirteen years or something like that.' After school he landed a job with ABC Television, before meeting Phil Yeend, an Englishman who had settled in California and set up Conway Studios. Talmy was soon offered a job there as an engineer. The young Talmy jumped at the chance. 'Three days later I was tossed into the deep and did my first session solo,' recalled Talmy. 'It was for a twelve-piece Latin band which I miked up OK and recorded OK, but then they wanted me to do some editing which I had hardly ever done. I was sweating bullets and trying to cut the tape freehand, and somehow I got it right, but to this day I don't know how.'

In 1962 he moved to London: 'I thought I should see something of the world before the world passed me by,' he said. 'I expected to be in London for a few weeks, I had a booking [at home in the USA] to produce four singles and I said I'd do them when I got back – but I didn't get back for seventeen years.' Once in Britain he talked himself into some recording work. 'The first person I saw [in London] was Noel Rodgers who was at Universal Publishing at the time and he made the call to Dick Rowe [at Decca] for me,' explained Talmy. 'It was as simple as that, I didn't have to pick up the phone and start calling people. I was never on staff at Decca, I was the first independent producer, to my knowledge, in England. I got a weekly retainer and they gave me bands.' Talmy had got the job by reeling off a list of records that, in reality, he had little to do with, and then playing some demos that had been recorded by Nick Venet, head of A&R at Capitol Records, who had generously told the aspiring young producer to pass them off as his own work.

Talmy settled on the King's Road, which had already established itself as one of the new decade's key creative hubs. 'It was unbelievable,' he said. 'In retrospect I was in the right place at the right time completely by accident. Right before the British explosion of everything and the King's Road was the hotbed of where it was happening. There must have been about four hundred people who all knew each other to some degree and whenever there was a party we would all go. Music, fashion, film – it all came out of that small group.'

Talmy's version of The Kinks' story is often different to Larry Page's, but their recollections of Wace and Collins match. 'They were public school stereotypes,' said Talmy. 'They were amusing and I suppose "chinless wonder" comes to mind, but they were very nice, I liked them. I got on with them fine, it was Larry Page I never got on with and nobody else did either.' It was Talmy, according to his account, who really got the band into Pye after hearing the demo while it was being played to Tony Hiller. 'I was at Mills Music in Denmark Street when Robert Wace walked in with the demo,' said Talmy. 'He said, "Is there anybody here who'd like to listen to this?" I said, "I'm here, I'll listen." I liked what I heard and we took it from there. I met them and we chatted and I thought this was a band that could actually make it.'

Ray Davies met Talmy for the first time in a Sloane Square pub shortly before their first session together. They chatted about music and the sounds they wanted to create in the studio, and seemed to get along well. The session took place at Pye's Studio One on 20 January 1964, using a three-track mono tape recorder for the five songs. It lasted six hours. Session drummer Bobby Graham joined the three bandmates. 'You Still Want Me', 'You Do Something to Me' and 'I Don't Need You Anymore' were reprised from the Regent Sound session and 'I Took My Baby Home' was also attempted. The final song was Little Richard's 'Long Tall Sally', which Arthur Howes had seen The Beatles perform in Paris earlier in the week and suggested they use for their debut single because everyone knew it already.

'I chose all the songs to be recorded, except for the first singles which Pye insisted I did,' said Talmy. 'From that point I said, "You know what? I'm choosing from now on."'

Ray Davies was quickly getting to grips with the craft of songwriting, rapidly increasing in both quality and quantity. 'Ray was certainly one of the most prolific songwriters ever,' recalled Talmy. 'He would come in with a dozen songs that he'd written the night before or something, and we'd go through them and I'd say, "That needs more work, that's great," and so on.'

Talmy made sure that the band had thoroughly rehearsed beforehand so he had a good idea of how things would turn out when they walked into the studio: 'It was a totally different mindset at that point in time. The shorter the time the band spent in the studio the better they were, which later became the reverse. So we had three-hour sessions and would cut a lot of tracks because no one was screwing around.' It was also in Talmy's own interest to get the songs recorded as swiftly as possible. 'I was charged for the studio time by Louis Benjamin,' he said. 'He was one of the biggest assholes of all time, I really despised *that* son-of-a-bitch! It wasn't a usual situation so I did the first stuff in mono because it cost me less. I thought if you're not going to play the game then screw you, I'll do it in mono.'

After management scrutiny, 'Long Tall Sally' was deemed to be good enough and The Kinks' debut single was given a release date of 7 February. 'Long Tall Sally', as The Kinks performed it, was much closer to The Beatles' R&B version than the frenetic Little Richard take. Again, the Davies brothers shared the vocals, before Ray pulled out his harmonica for a solo, and a few Lennon and McCartney-esque 'ooos' punctuated the chorus. 'I Took My Baby Home' found a place on the B-side.

The Kinks would have to promote the single with live dates and possibly some television appearances, and so needed to find a full-time drummer quickly. Mick Avory had been contacted by their managers and now it was time to meet him. 'I remember sitting in the living room with Pete and his girlfriend, a girl called Nicki Start,' said David Quaife. 'They knew they had a new drummer coming in who'd played with the Stones, but they were told they'd have to use a session man until the new drummer established himself with the band. Nicki said, "That's not fair is it?" and Pete replied, "Well it's not fair what happens to me either, is it!?" That was the first time I realised that the seeds had already been sown for Pete's dissatisfaction with how he was treated in the group.' Pete was already feeling squeezed out by the Ray-Dave axis, and while it had originally been Dave's project, leadership of the band was fast becoming Ray's, as both singer and now songwriter.

The first meeting with Mick Avory took place in the rehearsal room of an Islington pub. 'I was present at the Camden Head when he arrived for the audition,' said Quaife's long-time friend Jeff Bailey. 'Ray was impressed at the rock drummer. He fitted like the last piece of the jigsaw. I remember that he kept squinting and closing his eyes when he played, and he had huge hands.'

'So when I went down to the pub where I was to meet someone called Mick Avory, I got a bit of a turn,' recalled Dave Davies. 'He stood over 6ft tall, in suit, shirt and tie, and had the shortest hair I'd ever seen. "Ha, he's just got out of prison!" I thought. He looked amazed at my appearance and rather longingly at my shoulder-length hair.' Avory had thought the advert meant, 'smart' as in 'clean cut', so he'd worn his suit and had his hair cut short especially for the audition. 'We all got on well with Mick from the start,' said Dave. 'It was terrific having him around. A group's members really need to respect each other, both as musicians and as people. Otherwise the group's no good.'

After playing through a few songs with the three musicians, Avory was asked to come back the next day and play in front of the management. He arrived in a paraffin delivery van, and had to unload and set up his drum kit while the others looked on. This time, Grenville Collins grilled the drummer on his background and experience. With his upper-class elocution, Collins asked Avory what he did for a living. Avory replied in a working-class rumble that he delivered paraffin. Collins sniffed: 'Delivering paraffin? Do you see that as a career?' Avory replied that it was only until he could get into a band. 'Well, you're on a trial,' said Collins. 'Three months.'

Those three months were to become twenty years.

Mick Avory was born in the Hampton Court area of Surrey on 15 February 1944 to Charles and Marjorie Avory. He was one of three boys and went to school in nearby Molesey and Weybridge. He had taken music lessons before making his first appearance before a crowd at the Molesey Carnival in 1957. 'I went for some piano lessons when I was about 15, just three or four times,' he said. 'We didn't have a piano at home so I practised at my friends' [house]. The teacher was an old lady, but she was steeped in teaching people classical music. She played me this piece but it was all learning parrot-fashion with no continuity, when all I wanted was to be able to find my way round a piano, but she couldn't really teach that way and it would have taken me twenty years.'

Mick's musical tastes were influenced by his older brother, seven years his senior. Via his sibling, he got into West Coast jazz at the age of just 7 or 8 and, by 10, was listening to rock and roll. 'I discovered Elvis Presley at the same time as all my friends at school,' he recalled. 'I bought rock and roll into the house when I bought "Rock Around the Clock".'

By the age of 11, Avory was a member of the Boy Scouts, where he was part of a little band. The start of his drumming career came about by accident. 'The guy who'd played with a stick and a brush got disenchanted with it and left, he wanted to play mandolin of all things,' Avory explained. 'I'd been to the meetings and was allowed to go with the senior scouts because one of them lived near me so they let me join them on drums. I kept in time and I liked it, I was part of something, we had a washboard player, too. Someone got me a drum from a school and a cymbal, and then I got myself some proper brushes and sticks and it developed from there. The skiffling Scouts did a few gigs. I remember the local carnival at Hampton Court, one or two pubs. Trad jazz was quite popular so we'd get a few gigs on the back of that. Someone put us forward for Hughie Green's *Opportunity Knocks* [the television talent show] so we went up for that on Baker Street, but opportunity didn't knock!

'The worst problem when I first started playing was transport,' said Avory. 'I did two grocery rounds and a paper round to raise the money to get a drum kit, and when I finally bought it, it suddenly occurred to me that I had no way of carting it around. I solved it in the end, though. Every time I went to play on a date I used to strap the bass drum on my back and go pedalling off on a bicycle!'

Avory was keen and ended up sitting in with bands playing vastly different styles of music. At the age of 17, he had a long-running gig with The George Shearing Jazz Trio at a hotel on the Great West Road. At the same time, he started having lessons with a jazz drummer and, once again enchanted by the music, went back to his brother's records. He then took lessons with a friend of Tony

Kinsey, one of the older musicians his brother liked. 'He wasn't actually a drummer, he was a sheet metal worker,' said Avory, 'but he could really play. It was good for the jazz-feel stuff because that's what he knew. He didn't really help me with the rock and roll stuff, and I just had to learn that by experience really.'

A year later, Avory found himself playing with an unusual father-and-son duo: the boy played vibes and piano, while his dad acted like a booking agent, adding a bass player and guitarist as necessary to get work for his son. He used to advertise in *Melody Maker* and it was through this route that he got a call from a young man by the name of Mick Jagger, who needed a drummer. The job was passed on to Avory. 'I went to see what it was all about but they wanted a full-time drummer and I'd never considered it as a living,' said Avory. 'I was comparing myself with the famous jazz drummers I'd seen and I wasn't anywhere near their technique. Also, it wasn't seen as a good industry for regular work. It all seemed a bit precarious.'

Nonetheless, Avory wound up at the Bricklayer's Arms in Soho, in the summer of 1962, playing in an early, unnamed incarnation of The Rolling Stones with Brian Jones and Mick Jagger. 'I practised with them a couple of times and they said they wanted to do this gig at the Marquee,' recalled Avory. 'But I never actually played at the gig. Though Bill Wyman says I did and so does Keith Richards!' In 2011, Stones co-founder Dick Taylor told *Mojo*, 'I'm certain Mick Avory was with us when we made our debut at the Marquee that July [1962].' It wasn't until a year later when 'Come On' reached number twenty-one in the UK charts, long after he'd been replaced by Tony Chapman, who in turn gave up the seat to Charlie Watts, that Avory realised it was the same band.

When he left school, Mick Avory didn't have any idea of what he should do next, although he later came to feel he should probably have gone to art school. As it was, he soon fell into a series of short-lived jobs – draughtsman, carpenter and sheet metal worker among them – while playing in bands at weekends.

I didn't really have any direction, I never really did anything I was any good at . . . My dad was an artist through and through, he'd been to art school and had a fully comprehensive training for modelling, painting, wood carving, everything. The two wars interrupted his career so he didn't recommend art as a living, but that was what I was good at so I was steered in the wrong direction . . . My brother was a draughtsman, but that didn't suit me, free art was more my thing, not drawing lines with rulers. I did a year at a firm called DG Canon and Son in Merton, South Wimbledon, but they said 'you're not really cut out for this'. They made ventilation ducting and had a factory next door, I had three months in the factory so I understood exactly what they were doing, but it wasn't really that creative. I left there and my dad got me a job where he'd got stuck in a firm that made fireplaces. He designed the fireplaces from stone, brick and slate. He was the works director and they gave him a share of the company, but they were a small company and he was stuck with that for most of his working life.

When the fireplace firm was finally liquidated in the late 1950s, Charles Avory received just enough of a pay-off to buy a car and take up a job he actually enjoyed, joining the design team at Shepperton Studios. There, he made the ship's figurehead for the 1958 movie *The Vikings*, and designed the set for Richard Burton's *Beckett*. Tragically, while still in his fifties, he suffered a stroke and had to give up work, just as he had finally found something he loved. He passed away at the age of 59.

Mick was still doing manual jobs when he went to meet The Kinks for the first time, but his heart was set on music. 'I wanted to pursue it even if it wasn't going to be a career,' he said. 'I could earn some money and travel a bit. Playing eight hours a night in Germany would be better than doing a real job, but of course it soon became something much bigger. Wace and Collins talked big, big money and I thought, "Blimey what have I got into?"'

He quit his paraffin delivery job but didn't get a contract with the band straight away and so felt out on a limb. As soon as they started playing gigs, however, he would be paid £22 a week by Arthur Howes, and his first performance as part of the new line-up was just days away.

The band first played under their new name at Oxford Town Hall on Saturday, 1 February. The Rolling Stones had performed there a few weeks earlier but The Kinks and the opening act, R&B band The Downliners Sect, played unadvertised to a sparse crowd.

Next up was a television appearance to promote 'Long Tall Sally'. The BBC's upstart rival, ITV, which had gradually been extending its reach since 1955, had first broadcast its music show, *Ready Steady Go!*, five months earlier. With their opening catchphrase 'The weekend starts here!', hosts Keith Fordyce and Cathy McGowan could help send singles to the top of the charts. Just a couple of weeks before The Kinks' TV debut, The Beatles had appeared earning the show its highest ever viewing figures. Getting a slot was a huge coup for the former Ravens.

With their new name, the band felt they had to make a visual impression as well as a musical one. Fashion and pop music were becoming increasingly intertwined and John Stephen was one of the first to cater for London's growing market of up-and-coming rock musicians. He outfitted The Small Faces and The Rolling Stones from his chain of boutiques. 'Our manager said we needed really outrageous stage suits so we spent all our money getting John Stephen of Carnaby Street to make these awful itchy green suits,' recalled Ray Davies. 'The trousers were really tight with leather straps, so our Cuban heels could get through, and matching straps on the sleeves and collars. When they arrived they looked like they hadn't been finished, but it was our own design. We wore them with leather caps and looked like prats.'

Mick Avory, who, Dave Davies declared, looked like a navvy in his Sunday best, had a smart new drum kit with a Kinks logo on the front, a stylised spelling of the band's name with the 'K' and 'S' looking like they were wearing Cuban-heeled 'kinky' boots.

In the lead up to the show, Larry Page had booked a dentist appointment for Ray Davies to have the gap between his front two teeth fixed, but Ray got cold feet and left the waiting room. He did, however, agree to have removable caps fitted for TV appearances.

When the day came, the band mimed their way through the song, and Dave Davies was briefly interviewed on air by the boy-next-door presenter, Michael Aldred, who he would later get to know much better. Bruce Fleming was there to photograph the show and it was arranged that afterwards friends and family would wait outside to pose as rabid fans, mobbing the band. The picture made it into the pages of the *New Musical Express* the following week.

Despite their best efforts, the single charted at number forty-two and then dropped from sight. Reviews were favourable, though, with the *New Musical Express* approving of the band having brought the song 'up to date'.

In the days following their appearance on *Ready Steady Go!*, The Kinks finally signed formally with Boscobel Productions, this new agreement superseding the contract they had signed with Wace and Collins the previous autumn. Robert Wace and Grenville Collins would now take 40 per cent of the band's earnings, with Larry Page taking a further 10 per cent. Kassner were assigned all the music publishing rights. The Boscobel agreement was to last for the next five years, and the volatile mix of Wace, Collins, Kassner, Page, Pye, Talmy, Howes, and the band-members themselves, would cause problems down the road.

With bookings increasing and the distances between venues growing, Wace and Collins had splashed out on a decommissioned ambulance and converted it to carry the band and their equipment from gig to gig. Trips to Staffordshire, Wigan, Manchester and Birmingham were made and they were given a lunchtime slot at the prestigious Cavern Club in Liverpool. In front of a tough audience, the Londoners did well enough, playing a southern version of the native Merseybeat, to earn themselves further northern bookings.

After a dozen one-off dates during the rest of February and March, the first 'proper' Kinks tour was due to begin on 28 March. As was the vogue, they were to be part of a package of acts, with, on this occasion, The Dave Clark Five, The Hollies, Mark Wynter, The Trebletones and The Mojos.

Before setting out, the band headed back to Regent Sound Studios where they quickly recorded a trio of new demos that Ray had written. The titles – 'It's You', 'It's Alright' and 'You Really Got Me' – were all but indistinguishable from those of their previous recordings, but the music was shockingly different. Before anything could be done with these exciting new recordings, however, The Kinks were off on the road again.

The touring groups travelled together on buses, starting with Coventry and zig-zagged to Scarborough, Leicester, Cleethorpes, Carlisle and Newcastle-upon-Tyne in their first week alone. The Kinks were being paid £250 a week, but £100 of that went to Wace and Collins. While The Hollies and The Dave Clark Five had roadies, The Kinks had to do all of their own loading and unloading every night. By virtue of their television exposure, they were given the second slot in the show, appearing after The Mojos' opening act.

Dave Davies thrived on the travelling party atmosphere, and made friends with Graham Nash and Eric Haydock from The Hollies, but he wasn't a fan of The Dave Clark Five, who he found contrived. Hanging out backstage, he met up with Cilla Black, Sandie Shaw and The Searchers. Already he was living the rock and roll life that he had dreamed of but, musically, the band was yet to live up to its promise.

In the midst of the tour, Pye released 'You Still Want Me' as The Kinks second single. It flopped. Spectacularly. Scarcely reviewed (*Record Mirror* simply called it 'pounding stuff'), it failed to chart at all, even though Wace and Collins paid for an advert on the front page of the *New Musical Express*. As beat group The Mojos now had a single of their own in the charts – 'Everything's Alright' reached the top ten – and so they were promoted above The Kinks, who were relegated to the opening slot.

The Kinks' stage performances were so rough and ready that former Billy Fury road manager, the no-nonsense Hal Carter, was drafted in to sort them out. Carter had been warned by the label that the band had to be tidied up before the tour reached London or Pye would drop them, so he dragged them in for afternoon rehearsals and shouted out instructions about what to play, how to play and even where to stand. Dave Davies rebelled against Carter's instructions, seeing him as another has-been from the Larry Page era, but Ray listened. Never turn your back on the audience; keep the audience involved; don't talk amongst yourselves – these lessons hit home.

After they were described as looking like a gang of Dickensian characters, Wace and Collins tried to improve things further by purchasing new outfits for the band. They debuted the new look in Bournemouth, where The Kinks went on stage resplendent in red hunting jackets, frilly shirts and Chelsea boots. This would become the classic Kinks 'look'. Now they needed a sound to match it.

The song that would save The Kinks' career developed over the course of several months. Pye had agreed to release three singles, with an option to release more if they were successful, but if none of the three produced a hit, The Kinks' career was likely to be a very short one, as The Kalin Twins, Jerry Keller, Ricky Valance and B. Bumble and the Stingers could attest. There was a lot riding on the next record.

Allan Ballard would go on to have a famous career as a rock photographer, snapping classic images of The Kinks in hunting suits and riding on horseback, and much later taking iconic images of Adam and the Ants, Duran Duran and The Stray Cats. In the spring of 1964, he was an assistant to fashion photographer John Cowan, who was assigned to an early session with the group. Ballard and Cowan went to meet the band in Fortis Green. 'It was quite a small, pokey, Victorian terrace, a bit scruffy, and in the hallway they had an upright piano,' recalled Ballard. 'Ray sat down and plonked out, "Der-der, der, der-der!" He said, "What do you reckon to this?" It meant nothing to me at the time, but it ended up as "You Really Got Me".'

Ray also played the basic chords to Dave, initially thinking the song could be arranged as a more laid-back number. But after the younger brother heard it he immediately realised how powerful it would sound on an electric guitar. From the chords Ray tapped out on that beer-stained out-of-tune upright piano would emerge a genre-busting guitar tune that would break boundaries.

Early demos of 'You Really Got Me' had been discounted as being too 'bluesy', with Pye insisting on another pop R&B effort. When the tour finally wound its way to London on 2 May, The Kinks had grown in confidence, and started dropping 'You Really Got Me' into their short set. It was well received and these live performances revealed its raw energy.

Dave had been trying out some rudimentary customisation of his amp. He took a single-sided Gillette razor blade and sliced the cone all the way around, then plugged it in. He didn't know anything about electricity and got a terrible shock but, once made safe, the amp transformed his sound, producing a static-drenched crunch and the meanest power chords since Link Wray had first swaggered onto the airwaves with 'Rumble'. Dave later explained that it also gave him an emotional platform: this unruly, angry new sound gave body to all those simmering frustrations about his ruined relationship with Sue Sheehan.

The Kinks went in to record 'You Really Got Me' at Pye in June, although it would only see release at the cost of serious conflict with the label bosses.

Shel Talmy said, 'When I first heard it, I said, "Shit, it doesn't matter what you do with this, it's a number one song." It could have been done in waltz time and it would have been a hit.' It was the band who had their doubts, however. After hearing the playback of Talmy's production, they felt the producer had obscured the song's natural power, with Ray especially unhappy. 'It was a slower and much bluesier version, but it was an extremely good recording,' said Talmy. 'It would have gotten to number one.' But the band felt there was too much echo and that the guitar was buried too deep in the mix.

Ray hated it and wanted to record it again. Pye refused and Talmy, who was being charged for studio time, was understandably reluctant. Larry Page stepped in and asked Pye's Louis Benjamin to let the band try again, but having backed down on making the third single another R&B number, Benjamin stood his ground. At this point, Page pointed out that he was the song's publisher and issued a threat: he wouldn't let Talmy's recording be released. Pye and Benjamin countered by refusing to fund another session and the dispute looked like a stalemate. Ray also said that he would refuse to promote Talmy's version of the single, so Robert Wace and Grenville Collins were left to decide whether to let the band's Pye deal fizzle out or to fund a second session themselves. They chose the latter option and paid £200 (more than £3,000 in today's money) for the band to record 'You Really Got Me' again. For all the later acrimony between the band and their management, it was Page's backing and Wace and Collins' cold hard cash that set The Kinks on their way to stardom when they could so easily have slipped into obscurity.

If The Kinks were under pressure at the previous session, the stakes were even higher now, having forced their managers to pay for the session and fallen out with their label. This really was their last chance at a hit. The all-important session was booked at IBC Studios on Portland Place, with Talmy again producing; the four Kinks; and session drummer Bobby and pianist Arthur Greenslade performing alongside them. Mick Avory was relegated to tambourine.

Only two takes were needed. The lyric was really just about sex, and the music they produced that night sounded as insistent and raw as the act itself. Ray Davies sang like a man in the throes of passion, too. They knew from playing the song live what the looks on the teenage audience's faces meant when they danced to it, and managed to distil that sexual urgency to just over two minutes of tape.

Like all the great songs in rock history, 'You Really Got Me' announces its intentions within its first seconds. Dave Davies' repetitive five-note riff seems to spell out the five syllables of you-real-ly-got-me, you-real-ly-got-me twice before there's a snap of Bobby Graham's drums and Ray enters to tell the subject of the song of his overwhelming lust – that he 'can't sleep at night'. This is what the teenage girls at their gigs wanted their boyfriends to tell them, and this is what the boys wanted to feel. At each pass, the tension is ratcheted up a notch, first by the added background vocals and then by Ray's increasingly frantic singing. After the first chorus the singer regains his composure only for the tension to immediately start rising again. And this is all within the first forty-five seconds. By the end of the second chorus, when he screams 'Oh, no!', every listener knows exactly what he means.

'I made a conscious effort to make my voice sound pure and I sang the words as clearly as the music would allow,' said Ray Davies. 'Those thumping chords started playing down my headphones and in the first row of my imaginary audience I saw a girl. Every emotion I had was focused on that one image and nobody could deny me this moment.'

Another 'hook' is Dave Davies' short, stinging guitar solo, which is so good that he has spent the past decades fending off suggestions that he didn't play it. He did.

The whole single was over in just two minutes and eighteen seconds. Finally, Ray had recorded a song on tape in the way he had imagined it in his head. 'I was floundering around trying to find an identity,' he explained. 'It was in 1964 that I managed to do that, to be able to justify myself and say, "I exist, I'm here". I was literally born when that song hit.'

With The Beatles

By July 1964, Beatlemania had reached such a scale that The Beatles were starring in their own feature film, *A Hard Day's Night*, which made a profit of more than £2 million (roughly equivalent to £30 million today). They had even conquered the USA, the birthplace of the R&B sound they'd made their own, earlier that same year. Their work rate was amazing: they were about to start work on their second album of the year, *Beatles For Sale*, and seemed to be constantly on tour or on the television. The Kinks, on the other hand, had recorded what they desperately hoped would be their breakthrough single and so existed on the opposite side of a gulf from the world's biggest band. Nonetheless, on 2 August, the two groups came face to face, at the Gaumont Cinema in Bournemouth.

While it was a great opportunity to be on the same bill, not many bands were brave enough to play right before The Beatles, but The Kinks were expected to do just that, as they were scheduled to open the second half of the show. The Beatles arrived just as The Kinks were about to go on and, while the Londoners nervously fiddled with their equipment, John Lennon and Paul McCartney wandered onto the stage and peeked out through the closed curtains at the massed ranks of screaming Beatles fans. There was some chat and banter between the bands, and Lennon cheekily suggested to Ray Davies that if The Kinks ran out of songs, they could borrow some of his.

As the moment of the performance drew closer, Lennon was still on the stage, causing Ray some anxiety. Reminiscing about the evening in his book *X-Ray*, he says that he told the Beatle, 'It's our turn. You're on after us.' Lennon cut him down to size: 'With The Beatles, laddie, nobody gets a turn. You're just there to keep the crowd occupied until we go on.' Discussing the gig years later, Ray would say that The Kinks were acting like upstarts and seemed to bear no grudge for this needling.

During the 1960s, many pop and rock fans fell into one of two camps — Beatles or Stones. Ray Davies could see both sides of the argument.

> I like them both for different reasons. I liked The Beatles because their tunes were nice. They were very tight and I liked their records, which surprised me because I didn't think I would. But I'm closer to the Stones because I used to play in blues bands in England so maybe I'm a bit closer to them, in a geographic sense, than The Beatles. I think the Stones were more honest than The Beatles. Maybe that's what gives them the edge. Paul McCartney was one of the most competitive people I've ever met. Lennon wasn't. He just thought everyone else was shit.

In the case of The Kinks, Lennon would be forced to change his opinion of the unknown Londoners quickly. Though the audience began by screaming for The Beatles, they were won over when Dave Davies cranked out the opening chords of 'You Really Got Me'. He dashed around the stage throttling his guitar and, at least for a while, The Beatles were forgotten. 'Later I watched The Beatles play from the wings and actually heard some fans screaming "We want The Kinks",' said Ray.

'There was a six-month period when we were bigger than any

of those bands,' recalled Ray Davies, referring to The Beatles and The Rolling Stones, amongst others. 'We had three straight number ones in 1964.' Officially, 'All Day and All of the Night' only reached number two, although it did top some singles charts and, technicalities aside, it was a remarkable time for The Kinks.

Early comments on the new single were favourable and it seemed likely to be a hit. To prepare for the anticipated media attention, Wace and Collins enlisted the help of The Beatles' press man Brian Sommerville. Sommerville had previously worked on Fleet Street and fitted perfectly alongside Wace and Collins. His heavy-rimmed glasses, comb-over haircut and three-piece suit made him look more like a stockbroker than the rock and roll public relations men who would rise to notoriety as the decade wore on. In *Kink*, Dave Davies remembered Sommerville unkindly as 'an overfed politician' with an 'anxious, sweaty brow'. Nonetheless, he knew his stuff, and would become a lightning rod for the managers, the band and especially Ray.

Connections with the press were never more important than around the release of The Kinks' last-chance single, 'You Really Got Me', on 4 August 1964. It was backed by 'It's Alright', a harmonica-led romp with gang-style vocals and a laconic Ray Davies lead, and started out with favourable reviews on the TV shows, *Juke Box Jury* and *Thank Your Lucky Stars*. In the press the song was labelled a hit by *Record Mirror*, which hailed it as a 'a Top 50 Tip, it's a "riot raiser"', and in *Melody Maker*, it was reviewed by 'Crying Game' singer Dave Berry, who impressed Ray by observing that The Kinks sounded like a band who recorded exactly what they wanted to.

The first published interview with Ray, albeit an extremely short one, came in mid-August, in the *Record Mirror*, with 'You Really Got Me' well on its way up the charts. On Peter Jones's *New Faces* page, under the headline THEY LIVENED UP THE CHAMPAGNE CIRCUIT, Jones gave a brief run through of the band's story so far, ending with 'They deserve to get a hit on the strength of their name alone!'

One of the first full-band interviews appeared on 4 September in the *New Musical Express*. The band members had to pick their favourite acts and songs: Dave Davies chose 'You Really Got Me' and the Kingsmen's 'Louie Louie'; Mick Avory added Inez Foxx's 'Mockingbird' and The Beach Boys; Ray selected Joan Baez and 'Train and the River' by Jimmy Guiffre; and Pete Quaife chose The Beatles and Dionne Warwick. Together, they added tracks by Slim Harpo and Chet Atkins.

As the single ascended the charts, the band spent the late summer playing numerous gigs around the north of England. These had been booked before 'You Really Got Me' took off and couldn't be avoided, meaning that higher-profile shows in the capital would have to wait. As it happened, this was extremely convenient for Ray Davies.

In May, after a performance at the Esquire Club in Sheffield, Ray had met Rasa Didzpetris, a petite, blonde 17-year-old girl whose parents were Lithuanian refugees. A friend had dragged her along to the show and, afterwards, Rasa and Ray really hit it off. She was still attending a convent school, which made their early courtship difficult, but the band's gigs in the North allowed them to meet up during the school summer holidays, just as 'You Really Got Me' entered the top ten.

The Kinks' third single had been released in August and, by the middle of September, it had reached the very top of the charts. The song sat proudly atop the *New Musical Express* top thirty ahead of The Honeycombs' 'Have I the Right', 'I'm Into Something Good' by Herman's Hermits, and The Supremes' 'Where Did Our Love Go'. They had cut it fine but they had made it, and Pye were willing, for now, to keep backing them.

To understand their achievement, it's important to appreciate that this was a time when the charts comprised one legendary single after another: The Beatles' 'A Hard Day's Night', The Beach Boys' 'I Get Around' and Roy Orbison's 'Oh, Pretty Woman' were just some of those loitering in the lower reaches.

The Kinks' success prompted Louis Benjamin to call the band in to Pye to congratulate them, and a photo of him shaking hands with a decidedly sceptical-looking Ray Davies was published in the *Record Mirror*.

Not only did 'You Really Got Me' top the charts, but it also proved extraordinarily influential on bands of the time. In 1964, although Merseybeat was in vogue and being pushed heavily by the record labels, with 'You Really Got Me', Ray Davies was turning back towards the earlier influence of the American blues. Rather than try to emulate the feel of his sources, however, he sought to integrate elements of it into his own sound. The shift between keys lifted the twelve-bar blues into something genuinely new, and this mix of American blues with a European flavour enjoyed a rapid and wide appeal. In Memphis, Tennessee, Chris Bell (a future member of Big Star) and Bill Cunningham (a future member of the Box Tops) formed a band called The Jynx in The Kinks' honour. John Entwistle and Pete Townshend of The Who heard the song at Keith Richards' mother's house and went straight home to try and play it, the result becoming the main riff of 'I Can't Explain'. In Florida, a 14-year-old named Tom Petty also found himself inspired by 'You Really Got Me'. 'I heard that song for the first time at a dance,' he said. 'The DJ played it really loud and the whole room went still. Then everyone erupted in applause – for a record. That guitar break – I'd never heard anything that wild in my life.'

In later years, the song is variously said to have given birth to punk, heavy rock, metal and grunge, among other genres and sub-genres. In a Q magazine special edition, *100 Songs that Changed the World*, published in 2003, 'You Really Got Me' was named the fifteenth most important song of all time, behind the likes of 'Rock Around the Clock', 'Do They Know it's Christmas', 'Good Vibrations' and Elvis Presley's debut, 'That's All Right'.

'We just knew we were going to make a great record,' said Ray Davies. 'I was hyper-aware. But not just for those two minutes. I was going through a very aware stage. I was aware of everything being right. Of making the right call, being lucky and knowing it, riding it.' It wasn't quite Beatlemania, but The Kinks were creating quite an unmistakable stir, and beginning to feel both the thrill and inconvenience of fame.

In September, the band were playing a show in Bradford, and Ray arranged to meet Rasa in a nearby park when she got out of school. News of The Kinks' frontman arriving in town spread through the school and, when he got there, he found himself mobbed by fans. Mother Superior was not amused and Rasa was expelled from school. Undeterred in her affections, Rasa spent time that autumn at her sister's flat in London so she could meet up with Ray, and when The Kinks played up north the couple would stay at her parents' house, where the family spoke Lithuanian. She and Ray enjoyed long walks along the Thames when Ray had any free time, but that came less often as the band became more in demand.

As soon as 'You Really Got Me' had started climbing the UK and US charts a month apart (it finally reached the US top ten on Reprise Records), Pye asked Ray to pen a follow up. They made it clear that they didn't want a stop-gap single but a second hit. He was also required to write an album's worth of material to go with it. The band was given only four days of studio time to record a further ten songs for the record, and Ray had barely anything written. Partly because of the workload, he told the label that he wanted to include some cover versions, as he still saw The Kinks as primarily a covers band. Indeed, he was yet to recognise or accept his future as a songwriter. At that time it was a role that was being forced upon him by sudden success, just as the role of lead singer had fallen on him by necessity. Fortunately, Pye agreed that a mixture of cover versions would help fill the album, providing material with which record buyers would be familiar. Albums of entirely original material were still a few years away and the industry was very much singles-led.

Shel Talmy was under contract to produce for three years and so reprised his role behind the desk when the band came in to record their debut album. 'Once "You Really Got Me" was a hit everything changed and I wasn't charged for the studio time,' he said. His first job was to help the band decide which material to use: '[We picked] things that me or Ray or the band knew and thought would be fun.'

Two Chuck Berry numbers were chosen, 'Beautiful Delilah' and 'Too Much Monkey Business', alongside 'Long Tall Shorty', 'I'm a Lover Not a Fighter' and live favourite 'Got Love If You Want It'. Talmy also picked out a couple of traditional songs, 'Bald Headed

Woman' and 'I've Been Driving On Bald Mountain', which he arranged. In all, the fourteen-track album would feature only six numbers by Ray Davies, most of which had been recorded earlier. The most impressive new composition was 'Stop Your Sobbing', which had a new, chiming guitar sound and lyrics which, unlike the last two singles, were something other than an admission of lust. It was supposedly inspired by an old girlfriend who broke down in tears when she saw how famous Ray had become, worried that fame would ruin him, and it offers proof, if any were needed, that he was fast becoming a skilful writer.

With the songs chosen, the rest was done pretty quickly. 'I did some of my own engineering and mixing,' said Talmy. 'Mixing was super fast, we only had three tracks, so it was just a few tweaks and maybe a few studio tricks that I'd picked up to make something sound louder.' Session musicians were again drafted in. Bobby Graham provided drums for eight songs; Jon Lord (later of Deep Purple) added organ; and Perry Ford played piano. A pre-Led Zeppelin Jimmy Page, then a precocious session guitarist, provided twelve-string acoustic guitar for two or three songs. Even Rasa got to sing, on 'Stop Your Sobbing'.

'Pete Quaife was my favourite guy in the band,' said Talmy. 'He was the only one that I truly had any rapport with. Dave didn't say much. He and Ray would get into fights and I'd take a break and let them fight it out. Mick Avory didn't come till later [in fact he played on six songs] and I never really got to know him very well.'

This distance between Talmy and Avory may have been a product of the drummer's modest contribution to the album. 'Mick was our drummer and it was a great surprise to us to find that he was not allowed to play on most of the early recordings,' said Pete Quaife. 'In those days it was customary for the producer to use his own choice of drummer. The explanation was that "drumming and drums are hard to record and the producer always chooses the drummer that sounds right to him."'

There are differing accounts of Ray's relationship with the producer. For his part Talmy is clear: 'Ray, I think it's fair to say, probably resented the fact that there was a producer from day one. He thought he could do it better, but he was stuck with me.'

Davies, however, has described the situation more amicably. 'I got on well with him [Shel] 'cause he's a good-feeling guy that you like to have around,' said Ray Davies of the first album sessions. 'The only phrase I remember him saying to me was, "Oh shit, no one will notice."'

Pye gave the band an occasional slot to practise at the studios. Robert Wace would often drop by to see how things were going, but Grenville Collins tended to stay in the background. 'They found the band and got them to the right place but apart from that they had little involvement in the music,' said Talmy.

The Kinks were kept busy with promotional duties throughout September, including a flight up to Manchester to appear on *Top of the Pops*. It was Ray Davies' first time on a plane: 'We were in a 707 and when it roared and took off I broke out in a cold sweat. I was so terrified I forgot to be nervous about the show.' In all they played more than twenty shows that month. Many of the crowds were hysterical, some almost to the point of rioting. In Newcastle, a gig was abandoned after only three songs, when the crowd surged onto the stage and more than a hundred girls fainted. The performances were exhausting and the journeys in between no less so: four nights later, driving home from a show in Rochdale in a brand new car, the band, with Rasa crammed in as well, had a collision with a truck, though no one was seriously injured.

Amidst all of this frenetic activity, the band were called back in by Pye to record a stand-alone single. Talmy described the selection process: 'Ray used to come in and play me the stuff on piano, or guitar, and, we'd go through the songs and decide which ones to use and then talk about arrangements.' Ray, however, still believed that his songwriting would be short lived and when he did write, he aimed to capture the sound that he and Dave had created in Fortis Green. He managed this with unforgettable success in The Kinks' next song, 'All Day and All of the Night', but, before that musical milestone was unleashed, the band's debut album was released, on 2 October 1964.

Simply titled *Kinks*, with a band portrait on the cover and a large 'K' on the back, the record came in at thirty-two minutes. The first song on the debut album was sung by Dave, doing his best Chuck

Berry impersonation, but most of the first side struggled to rise above the level of a derivative Merseybeat combo until 'You Really Got Me' closed proceedings. Side two opened with the high-speed 'Cadillac' and included more Chuck Berry, and the instrumental 'Revenge', sandwiched by the twin traditional songs 'Bald Headed Woman' and 'I've Been Driving on Bald Mountain'. Towards its end, the album showed more promise with the new 'Stop Your Sobbing' and the last track, a polished rendition of 'Got Love If You Want It'.

Record Mirror gave the new album a half page of coverage with Norman Jopling exclaiming, HOT NEW KINKS LP! and calling it 'one of the most authentic British R&B albums I've heard to date'.

As *Kink* hit the shops, the band headed out on tour with Billy J. Kramer, supported by Cliff Bennett and the Rebel Rousers, and The Yardbirds, among others. Their schedule showed no signs of slowing – more than twenty shows were packed into October.

'A few months ago we thought we were a closely knit unit,' said Ray Davies at the time. 'We realise now that we weren't. If one of us had left we wouldn't have broken up. It's different now. We've got a sound and we're successful. The group couldn't go on if any changes were made. When I walk on stage and see rows and rows of people who have paid to come in and see us, it makes me work very hard for them. That's the precise moment every night that makes me determined to give a good show.'

In late October, at the end of the tour, 'All Day and All of The Night' was released as the follow-up to 'You Really Got Me', amidst great expectations. Following up a number one single ensured much press coverage. CAN THE KINKS HIT JACKPOT? asked *Pop Weekly*. Answering their own question, it appeared the answer was 'yes': 'They seem to take every number and manage to get something different. The Kinks, anyway, will in my opinion hit a fortune whether they hit in America or only in Great Britain. They don't have to be great singers if they can produce a distinctive style.'

And that style was much in evidence. Another crunching guitar riff from Dave Davies, another understated vocal from Ray, and another tension-building verse that exploded in the chorus; the formula was perfect, and the band topped charts again, as well as reaching the US top ten.

The need for new product was never ending: a US version of the album, three songs shorter than the UK version and retitled *You Really Got Me*, was released in late November and, in the UK, a new EP, *Kinksize Session*, led by a cover of 'Louie Louie', topped the UK EP charts. Ray wasn't proud of these efforts. Having been rushed to write three new songs, he finally penned the lyric to 'Things Are Getting Better' in the pub during a lunch break. 'The whole EP was pretty dreadful,' he said. 'That's the sort of thing we shouldn't have done.'

It had been a hectic three months, from the uncertainty and near failure of the summer to vindication and trans-Atlantic success before the year was out. Dave Davies took particular delight in their achievements. He liked being recognised in clubs and in the street, and already had more money than he had ever dreamed of. In *Kink* he admitted to getting involved with drugs around this time, namely 'purple hearts' and amphetamines. There were new girls every night and he enjoyed the company of as many of them as he could. Eager to enjoy his newfound freedom to the full, he moved out of the family home to nearby Connaught Gardens.

Around the same time, Grenville Collins and Robert Wace moved their Boscobel operations to Kingly Street, parallel to Carnaby Street, the evolving epicentre of London fashion. Wace opened a clothes boutique in Soho and more were planned for Carnaby Street. Not long after he had a visit from an insurance agent saying other shops in the area had taken out 'special' insurance and left a card bearing the name Kray Enterprises. A few weeks later, the shop was smashed up and Wace closed it down.

For Mick Avory it had also been a life-changing year. 'I'd gone from £9 a week delivering paraffin,' he said. 'It was a real turnaround, I was thrown in the deep end and didn't really know what was going on.'

Another package tour took up a large stretch of the autumn, ending in December. 'I really enjoyed that tour with Gerry and the Pacemakers and Gene Pitney,' said Avory. 'We were really confined to the theatre, two shows a night, and if you went outside you'd get ripped to pieces, so we got to know the other acts by sitting around inside a lot of the time. It was a really diverse line-up, with people like [Motown drummer] Earl van Dyke and [soul singer] Kim Weston. The other drummers would share tips and I'd learn from them. Uriel Jones was part of the whole Tamla Motown scene and he used to tell me, "You just need to practise some bar fills. Do a bar and a half then do two bars and do variations on what you know is two bars until you get the feel of the structure of the music, rather than just playing rhythms."'

The tour ended in Oxford on Friday, 11 December, and Ray immediately headed north to Bradford after the show. In typical fashion, when everyone was expecting him, like Dave, to go wild and enjoy being a pop star to its fullest extent, Ray did the exact opposite: he got married.

Rasa was pregnant when they tied the knot at St. Joseph's Church in Bradford on 12 December. Brian Sommerville, Robert Wace, Grenville Collins, Larry Page and Dave were in attendance, as well as hundreds of screaming fans outside who had earlier been alerted to the marriage when the couple's banns had been read out. Mick Avory and Pete Quaife were not invited. The wedding reception took place at the bride's family house, a small terraced affair much like the one in which Ray had grown up. Dave was the best man, but he was upstairs having sex with one of the guests while he was supposed to be giving his speech. His sister, Peggy, caught him in the act, much to the displeasure of Rasa's family.

The newlyweds moved into a flat just a few hundred yards from the Davies' family home on Fortis Green. As The Kinks were about to hit the big time, and London was poised to explode as the most exciting city on the planet, 20-year-old Ray Davies was settling down.

New Equipment Needed

'You Really Got Me' would go on to sell a million copies and, in the coming months, The Kinks would have a record in the British top fifty for fifty-four out of fifty-six weeks, putting them firmly in the first rank of British bands.

One of the last things they had done in 1964 was visit Shepperton Studios, where they filmed performances to be broadcast on *Shindig!*, the most important American music television show of the day. Broadcast on the ABC network on 20 January 1965, live (not mimed) performances of 'You Really Got Me' and 'All Day and All of the Night' announced the band's arrival into the homes of mainstream America.

A US tour was being arranged for later in the year but, first, The Kinks set off for the Far East and Australia, and the first major tour of their lives, which, apart from a very brief trip to France, was also the first time any of them had left the UK. It was also further than The Beatles had travelled – the Fab Four never played live in Australia. Flying out from Heathrow on 16 January, Ray left behind his new wife of only five weeks and also Shel Talmy, who was working with a new band called The Who, whose debut single 'I Can't Explain' was influenced by The Kinks' vibe and sound.

Travelling first class was a new experience for all. They stopped over in India during the trip and the single night they spent in Bombay was, according to Ray in *X-Ray*, one of the most memorable nights of his life. Unable to sleep, he went down alone to the beach where he could hear the chanting of the working fishermen as the sun rose. It was a sound he was determined to incorporate into his songwriting.

Ray was already experimenting with new musical directions, as was made clear on the new single 'Tired of Waiting for You', which was busy climbing up the UK charts. It had been recorded back in August 1964, but Talmy had wisely suggested they hold it back from the album and release it separately at a later date. Talmy and The Kinks were of a similar age and Dave Davies later joked that neither the producer nor the band knew what they were doing in the early days, but, at the very least, the shrewdness of this decision suggests an intuitive feel for the group's future development. Not only did 'Tired of Waiting For You' keep The Kinks at the top of the charts and in the public eye, it proved they were something other than a one-trick pony. The song was a vast departure from the previous two hit singles. Instead of driving guitar riffs and lyrical tension, it presented a gently rolling guitar sound and understated vocals; this was a song of longing rather than lust, resignedly imploring the object of the singer's affection, 'It's your life and you can do what you want'.

The Kinks' tour opened in Perth, the western capital of Australia, to a generous reception in a stifling 50°C heat. 'At the end of the show they stood up and clapped, a sort of special thank you, and we felt quite moved,' said Dave. 'When we got back to the dressing room we were very quiet, each scared to say how he felt in case he sounded soft.'

They moved swiftly on to Adelaide, in the south. This was the show that the Davies brothers had most been looking forward to, as their sister Rose had settled there the previous year. The blue skies were what impressed Dave the most on first arrival. Coming from cold, grey London to a country bursting with colour proved an almost magical experience for the 20-year-old. He visited Rose with Ray and wrote about the experience for *Rave* magazine. 'Despite the glorious climate and friendly people, it is lonely here sometimes,' said Rose. 'There is no running around to Mum's to borrow a packet of tea, or having my little brothers drop in. Sometimes it rains; when it does I get really homesick. Looking back it seems it rained all my life in England.'

Ray and Dave were pleased to see that Rose, Arthur and Terry had done well in Australia and lived in a nice detached house. They talked long into the night about the old days and Rose pulled out an old tape recorder to play back some of Ray's earliest experiments on the piano. She was shocked to be told that one of the simple tunes she had on tape was the basis for 'Tired of Waiting for You'.

The tour saw The Kinks play venues holding between 2,000 and 6,000, and full houses in Melbourne (where the band was showered with wild heather), Brisbane and Sydney. The Rolling Stones were in Australia at the same time and seemed almost to follow The Kinks around the country. 'One night in a Brisbane hotel Pete Quaife and I were in Mick Jagger's room talking about music,' said Dave Davies. 'Mick never gave much away; he always seemed to be on his guard . . . there was an obvious rivalry between the Stones and The Kinks, and Mick especially appeared a bit wary of us.'

From Australia, The Kinks went on to New Zealand, Hong Kong and Singapore, where Ray received a call to say that 'Tired of Waiting for You' had topped the charts. Alone in his hotel room, he called room service and ordered a bottle of champagne for himself.

They travelled home via New York, where a three-night stopover was just long enough for the band to record a couple of lip-synched performances for the *Hullabaloo* TV show on NBC. The rest of their time in the US was taken up being rushed between radio DJs by representatives of Reprise, their American label.

The band landed back at Heathrow on Sunday, 14 February, and had to be in Pye's Studio Two first thing the following morning – they had been given just three days to record their second album.

Pete Quaife enjoyed the overseas touring but he was also happy to be back home under grey English skies. More outgoing than Ray, but reserved compared with Dave, Quaife's contribution to The

Kinks was more than musical. '[Pete] liked meeting people and he was a bit cheeky,' wrote Dave. 'He always seemed to know what to say. Pete was a diplomat, he was more charming and he was the glue between me and Ray.' And, of all the band members, Quaife was the most interested in fashion, even though Dave often courted attention by dressing outrageously.

Quaife immersed himself in the mod movement and would go about everywhere in his green fish-tail parka. The mods reached a peak in the mid-1960s, infiltrating fashion, music and film. They gave working-class men the opportunity to dress in smart suits and aspire to a middle-class lifestyle, while appreciating a range of music from ska to soul to R&B. Along with the trim suits and parkas, the scooter was one of the mods' most iconic symbols. When The Kinks played locally, Pete Quaife liked to travel to shows on his own new Vespa scooter, stopping at mod cafés along the way. Often he arrived with his face dirty black from exhaust fumes, peeling off the parka to reveal the hunting jacket and frilly shirt underneath.

At shows in the London area, Quaife would get support from his whole family. 'Everyone would be there,' said David Quaife. 'Grandmother, granddad, uncles, aunts, and everybody watching, it was fantastic. Nanny Kilby, from my mother's side, enjoyed it so much she was promptly sick on the way out, she was well into her seventies!'

If Pete Quaife was taking fame in his stride, Mick Avory felt like he was caught up in a whirlwind and Dave Davies, the youngest member of the group, just went wild. Perhaps unsurprisingly, the pensive and sensitive Ray felt as if the weight of the world had descended on his shoulders. The only band member to be married, he was also about to become a father. He was still The Kinks' lead singer, a job he had never really wanted and which made him the reluctant focal point of most of their fans and the media's attention. And, of course, he was now the principal song writer, and felt under mounting pressure to keep churning out hits. In both his personal and professional lives, a lot of people were depending on him. He wrote in *X-Ray* of 'a feeling of dread' thinking about the baby that Rasa was carrying: 'Suddenly part of me belonged to somebody else. I felt both elated and cheated. While Rasa slept I watched her and wondered why she was there.'

For the new album, which commenced recording on 15 February 1965, Ray had written ten new songs which would be supplemented this time by only two cover versions, 'Dancing in the Street' and 'Naggin' Woman'.

In the safety of the couple's small flat at the Muswell Hill Broadway end of Fortis Green, Rasa would be the first person to whom Ray played his new songs on his piano. When the band headed into Pye for the new recordings, it seemed only natural that she should accompany him and even end up providing backing vocals on four tracks. Although this sat uneasily with some of the other Kinks, Pete Quaife in particular, as long as Ray wanted her there, she would stay.

Such was the turnaround of albums in the mid-sixties, the sessions were completed on 18 February, and the record was in the shops less than three weeks later. Few bands are capable of sustaining high quality across an entire album and, back then, when the industry's chief output and focus remained the 7 inch, albums were simply made too quickly, the best songs omitted, reserved to be released as singles. The Kinks' second album was titled *Kinda Kinks* and, compared with their singles output of the time, pales into insignificance.

Dave Davies had been working on songs with Ray in the front room at Fortis Green, which resulted in a co-writing credit for 'Got My Feet on the Ground'. He also took over lead vocal duties on three songs. 'Naggin' Woman' was a traditional blues take and 'Come On Now' was an upbeat rocker. 'Nothin' in the World (Can Stop Me Worryin' 'Bout That Girl)', however, showed a new dimension to Ray Davies' writing, being a blues-influenced, finger-picking song, indicative of a folk movement that had yet to take hold in the British charts. 'Tired of Waiting For You' closed side one on a high, but 'Dancing in the Street' opened side two with a corresponding low. While it was admirable that the band were trying numerous musical styles on the album, this cover of the famous Martha Reeves and the Vandellas hit was misguided: sludgy and clumsy, it was little more than low-quality filler, and would never have made it onto the band's later albums when LPs came to be seen as complete works.

Despite the patchy nature of the album, it reached number three in the UK charts, and then The Kinks were sent out on the road again. It was a hard schedule, and cracks were starting to show. In mid-March, there were rumours of the band breaking up. Ray and Pete spent time explaining to the press that it wasn't true, although Pete did let on that there had been a punch-up in America on the way home from Australia. 'As far as we were concerned it was a right old laugh,' Pete Quaife told *Disc Weekly*. 'But everybody there thought it was for real. It just didn't mean anything. It was a blow-up for five minutes and then it was over.'

The next single, the jaunty 'Ev'rybody's Gonna be Happy', was also a relative failure. It only scraped to number twenty in the UK and did even worse in the States, where it only just managed to get into the top forty before dropping away.

Shows around this time were fraught and the band often got bruised, buffeted and had their clothes torn off by hysterical fans. At one gig in Stirling, Ray collapsed from exhaustion; Dave then came down with bronchitis and several dates were cancelled. During this hiatus, Pete passed out on a trip to the cinema, collapsed and gave himself concussion. With only Mick Avory being fit and well, various valuable television and radio performances also had to be cancelled. But, rather than take an extended rest to recover, The Kinks instead flew off to Denmark on 8 April for a busy weekend of shows. They were due to return to London for the *New Musical Express* Poll Winners' Party at the Empire Pool (later known as Wembley Arena) on Sunday, 11 April. This insane schedule would prove to be a terrible mistake.

The Kinks landed in Copenhagen on Thursday morning, held a brief press conference and then headed to Nykøbing for that night's show. The gig was well received and passed without any incident. The band returned to the Danish capital for their Friday night show at the Tivoli Gardens. Among the eight bands playing that night, The Kinks were the headliners and, of the others, only The Honeycombs had tasted any success. Compared with what they'd grown used to in Britain and on their tour of Australia, the band found the audience far from wild, until, mid-way through their set, some girls ran down to the stage. The police overreacted: around forty riot officers, with batons drawn, rushed into the auditorium and instructed the band to stop playing. The promoter pulled the group off stage and fights broke out between the two thousand strong crowd and the police. The theatre was trashed in the ensuing riot. Once the place had been cleared, the band were led out, and were unable to believe the scale of the devastation. Seats had been ripped out, mirrors smashed and ornate furniture had been destroyed. 'We were innocent bystanders really,' said Ray. 'The kids broke up the auditorium and we got the blame.'

Things got worse once The Kinks returned to their hotel. A clearly drunken Dave smashed a mirror in the hotel bar with a bottle and then got into a scuffle with a member of staff. The police arrived and he was whisked away for a night in jail, despite the protests of Grenville Collins. The next morning he was bailed and joined the band for a press conference. Although the night's second show at the Tivoli had been postponed it was the police, not The Kinks, who were widely blamed for causing the riot by the local newspapers. And if their trip to Copenhagen had turned out to be a dismal failure professionally, for Dave Davies and Peter Quaife, at least, there was to be a personal silver lining: it was here that they met two local girls who they would later marry – Lisbet Thorkil-Petersen and Beden Paustien. More immediately, though, The Kinks had to board a plane back to London, where they would arrive late for their slot at the *New Musical Express* Poll Winners' Party.

Broadcast for television by ITV, the Poll Winners' Party was a large, high-profile event with more than twenty acts performing in front of ten thousand fans – hosted by Jimmy Savile, Cathy McGowan and Keith Fordyce. The lead acts in 1965 included The Beatles, The Rolling Stones, Herman's Hermits, The Searchers and The Animals. The Beatles were scheduled to close the show but The Kinks' late arrival from Denmark meant the rival foursome would go on last. Tired and on edge, The Kinks were in no state to produce a great performance and, when Ray found out The Rolling Stones had won best new band, his mood turned to fury. As the Stones had performed at the show twelve months earlier, he couldn't understand how they counted as a 'new' band. 'I felt this was a total deception,' Ray wrote in *X-Ray*. 'Tantamount to a slap in the face from the music business. From that day on, I re-named the *New Musical Express* "The Enemy".'

The Beatles gave a masterful performance and debuted their new single, 'Ticket To Ride'. In their wake, The Kinks stumbled badly. They sounded bad and played poorly on one of the biggest stages of their career to date. Afterwards, John Lennon quipped to Grenville Collins: 'That's for Bournemouth!'

Ray had reached breaking point. The next day he was supposed to travel down to Southampton with the band for a television recording, but refused to go. 'I sat down and said, "I can't do this anymore."' he recalled 'I said, "I won't stand for this shit anymore. I don't want to do it. I've just had enough of doing publicity."' It wasn't just the constant travel or the questioning from interviewers – his answers were being pulled apart, too. He had made an off-the-cuff remark that he could sing 'You Really Got Me' better than Frank Sinatra. So, of course, someone piped up with, 'Who is this guy who thinks he can sing better than Sinatra?'

'I'd had all the praise for the first three records and I was getting the backlash,' said Ray. Brian Sommerville tried to give him a pep talk, saying that he had either to be in show business or out of it. 'I said I wanted to be out of it,' Ray told *Q* magazine in 1989. 'I didn't do press for a long time, and maybe that's why I've had a mixed reception; press people think I'm difficult.'

Ray was happiest back in the studio, away from marriage about which he was already having second thoughts, and safe from the mauling fans and hounding press pack. At Pye, in June, the band put down versions of new songs such as 'Set Me Free' and the Indian-flavoured 'See My Friends'. The latter showed The Kinks experimenting with and expressing Eastern influences at an earlier stage than their contemporaries. The Beatles' 'Norwegian Wood' is now famous for featuring George Harrison playing sitar, but wasn't recorded until October 1965.

*

Because of their chart successes, The Kinks were given the headline spot on the next package tour. This time, they were joined by Mickey Finn, The Yardbirds, The Riot Squad, Val Mckenna and the American all-girl group Goldie and the Gingerbreads. The latter had experienced some chart success with 'Can't You Hear My Heartbeat' and had previously opened for the Stones, so they knew their way around the UK circuit. 'We were a good band for the "hot seat",' said lead singer, Genya Ravan. 'That's a position on the bill that is usually the hardest, because it's right before the headliner and we always managed to keep the audience from getting too rowdy.'

There were very few girl bands around at the time and it is unsurprising that The Gingerbreads attracted a lot of attention. 'I know that the drummers kept an eye on Ginger all the time,' said Ravan. 'Not only because she had a great foot, but she was beautiful.' But there were few allowances made for gender and Ravan found the touring hard work, with seventeen gigs played over nineteen days. 'It was very draining, particularly for us girls, but it was hard on the guys as well I'm sure. The thing is, we did like our showers and sometimes that was impossible.' The travelling between venues was especially gruelling, although leavened by the camaraderie created by the bands' shared conditions: 'We watched the driver all night, so he wouldn't fall asleep, and we took turns to entertain him with jokes and sometimes we would even flash trucks passing by just to keep him laughing. The atmosphere was great, they always wanted to hear more about the States.'

The tour started in Slough and wound its way through the Home Counties and the Midlands, before heading down to Taunton in the West Country on 18 May. There had always been an underly-ing aggression and friction within The Kinks and, although it was one of several factors that gave the band their energy, it also held them back from even greater fame and fortune. Throughout the sixties, when they were almost constantly on tour or recording in the studio, they were four young men variously enjoying or strug-gling with the fame and adulation, often cooped up together all day, every day. Such pressurised proximity was a recipe for egos to clash. Fist-fights broke out during practice sessions and even mid-concert, and not just between the volatile Davies brothers: Dave Davies and Mick Avory came to blows more than once.

After the show in Taunton, Dave was in high spirits and asked Mick to give his opinion on some long-forgotten debate. Mick did not have an opinion and didn't want to get involved. Dave wouldn't let it go and kept on at the drummer until the confrontation turned physical. This time Avory got the better of the guitarist — after the band's managers broke up the fight, Dave was left with a pair of black eyes.

The next show was in Cardiff, where Dave took to the stage wearing sunglasses to hide his shiners, but his anger was still simmering away. What happened next has gone down in rock lore. Mid-show, Dave told Avory that he would sound better if he played the drums 'with his cock', and then kicked over the drums. Avory retaliated by smashing Dave over the head with a drum pedal, sending the younger Davies brother down onto the stage. The big drummer panicked when he saw Dave laying there motionless and ran right out of the theatre, disappearing into the Welsh night with his frilly shirt and hunting jacket flapping about him.

At the time, The Kinks' closest ally in the press was Keith Altham from the *New Musical Express*.

We got on well when I talked to them, and they were always very chatty and we built a relationship . . . What happened on the *NME* in those days was you became like 'The Kinks person', or 'The Rolling Stones person' and you stayed with that band, which was good in some ways and not so good in others. Andy Gray, this old Canadian journalist, would come in at the beginning of the week and read out the charts, and you had to go out and do an interview based on who was in the charts. 'OK, who knows The Animals? Who knows The Kinks?' We each covered hundreds of bands on that basis. With each band you would have to interview them three times in each period. Once when they entered the charts, again when they reached the top twenty and again if they went to number one. There was a new single every three months so you'd really do a lot of interviews with these bands.

Aside from the interviews, Altham would run into members of the bands at clubs like the Speakeasy or the Ad-Lib, where they would chat about the usual young men's topics – girls, music, football. 'We were all the same age it gave us a kind of affinity,' said Altham.

In the aftermath of the Cardiff brawl, it was Altham to whom Mick Avory turned. 'On the night of the incident, Mick rang me up and said he'd had a major falling out with Dave,' recalled Altham. 'I lived just outside Kingston and he said could he come and stay? I was a bit taken aback, I'd only just got married, so I asked my wife and said, "Do you mind if a mate comes to stay?"' When he arrived, Avory told Altham what had happened. He thought the police were after him and he didn't know how badly injured Dave was. 'Though everyone says he threw a cymbal, he didn't,' explained Altham. 'The police had been called because Dave had been knocked unconscious.'

'The Kinks were a great bunch of guys,' said Genya Ravan. 'The two brothers were very close and loving even if it didn't look like it. Ray loved Dave so much and I'll never forget him crying backstage, "My brother, my brother".'

'The incident with Dave and Mick horrified me,' said Ray. 'I was scared it was going to happen again. Seeing people reduced to that level and talking to the police afterwards who wanted to arrest Mick for GBH. It was a pretty horrible time.'

Dave later remembered only kicking over the drums and then waking up in the dressing room covered in blood. He had sixteen stitches to a head wound and was packed off to hospital before he could return home to London. The final four shows of the tour were cancelled. 'Not many live to tell the tale,' said Dave. 'That was outrageous, that was very funny. Though not at the time. Imagine Mick trying to hide in the crowd thinking he'd killed me, with that pink hunting jacket and frilly shirt he used to wear.'

'I'm not sure if there was a warrant out for his arrest or not,' said Keith Altham, 'but the papers said there was and Mick certainly thought there was so he ran scared and came to stay for the night. The following day he made a few phone calls and realised he hadn't killed Dave and they had to repair it.'

For a while, no one knew where Avory was staying, and the future of the band was questioned. 'Everything was a bit upside down,' said Pete Quaife. 'Nobody really knew what was happening. Had we split up? Had we decided to go our own different ways? For about a week it was total confusion. I personally had no contact with anyone. I just stayed at home and counted my losses.'

Ray used the downtime to go back into the studio, on 24 May. With The Riot Squad's Mitch Mitchell on drums and an unknown bass player (Pete Quaife had decided to stay away), Ray recorded versions of seven new songs. Among them were a mesmerising track called 'This Strange Effect' and another titled 'I Go to Sleep'. The latter had been composed while he was at his parents' house waiting for news from the hospital where Rasa had been admitted to give birth to their daughter Louisa on 23 May.

The first time Mick and Dave set foot in the same room together after their fight was when Larry Page called the band to his office to discuss plans for the upcoming US tour. Page decided to try and bluff his way through the group's lingering resentments, completely ignoring the fact that Dave was sitting there with a bandage round his head. Page began by outlining the tour dates, the percentages, the running order of the shows and the position of the new single in the US charts. Then, after about twenty minutes of monologue, he paused and said, 'Right, are there any questions?'

'Yeah,' replied Mick Avory. 'I'm gonna need a new drum pedal.'

A Recipe for Disaster

Within days of the Cardiff incident, 'Set Me Free' was released as The Kinks' sixth single. The *New Musical Express* noted 'a characteristic raucous guitar introduction'. That it was 'characteristic' was no accident: Ray had been asked to write a 'Kinks-sounding' song. 'It was the first time I felt uncomfortable [writing],' he said. 'I had to write something that sounded like us. It was designed for "The Kinks" rather than for me.' The use of session musicians in core roles was being phased out so the song was played by the four Kinks themselves. Mick Avory had played on his first Kinks single, 'Ev'rybody's Gonna Be Happy', earlier in the year, and proved he could handle complicated arrangements. 'Set Me Free' opened with a rolling guitar riff; the song was slower and quieter than The Kinks' big hits so far; and Ray's vocal performance was understated, with a quite straightforward lyric. The single made it to number eight in the UK and just failed to break into the US top twenty.

Dave Davies reckons that the band, and Ray in particular, were so successful in 1965-66 because the two brothers were giving each other great emotional and creative support during this time. They were the main songwriters and made most of the decisions. While Mick Avory wasn't overly concerned about this arrangement, and was happy to go along with whatever they decided, Pete Quaife was frustrated that he didn't always get a say in matters, or was simply overruled. But from the outside it seemed that, despite the occasional bust-up between band members – apparently easily smoothed over – everything seemed to be going well.

Having so much contact with the band in the mid-sixties, Keith Altham of the *New Musical Express* had an up-close view of what was going on between the musicians and their management. 'Larry [Page] fell out with them and the relationship somewhat soured, but later he got back with them so he couldn't have been as bad a manager as they made out,' he said. 'Grenville [Collins] always struck me as someone who was better suited to the Stock Exchange and Robert [Wace] was the enthusiastic one, but he didn't really know anything about the business.

The differences between Page's approach to running the band and that of their management were soon to become apparent as The Kinks headed over the Atlantic for their first long tour in North America. Wace and Collins decided not to go, and the band would only have Larry Page on hand for Stateside management duties. Consequently, he had full control for what was going to be a rough trip.

Ray Davies didn't even want to go because Louisa had just been born, though he eventually agreed once he had assurances that his father would keep an eye on Rasa and the baby. All four members of the band entertained a view of the USA that had little connection to reality. Vast swathes of America were unprepared for, and uninterested in, a group of hairy English youths. Promoters and the authorities had read the press accounts and expected trouble from the notorious Kinks. This in turn put the band on edge from the start, and further ratcheted up the tension. Page would soon find himself trying to manage a catastrophe.

The British Invasion of the USA had kicked off a year earlier when, for the first time, the tides of rock music had turned back towards North America. Since the Second World War, the US had become the dominant world force in popular culture. European teenagers were easily seduced by images of hamburgers, Cadillacs and never-ending Californian sunshine. Rock and roll, as represented by Elvis, Jerry Lee Lewis and Chuck Berry, had been exciting, new and rebellious but, by 1963 the US charts were being topped by safer sounds from the likes of Bobby Vinton.

All this changed on 7 February 1964 when The Beatles landed at New York's JFK airport. The Fab Four may have had modest expectations as they flew to the USA for the first time, but they were met by a screaming mob at the airport, and that set the tone for all that was to come. They needed police escorts everywhere and, when they appeared on the *Ed Sullivan Show*, they sent shock-waves countrywide as a staggering 70 million people tuned in. They were the most exciting thing the youth of middle America had ever seen and, by April 1964, The Beatles occupied the top five spots in the US top 100. The door was opened and the invasion followed.

The Zombies, The Dave Clark Five, Peter and Gordon, Herman's Hermits, The Yardbirds and The Searchers all took advantage of this eager new market. By the time The Animals landed, the atmosphere had reached such an intensity that a ban on airport welcoming crowds had been imposed, and the Newcastle five piece arrived to a deserted terminal. Donovan, however, got the chance to meet Salvador Dali and Andy Warhol, and The Hollies visited tiny jazz clubs to see Miles Davis and Charles Mingus.

New York was the city of the movies they had all grown up watching, but the reality proved even better than they had imagined. Most of the English bands had never eaten pizza, and take-out food was unheard of amongst a generation which had grown up on rations. As soon as the bands ventured away from the east coast, however, the America they encountered was a less pleasant surprise. They found that real-life cowboys still roamed Oklahoma and the Midwest, and that racial segregation was prevalent in the south.

For their part, many Americans had only sentimental ideas of what quaint little ol' England was like. They thought that every band must be from Liverpool, which they imagined to be a magical place, rather than a tough northern city. Gordon Waller, of Peter and Gordon fame, a Scot educated in London, didn't object: 'They referred to us as the "Liverpool sound", I just went with the flow. If that made them happy and made the kids buy records – solid!'

The Beatles themselves believed that US youth culture was behind its British counterpart by about a year. Dave Davies thought it even worse. 'I was surprised how old fashioned Americans were,' he said. 'They didn't play anything on the radio that was any good, it was all poppy, croonery, fifties kind of stuff. I expected to hear Leadbelly.' But he was to be disappointed: 'No one knew who he was!'

Those who weren't excited by British pop hated it, and a certain type of macho American male felt threatened by the long-haired groups colonising their pop charts and airwaves. Resentment brewed.

It was into this atmosphere of hysteria and backlash that The Kinks arrived on 17 June 1965. The following night was their first show, at the Academy of Music in New York. Promoter Sid Bernstein introduced them as 'The Kings', and things went dowhill from there.

'Once The Beatles had opened the cornucopia of America everyone poured through it,' said Keith Altham. 'But once through the door they had no real comparative examples to work from in terms of what to ask for in percentages, merchandising, agency fees, because no one had done it before on that scale. A lot of people were quickly out of their depth.'

Nothing had really been worked out in any detail. The Kinks were bundled into a van and told, 'There's New York, now go and do the gigs.' They soon discovered that they were expected to travel vast distances by road, and driving for eighteen hours immediately before going on stage made delivering great performances a challenge. 'We had been moving so fast we still hadn't recovered from jet lag,' said Ray in *X-Ray*.

Many different acts appeared with the band on this tour, from big names like The Dave Clark Five and The Supremes, to now long-forgotten bands such as Fish & Chips and The Fugitives. There was also a wide, and occasionally chastening, variety in the size and status of the venues at which The Kinks played. 'It certainly wasn't the American tour we'd been promised,' said Pete Quaife. 'We'd had big hits over there, so it should have been a good tour, and we started out doing nice big theatres. Then it degraded into silly little TV shows, smaller venues, crappier hotels.'

Even the bigger bookings could prove disheartening. 'It was like landing on another planet,' said Mick Avory. 'A package tour, but it was slightly different. We were playing larger venues and it was a bit of a recipe for disaster. We'd never played such large venues and I used to hate it because the drums weren't miked up in those days, and being stuck at the back of the stage I couldn't hear it properly. I just didn't really enjoy it at all from the playing point of view.'

Events took an ominous turn when Larry Page was arrested for non-payment of an obscure local tax of which the band were unaware. The oversight was resolved and Page released, but the tone had been set. In one small town, Ray Davies was later threatened by a local with a pistol. 'Are you a Beatle or a girl?' he was asked. In another, he went to his hotel room to discover he had been set up with a 14-year-old girl, and that the local sheriff was waiting just outside. 'The one thing I noticed was that in certain towns the older generations seemed fearful of change,' wrote Dave Davies in *Kink*. 'They didn't like us with our long hair and nonconformist attitude. The Beatles, you must remember, had a very smart clean-cut image and a very organised PR team.' Ray echoed his brother's views: 'We had fairly long hair, we were called The Kinks, we were upstarts and we didn't play the game that lots of other British Invasion people [did].'

When they weren't battling the locals, the band were fighting amongst themselves. On the bus journeys between shows, Mick Avory and Pete Quaife sat at the front, Larry Page and the crew would sit in the middle, and Ray and Dave would sit at the back. Insults would be traded back and forth, with fights liable to start at any moment. Local radio and television shows wanted them to be funny and witty like The Beatles, but that simply wasn't their style, even if they hadn't been exhausted and irritable.

On one leg of the tour, which was fast taking on the atmosphere of a trial by ordeal, the band drove to Philadelphia and then flew to Peoria. Mid-flight the plane was hit by lightning and when they arrived they ended up having disputes with local agents about underpayments. Next up was Chicago.

'When I turned 21, I spent it alone in a Sheraton hotel in Chicago,' said Ray. 'I was too scared to go out because we had screaming fans outside and there were all these security men with guns.' The show was billed as Summer of Stars '65, but The Moody Blues dropped out at the last moment, leaving only The Thunderbirds and The Blue Knights, while The Kinks set was halted due to a power cut.

The band had a day off after the Chicago show and then moved on to Springfield, Illinois. There they discovered the middle of America was far from ready for, and didn't want, long-haired rock stars corrupting their children. Even years later, the likes of the Velvet Underground got short shrift travelling cross-country, and they were, at least, American. A bunch of Limeys inside the gun belt of America didn't stand a chance. The promoter of the Springfield show, at least, seemed friendly enough – though maybe a little too much so. He drove the band around to the hotel, to the sound check, back for the gig, and then afterwards to his house for drinks. Something didn't quite seem right and, at around 4 a.m., when the band decided to leave, the promoter got agitated and upset, and wanted Dave, in particular, to stay. It was only much later that they found out he was notorious serial killer John Wayne Gacy, who killed at least thirty-three people between 1972 and 1978. He committed his first known sexual assault upon a teenage boy two years after The Kinks' visit in August 1967, using a crawl space under his floor to store the bodies of around twenty-six victims. He was executed in May 1994.

Keith Altham heard all of the road stories once the band got home.

There was some concert they did which was a showcase concert to which all the major DJs from all over America were invited. So the first few rows were filled with people who were going to play their records for them, and Ray called them a bunch of that little word beginning with 'c' and it didn't go down very well. Ray was pretty unhappy out there, there was a lot pressure put on you and a lot of name calling from certain factions. All the groups got fed up with it and there was a lot of prejudice about the length of your hair, which seems funny now but was real back then. You could laugh it off for a bit but when it kept on and on, and you were under stress and you'd been travelling, you'd have enough of it, so I can understand why people like Ray cracked, and he did, he was a particularly sensitive individual anyway and prone to that.

In Reno, Nevada, the venue was under-prepared, with too few security men, and, as the crowd rushed onto the stage, the band feared they might be about to suffer a repeat of the Copenhagen riot. By the end of June, The Kinks were fed up. Ray asked Larry to fly Rasa over to California and Pete Quaife asked him to do the same with his girlfriend, Nicki Start. Problems with visas, because Rasa's family were from what was then a part of the Soviet Union, meant delays. The band was unhappy and frustrations were about to boil over. Ray barged into Larry Page's hotel room and demanded some action. 'I knew it would all boil up inside and erupt sooner or later,' said Ray. 'And it did.'

The band spent a week in Los Angeles leading up to a prestigious gig at the Hollywood Bowl on 3 July. They were booked for television and press appearances, and Larry Page tried to use the time to his own advantage. He had persuaded Sonny and Cher, who had supported the band in Reno, to record Ray's song 'I Go to Sleep', and then took The Kinks into a local studio to record 'Ring the Bells', which he thought could be their next single.

'Larry Page went with us to one of Dean Martin's recording sessions,' recalled Mick Avory. 'We just dropped in with a guy from the record company, and Mel Tormé was there and we had a little chat, listened to one of his songs. I don't think he'd really heard of us. I went to see Dave Brubeck at the Hollywood Bowl and met Joe Morello the drummer, one of my heroes. I told him that we were an English band in town and we were also going to be playing there in a few days' time. He said it was a shame that he'd be out of town because he'd have liked to come along, I said, don't worry you won't learn anything.' Avory also met his jazz-drumming hero Shelley Manne.

On Friday, 2 July, the band recorded half a dozen songs for Dick

Clark's brand new television show, *Where The Action Is*, the title of which proved to be apt. The band were tired and on edge, and those around The Kinks knew that something would explode before too long. At the recording, words were exchanged between Ray and a union official from the studio. Over the years, there have been various versions of what was said and by who, but there seems to be broad agreement that the official made various digs at Ray, who snapped and punched him in the face. Three times. It was a loss of control that would have long-lasting implications. Surprisingly, Dave Davies failed to mention this event at all in his autobiography, but in *X-Ray*, Ray recalled 'being pushed and swinging a punch and being punched back'. Afterwards, Ray headed back to his hotel room, locked the door and stayed there.

The next day, he was feeling no better and refused to play that night's show. It was due to be the biggest performance of the tour with The Kinks appearing alongside, amongst others, The Beach Boys, The Righteous Brothers, The Byrds, Sam the Sham and the Pharaohs and Sonny and Cher. Larry Page eventually persuaded him to go to the venue and they did a sound check, but, once again, Ray insisted he wouldn't perform. Page had had enough. He had been with the band since they couldn't get a record deal, had just about got them around the USA in one piece, and now Ray was threatening to scupper the event to which the tour had been building up. Although Ray eventually agreed to play, Page couldn't take anymore. The next day, he flew back to England with Sonny and Cher, without telling the band. In 1982 he told writer Johnny Rogan that if he hadn't left, he would have had a nervous breakdown. 'When we asked where Larry had gone, they brushed aside our enquiries,' said Ray. 'Simply saying that he'd had to go somewhere on business.'

The Kinks were lost in America. They still had six shows to play and no management to guide them. Reeling from the loss of Page, they headed north to San Francisco for a show at the Cow Palace, which had a capacity of more than 16,000. Fewer than 4,000 tickets had been sold and, on arrival, The Kinks' payment was disputed, most likely because the promoter hadn't sold enough tickets to pay everyone as agreed. The Kinks were eventually prevented from appearing at all and found themselves in a strange city with no one to back them up. A temporary tour manager, Don Zacharlini, turned up, apparently from nowhere, and took over as the tour limped on to its ignominious conclusion. Zacharlini was a Laundromat entrepreneur with little experience of band management, and drove the band around California in his pink Cadillac.

Two days later they all flew to Hawaii, playing for US troops in the afternoon, and another show that night. At least Rasa had joined them but, when Ray had the audacity to kiss her at the airport coffee shop in Spokane, he was threatened with arrest after someone complained. The land of the free indeed. The remaining contracted shows were completed after performances in Tacoma and then Seattle, on 10 July.

Looking back, there was little about the tour that can be said to have worked out in The Kinks' favour. In amongst a few good shows many more were riddled with problems, on and off stage. 'Our biggest problem, it seemed, was management,' argued Dave Davies in *Kink*. 'I never understood why Robert and Grenville stayed in England, when this was potentially one of our most crucial career moves.' Yet Larry Page, an undeniably experienced presence, had accompanied the band to America, and, as his subsequent decision to leave suggests, at least some of the tour's disappointments were a product of The Kinks' own behaviour and temperaments. Moreover, they had been the unwitting victims of a culture clash that received little attention amidst the heady hyping of the so-called 'British Invasion'. As Ray put it: 'All this turned me into a less innocent person than I had been before I arrived in America.'

The Davies brothers could not get home to Britain fast enough but, despite all the mishaps and hostility, Mick and Pete stayed on. 'Visiting America and LA was great,' said Mick. 'I had a little holiday there with Pete for about two weeks, it was awesome for me. Drive-in movies, fast food, cars covered in chrome. It was so different to the UK and, with the sunshine, I thought why would anyone want to live anywhere else?' By staying in California, Avory and Quaife remained oblivious to the new dramas unfolding at home.

*

Larry Page had arrived in London carrying the masters of 'Ring The Bells'. He was intent on releasing it as the band's next single but, by then, Shel Talmy, suspicious of Page's actions, had already started legal proceedings to block the release of any Kinks material that wasn't produced by him. A stand-off ensued with Page saying 'Ring the Bells' would be the next single and Talmy saying it should be his own recording of 'See My Friends'. Talmy had the law on his side and won the battle.

Page did himself few favours by releasing *Kinky Music,* an album of instrumental takes of Kinks songs played by the 'Larry Page Orchestra', without Ray's permission, and much to his irritation. The opening track, 'Tired of Waiting', sounds like it's going to be a straightforward cover version until the point where the vocals should begin and the words are replaced by brass instruments, with a string backing. Other tracks used musical fill-ins in place of the lyrics. It's all very much of its time but, to modern ears, sounds like the soundtrack to a spoof of the decade in the vein of the *Austin Powers* movies. Page also included 'Revenge', which was credited to him and Ray Davies, along with a previously unreleased Dave Davies song, 'One Fine Day'. In notes for a 2006 CD re-issue of the album, he claimed that Jimmy Page and John Paul Jones, both later of Led Zeppelin, had played on the record; its version of 'You Really Got Me' certainly features a memorable guitar solo.

Another Ray Davies composition was already in the charts with Dave Berry's version of 'This Strange Effect'. Sheffield-born Berry had previously written about The Kinks in *Melody Maker.* 'I said they sounded like a proper band playing live,' recalled Berry. 'They appealed to me because they weren't over-produced and just sounded like we all sounded a bit later when punk came along. They sounded raw and back to our roots.' Berry had done one-off shows with The Kinks, but not a full tour. They would meet on the many regional TV shows every few months and then do one-off Sunday concerts. 'I'd be at the Sunderland Empire with say, The Who, and someone else and then you'd be off and see them again a few months later somewhere else,' said Berry. 'Ray says he wrote 'This Strange Effect' with me in mind . . . We have similar styles of presentation, neither of us are good singers – he says that! – and we tend to slide up to the notes. It was at somewhere like *Ready, Steady, Go!* that he just gave me the demo.'

Ray had recorded a version of the song on piano with just his vocals, a very basic take, as he had with 'I Go to Sleep'. 'At that time, with hindsight it might seem strange to give songs away,' said Berry. 'He was just starting out and wanted people to record his songs.' This was the song with which Berry broke through at the 1965 Knokke-Heist Song Festival – a contest which ran from 1959 to 1973, with entrants from the Low Countries, Germany, Italy, France and the UK. In Holland and Belgium, the song topped the singles charts, ironically knocking The Kinks off the number one spot. 'It was massive,' recalled Berry. 'It's still the all-time biggest selling song in Holland and Belgium.'

In the midst of fallout from America, Ray and Rasa headed away to Torquay on the south coast of England for some much needed respite. 'I was staying in a hotel, a hotel which was a bit snobbish,' said Ray. 'I felt a bit sick – even though I was paying the same money as all the businessmen who were also there. But I was wearing jeans and so on . . . I wanted there and then to be respected, which is nothing to do with money . . .' He resented the idea of being the pop star invited along to play golf just so the bankers and businessmen had a story to tell when they went back to work; again, Ray's acute working-class consciousness was coming to the surface.

When he got home to 87 Fortis Green, he sat down and wrote 'A Well-Respected Man'. This was the first of Ray's truly incisive character studies. It depicts a conservative commuter with an upstanding mother, waiting for his father to pass away so he can inherit the family fortune. In lines such as 'He goes to the regatta / He adores the girl next door / 'Cos he's dying to get at her', Ray's songwriting reached new heights, comparable with the turn to character and vignette that The Beatles were then exploring in songs like 'Norwegian Wood', and that Paul McCartney would later perfect in 'Eleanor Rigby'. Humorous, to the point and a perfect evocation of the song's central character, these lines were even performed with an upper-class lilt that was probably an amalgamation of the voices of Robert Wace and Grenville Collins. The song was included on the *Kwyet Kinks* EP in September.

Meanwhile, Talmy and Davies had their way, and the summer's new single was 'See My Friends' (sometimes mistitled 'See My Friend'). '"See My Friends" I really liked,' said Shel Talmy. 'We were so far ahead of the market that it was one of the lowest chart placings we had.' To realise the song's Indian influence, Dave Davies used an old twelve-string guitar to create a drone-like sound. Both Mick Jagger and Paul McCartney sang the praises of the song to Dave and their bands both went on to use Indian sounds in their own new songs: The Beatles' 'Norwegian Wood' arrived seven months later and the Stones' 'Paint It, Black' was issued in May 1966. Soon it seemed like every aspiring rock act in Britain was rushing out to buy a sitar.

'I got that idea from being in India,' said Ray. 'I always liked the chanting. Someone once said to me, "England is grey and India is like a chant." I don't think England is that grey but India *is* like a long drone. When I wrote the song, I had the sea near Bombay in mind. We stayed at a hotel by the sea, and the fishermen came up at five in the morning and they were all chanting. And we went on the beach and we got chased by a mad dog – big as a donkey.' The song peaked at number eleven in both the UK and the US. The Kinks had conquered Merseybeat, pop, R&B and garage, and were pushing their range even further, creating records that didn't fit into existing categories.

In the wake of Larry Page deserting the US tour, Robert Wace and Grenville Collins met with lawyers during August to discuss terminating Boscobel's contract with Denmark Productions and, by early September, their representatives were serving papers. Further legal tussles ensued when Ray signed a five-year publishing contract with Belinda Music, which provoked Eddie Kassner to sue. This in turn led to Ray's publishing earnings being put into escrow, which is where they stayed until 1970, when the court case was finally decided.

While Ray was settling down to life as a married family man, Dave was living it up more adventurously than ever: getting high, wearing outrageous clothes and sleeping with whoever he wanted to. As he wrote in his book, *Kink*, Dave was not averse to trying on his girlfriends' clothes and, during this time, used the Ashburn

Hotel in London for late-night meetings not only with girls, but also with men. In *Kink*, he describes going there with blues singer Long John Baldry, booking a room with two single beds to try and diffuse any suspicion. Davies also had an affair with a designer known only as 'Allen', but in *Kink* it's the sleeping around with women which takes up the most space. 'My sexual relationships with men were not nearly as satisfying to me as my liaisons with women,' he wrote. 'I was an angry rebellious kid and I wanted to try everything.' His stories sometimes go into too much detail as sexual accidents and embarrassing moments are recounted. There was no holding back for Dave: there is even a tale of his learning hypnosis and trying it on girls in hotel rooms before he got scared he might not be able to bring them back out of the trance.

His indulgences were not without consequences, however. That autumn, a girl called Eileen Fernley quietly filed a paternity suit against him. They had met on the same night that Ray first encountered Rasa, and she was the girl who had been found upstairs with Dave at Ray's wedding party. The case, which Dave disputed, would be heard the following year.

Around the same time, Mick Avory moved into a house on Connaught Gardens with Dave. Dave had been having an affair with *Ready, Steady, Go!* host Michael Aldred and, for a while, all three lived in the same digs. The arrangement was short lived. Fights between Aldred and Dave, often developing from Dave's lifestyle of staying out partying and drinking, led to Aldred leaving, and renewed tensions between Avory and Davies sprang up from the two bandmates spending too much time together. Dave moved briefly back to his parents' house and Mick returned to Molesey.

The Kinks played mini-tours of Scandinavia in September and mainland Europe in October, with the new EP, *Kwyet Kinks*, being released on 17 September. It topped the UK EP chart and featured 'Wait Till the Summer Comes Along', 'Such A Shame', 'A Well-Respected Man' and 'Don't You Fret'. The opening track was written and sung by Dave and is a proficient, quasi-country jaunt, but with an odd title for an end-of-summer release. 'Such A Shame' told an end-of-relationship story, while 'Don't You Fret' was an acoustic shanty that might have made a young Shane McGowan proud.

This gentler material found favour with the *New Musical Express* which reported, 'They're just as attractive as softies! You can listen to the words on this one and the singing is good.' In late November a new single, 'Till the End of the Day', was released a week ahead of the next album, *The Kink Kontroversy*.

Studio engineer Alan O'Duffy, soon to be known to everyone as 'Irish', had a strong musical pedigree, his father having recorded at Abbey Road in the 1950s: 'He was an Irish tenor in the same genre as Andrea Bocelli,' said O'Duffy, 'but Bocelli is an operatic tenor and my dad is a lyric tenor. Paul McCartney is a lyric tenor, the same as Don McLean, with a high melodic voice, so I grew up to my dad's records that he was making.' Alan himself had initial thoughts of being a singer, too, always taking the lead in plays and school musicals. Through his father, he got the chance to see the inner-workings of a recording session. 'When I was about 12 I was dragged along to Pye Studios and watched my dad make an album,' he said. 'It was the days where you'd record three tracks in a single session with session musicians.' Years later, O'Duffy got an interview at Pye and started there in 1965.

'The first band [I worked with] was from the Midlands,' recalled O'Duffy. 'They arrived in a van with sandwiches made by their mum and the piano player asked me if he could play the grand piano during the lunch breaks.' That band was The Spencer Davis Group featuring a teenage Steve Winwood. The second band he recorded in his long career was The Kinks.

Like everyone else, O'Duffy had heard 'You Really Got Me', and he liked the idea that he lived just along the road from the Davies' in Harringay. He has strong memories of his first sessions with The Kinks. 'I remember that the playback in the control room was very loud through Lockwood speakers,' he said. 'We were recording mono to mono. The backing track would be put down onto a mono machine and you would take the tape off the machine and onto a playback, and then you would play back the backing track through a Lockwood speaker which sat on the top of the microphone cupboard in Studio Two. You would play it back quite loud and Ray Davies, or whoever, would sing along, then Dave would do a guitar solo or whatever. That was the only way to work . . . The Kinks didn't get the use of the three-track; they were only allowed to work mono to mono.'

These sessions showed The Kinks diversifying, and Ray gaining confidence and becoming more prolific as a songwriter. This time, only one cover would be used on the record – the Kokomo Arnold rocker 'Milk Cow Blues', which Dave sang to open the album in a typically frantic manner. The whole album was put together in about a week, including mixing.

Though The Kinks didn't have an 'entourage' hanging around their sessions, there were a few characters populating the studio. Sometimes, Jimmy Page and Andrew Oldham might appear and stand around watching. 'I was the new boy in the room,' recalled O'Duffy. 'It was Shel and Alan, there wasn't a lot of direction, it was well, "We'll record this." Ray would say, "I've got this song and we're going to record it," and Shel would say, "Take one."'

'Alan' was Alan MacKenzie, a Scottish former television sound supervisor. His broadcasting background meant that he was used to doing everything live, something he tried to carry over into his work with The Kinks. Alan O'Duffy was his engineering assistant on the *Kink Kontroversy* sessions, while Shel Talmy produced.

'Shel Talmy was the first man I met who really drank serious coffee,' said O'Duffy. 'He was going a bit blind and he had the American "gloss" about him. A bit of showbiz. He used to wear black Fred Perry shirts and dark glasses inside, under the florescent lights. I used to think that was because he was in show business, not because he was going slightly blind. He used to smoke like a chimney and so did everyone else, but I didn't. I hated the smoke.'

Things were fairly straightforward. 'We didn't do many takes,' said O'Duffy. 'We would arrive at 10 a.m. and by five past we were recording the first song, it was very business like. In those days studio work revolved around the Musicians' Union, so it was their times. If you booked Jimmy Page for a guitar record the sessions would be ten till one, two till five and seven till ten.'

The album had a subtle country influence running through

it. The gentle 'Ring The Bells' was reworked from the American session with Larry Page. Elsewhere, session pianist Nicky Hopkins was all over the record, right to the fore on the desolate 'The World Keeps Going Round'.

'Nicky Hopkins looked so thin and pale,' said Ray Davies. 'It was as if he had just been whisked out of intensive care and dragged in on a stretcher so he could play piano on our track. Shel Talmy thought we should hire someone who could contribute more than just background chords.'

The band had also upgraded their instruments from the budget equipment of the early days. Dave Davies was using a flash 'Flying V' guitar, which he'd purchased in the USA, and they also had acoustic Fenders, a Gretsch and a Gibson to play with.

'We all, with the exception of Mick, participated in forming the harmonies,' said Pete Quaife. 'We would sit in the control room, and quickly rehearse the various parts and then record them. It was not as important to get them as right as The Beatles. It wasn't that kind of music.'

'There was none of the sort of scatter cushions or any of that,' recalled O'Duffy. 'It was semi-industrial and the walls were covered in wood, with stripes in the wood, and the stripes would have a slot which would go in and turn right so the sound would get lost in the absorption of the wood panel.'

The business-like nature of the sessions was only broken slightly when Rasa was present. 'Rasa is a very sore point with me,' admitted Pete Quaife. 'I'll make no bones about it, I didn't like her and felt that she was just a jumped-up groupie that had no right to be there. But it was Ray's [wife] and we had to respect that . . . As always happens, when a girl enters the group, the group always suffers. With Rasa tagging along with us all the time, tempers began to sizzle and eventually the group began to splinter.' Quaife's objection to Rasa was not shared by other members of the band. 'She used to fancy herself as a bit of a singer and we'd include her,' said Dave. 'She'd sing the top harmony or an octave, Rasa was really important.'

The new songs reflected what had been happening recently. 'Gotta Get the First Plane Home' sounds like it was inspired by events that summer, and the raucous chugging of 'Till the End of the Day' closed side one in a throwback to The Kinks' early singles. Homesickness and dislocation run through several songs, such as 'I'm on an Island'.

Ray had felt cornered during the writing of the record and, in an attempt to cheer him up, Wace and Collins had pulled in a favour and sent Mort Shuman round to give him a pep-talk. Shuman was most famous for his songwriting work with Doc Pomus in New York, which included songs such as 'Can't Get Used to Losing You', 'Teenager In Love' and 'Viva Las Vegas', but he also penned hits for The Hollies and The Small Faces, to name but two. 'This mad, druggy New Yorker came round to my little semi-detached house in London,' said Ray. 'He said, "I'm here to find out what you're thinking about. I'm not interested in what you have written."' Ray then wrote 'Till the End of the Day', which he explained was about freedom for someone who had been a slave or locked up in prison. He also came up with the more mature 'Where Have All the Good Times Gone'. This was the song of an older man reminiscing, not someone in their early twenties, and it demonstrated the ease with which Ray could now take on a character.

'At this time, because we were still trying to get used to recording, we just let everything go and happily banged away at our instruments, hoping that the producer could put it all together again,' said Pete. 'So the strange bassline in "Milk Cow Blues" was simply me showing off and trying to be nothing more than the lead guitarist. I cringe now when I hear it as far as arrangements go — there were none! Nothing serious anyway. We knew the numbers off by heart and we simply started each one and then did anything we could possibly think of to make the number more exciting.'

In the USA, The Kinks had managed to strike a chord with a host of teenagers destined for musical careers of their own. Tom Petty, Iggy Pop, Chrissie Hynde and Steven van Zandt were just some of their American fans, but it would be a long time before the chance to see The Kinks play live in the US came round again: it became apparent that the group had been banned from travelling to America. No official reason was ever given, no announcement was ever made and it was never explained to the band or their management. Was it because they hadn't lined the pockets of the right people? Was it due to Ray's punch-up at the television studio? Had they upset someone of influence along the way? Though it puzzled him for many years, by 2005, Ray had come to believe that the ban was inevitable: 'There was something in the air that a British band was going to be banned, and with the way we looked and sounded, we were the ones.'

'Everyone had roots in England but we might have moved there,' says Mick Avory. 'We'd have needed to change to suit the bigger venues, a lot of the songs weren't really suited for large arenas, but we'd have got caught up in Woodstock and things might have been different.' Financially it was certainly a set back; musically it represents one of rock and roll's great 'what ifs'. For a lot of their American fans, however, The Kinks simply vanished, with new bands taking the place they might have occupied. '[The ban] took away our best years,' said Ray. 'We were having hits around the world but couldn't get on the radio there, there was no music TV.'

Creatively, however, the US ban was a crucial turning point. Without the pressure to 'break' America, Ray Davies' songwriting was set on a different path.

On the Razor's Edge

The Kinks found themselves at the centre of London's cultural revolution in the 1960s. More than any other band, The Kinks were pointedly 'English' just when England was setting the global scene alight: when everyone else wanted to sound American, Ray Davies took on the roles of upper-class fop or working-class Londoner with ease. Ray sat back with a nice cup of tea and watched pop culture explode around him.

An obvious shift was in the world of fashion. Girls' hemlines were rising and it wasn't a shock to see shop window mannequins dressed in space-age silver foil or plastic dresses with Mondrian-inspired patterns. Fashion designers like Mary Quant and Paco Rabanne, models such as Twiggy and Jean Shrimpton, as well as hairdressers and make-up artists, were part of the new zeitgeist – popular icons, even stars. Ray Davies couldn't have written 'Dedicated Follower of Fashion' any earlier than 1966 because it wouldn't have had any resonance. By then, the number of dandy-dressing young men on the streets of London was growing dramatically and, although The Kinks weren't averse to wearing their hair long and appearing with a few frills here and there, Ray was upset by the sheep-like following of new fads and trends.

Dressing up was fine, but doing it for the sake of individuality was the important thing.

Close to home, Dave Davies enjoyed camping it up in pink floppy hats and Edwardian jackets; he grew his sideburns long; and spent his free time tramping up and down the King's Road, and through Soho. But, although Ray's latest composition was directly inspired by yet another fight, the song wasn't aimed at his brother: it stemmed from Ray having an argument that ended with the elder Davies rolling around on the floor trading blows with a fashion designer at a party. 'I got pissed off with him always going on about fashion,' said Ray. 'I was just saying you don't have to be anything; you decide what you want to be and you just walk down the street and if you're good the world will change as you walk past. I just wanted it to be the individual who created his own fashion.' Ray had been fearful of 'central control' since reading Orwell's *1984*, and a sympathetic view of his actions might be that this was an attack on that kind of thinking and a defence of individualism. It could also be read that Ray was a natural curmudgeon and contrarian. 'A terrible brawl,' recalled Ray. 'I kicked him, and I kicked his girlfriend up the arse.'

The next day, still fuming and perhaps unnerved by his own turn to violence, he decided to channel his anger through work and typed up a lyric which shone the dual lights of satire and social commentary on to the Carnaby Street scene and its followers, upon whom Ray bestowed the moniker 'the Carnabetian Army'. The genius of the song is that, even today, most people know someone who fits the character within it.

The band had spent much of January playing sporadic dates up and down the country, traveling as far as Scotland, and then went back into the studio in early February. They had already recorded a version of 'Dedicated Follower of Fashion' in which Ray launched straight into the lyric accompanied by just an acoustic guitar, but he didn't like those first attempts.

'That guitar clanging at the beginning,' said Pete Quaife. 'We did it over and over, changed guitars, tried it with a piano. Ray was after a sound and he didn't get it. When he realised he wasn't getting it, he took the tape, rolled it across the floor and set fire to it. The next day we started again and he settled for that. But I know he wasn't happy with the final result.' Engineer Alan O'Duffy doesn't remember the session that way but recalls issues with the vocals: 'It was a fairly straightforward recording . . . there was a lot of slagging-off that went on against Alan MacKenzie. It was unfair because the voice was a very "telephone" voice and edgy sounding and Alan wanted to do that. I remember someone criticising Alan saying, "Oh, was the jack-plug not plugged in properly?" It was that kind of slagging, but the record still stands up and sounds fabulous today. Those extraordinary records were made in a "live" way, there was no question of replacing, say, the third verse.'

'There's a lot of venom in that song,' said Ray Davies. 'You don't have to be Metallica to write venom. It's as venomous as satanic heavy metal, but it's done with humour.'

After its release at the end of February 1966, there was some press tittering about the song sounding like a pre-war ditty, and the band were mockingly referred to as 'The George Formby Quartet'. Ray Davies didn't care, he told Keith Altham for the *New Musical Express*: 'I feel complimented when people say it sounds like Formby, he made a lot of bread!'

With some irony, as fashion became more mainstream, much coverage was given to what the 'stars' were wearing, and The Kinks, despite their sneering, didn't escape scrutiny. In her 'Pop Mirror' column, Betty Hale followed The Kinks on a shopping trip along Carnaby Street. She fascinated readers with a report that said, 'Pete bought some jeans, Dave bought some five-guinea slacks at John Stephen's and four shirts . . . Mick had a brown-striped mohair suit made . . . and Ray says he's bought "nothing".' In an ironic twist, Mick Avory was soon modelling for John Stephen, in a range of gaudy suits, plastic Macs and futuristic-looking jackets. The photo shoots were arranged through Michael McGrath who did John Stephen's publicity. '[I would dress up] with these girls that he used to get round his [McGrath's] flat and took some pictures. They used to dress me up in these costumes that were the last thing I'd ever wear!' said Avory.

The B-side to 'Dedicated Follower of Fashion' was 'Sitting on My Sofa'. 'I came up with a line, a riff or two and a series of chord changes, and Ray embellished them and wrote a song based on them,' said Dave Davies. 'Ray took all the writing credit [it's actually listed as a co-composition]. It didn't bother me at the time – after all, it was family – and we were enjoying phenomenal success. The adulation we received seemed more than enough for me. I never thought about the fact that the publishing rights would be so valuable or even cared about it. In fact, I never thought about money much at all, unlike Ray, who has to be one of the most thrifty people I've ever known.'

Still only 21, a lot of responsibility had settled on Ray Davies' shoulders. The band were almost entirely reliant on him to write new material and the label wanted hit single after hit single. He had a wife and child, and yet he was expected to be on tour almost constantly. What space or time remained for his own hopes and aspirations? Or, indeed, his peace of mind? After another trip to Denmark, and then shows in Switzerland and Austria, Ray was unsurprisingly exhausted. On his return to London, his doctor diagnosed nervous exhaustion and a handful of imminent appearances were cancelled. Dave took over all of his brother's press duties.

There were some well-paying gigs lined up in Belgium during March, and Wace and Collins told the band that the contracts had to be honoured. Dave protested: they couldn't go to Belgium without Ray. Ray, however, insisted that they should and picked his own replacement for the tour – Mick Grace, from local band The Cockneys, who was told to keep his head down and bluff his way through. Dave did most of the singing and, apart from some puzzled looks from a few fans, they got away with it.

While The Kinks continued across Belgium without him, Ray was suffering at home. He was now prone to paranoia, and in his strung-out state, the tendency worsened markedly. One day, he asked a friend to drive him home in case he had left a tap dripping. When it got cold, he worried about pipes freezing. He had fights with Rasa and his sister Gwen. His mother visited every day and brought him food.

One one occasion his strange behaviour escalated to violence, albeit of a rather peculiar variety. While delirious, he had an argument over the telephone with the band's publicist, Brian Sommerville, during which he suddenly dropped the receiver, ran several miles to the publicist's office, and promptly tried to punch Sommerville in the face, before running off again. Robert Wace tracked Ray down with the help of a doctor who managed to convince the police that Ray was having a medical relapse, whereupon he was allowed to go home. Sommerville resigned the next day. More recently, Ray has denied that the punch actually made contact with Sommerville. 'If I'd made contact I wouldn't have got away with it,' he said. 'He would have done me for assault, no doubt. The joke was that I missed. I think his dignity wants to think he was hit, because he actually ducked and fell off his chair.'

Wace tried to keep a lid on things and took Ray out for a drive outside the city. During their excursion Ray was taken by the idea of buying a house in the country and was inspired to write a song about it.

Around the release of 'Dedicated Follower of Fashion', and following the departure of Brian Sommerville, Allan MacDougall, a Scot, was brought in as press secretary. 'Ray was on the razor edge between genius and insanity,' said McDougall. 'I think he was a true genius, but with definite tendencies towards going nuts.'

As he recovered, Ray started writing new material, but was reluctant to sign up for any long tours. A ten-day trip to play in New York was cancelled without any explanation. 'Stuck in England I just wanted to write for us,' said Ray. 'I wanted to break storytelling ground, I wasn't afraid to fail like a lot of my contemporaries. I had a stubborn desire to do something different. I wanted out of the music business. I had a one-year-old daughter and I wanted to be normal. I wanted to write something that could be sung in pubs.' Ray would write late at night when Rasa and Louisa went to sleep and, in order to avoid waking them, he moved towards writing quieter tunes.

When the band returned from the continent, Ray called Dave to come and listen to his latest work. Ray played him an embryonic version of 'Sunny Afternoon' and Dave picked up his guitar to play along while Ray sang him the first verse. Ray had the vision of a broken-down aristocrat being heavily taxed by an all-consuming government (the 'big fat mama'). The protagonist feels sorry for himself having come off worst in a brush with 'the man', and, having lost his wealth, is looking for sympathy from his middle and working-class listeners.

'At the time I wrote "Sunny Afternoon",' said Ray, "I was only playing *The Greatest Hits of Frank Sinatra* and Dylan's "Maggie's Farm". I just liked its whole presence, I was playing the *Bringing It All Back Home* LP along with my Frank Sinatra, Glenn Miller and Bach, it was a strange time. I thought they all helped one another, they went into the chromatic part that's in the back of the song. I once made a drawing of my voice on "Sunny Afternoon". It was a leaf with a very thick outline, a big blob in the background, the leaf just cutting through it.'

Ray Davies wasn't rebelling, like other songwriters in the 1960s, or at least, if he was, his rebellion took an elliptical form. While other bands aimed their songs at the youth movement and revelled in alienating the older generations, Ray took issue with that very sentiment. As highlighted by 'Sunny Afternoon' he was writing a kind of new English folk song — something that his granddad could sing. 'I didn't exclude adults from my audience,' he said. 'I basically wrote for my family, because I came from an environment where everybody sang and was musically inclined. I never had this hatred of adults that everyone said they had. I don't believe that Pete Townshend hated old people and wanted to die before he got old, because he got along really well with his dad. I think the generation gap was blown up by the press more than by the individuals involved.'

Ray Davies wasn't the only Kink having problems: Pete Quaife was becoming frustrated, and felt his input was being ever diminished. 'Nothing was really planned very much back then,' said his brother, David Quaife. 'I know that Pete was complaining about the managers and Larry Page. Even when it was arranged it was done badly. They'd be up to Liverpool, then down to Birmingham then back up to Liverpool, it was all over the place and it really, really tired them out, and I don't think they got paid that much.'

Despite being much younger, David Quaife was quick to see the opportunities of having a famous sibling. 'I always wanted to be a mod when I was growing up,' he said. 'I used to steal his clothes and later his scooter, and then I got a better scooter than him. I was driving around when I was about 14. He was this ultra-mod and I was jealous. He'd get these letters asking him to go down to Carnaby Street, saying he could just turn up and have £15 worth of clothes, which was a lot of money in those days. I used to pinch those letters and go down there and . . . stock up with clothes. He started to travel to gigs separately from the band. He would drive back with Pete Jones because even then there were arguments and bad feelings.' Through his separate travel arrangements, Quaife was unwittingly making himself more of an outsider in his own band.

Ray made his return to the stage in Paris after a six-week break. He was sporting a new moustache, which was only a couple of snips away from being a full Mexican 'Zapata'. Mick Avory had tonsillitis, so legendary session musician Clem Cattini sat in on drums.

Next, Dave Davies was dragged into court, for a hearing about the Eileen Fernley paternity case. After seven hours of deliberations, he was cleared of any responsibility by three magistrates.

In mid-May the band recorded a batch of new material, including 'I'm Not Like Everybody Else', 'This is Where I Belong', 'A House in the Country' and 'Sunny Afternoon'. These were songs with a distinct autobiographical character. 'I'm Not Like Everybody Else' was the first time that Ray really put down on tape a song that could be interpreted as an expression of his own deepest feelings, which is perhaps why he got Dave to sing it — it was too close to home. 'This is Where I Belong' was Ray adapting to, and enjoying, married life ('I can't think of a place I'd rather be/ The whole wide world doesn't mean so much to me' he sang), while 'A House in the Country' stemmed from his day trip with Robert Wace.

The band would convene more and more frequently at Ray's Fortis Green house to practise and be introduced to his latest new songs. Ray would play them his compositions on the piano. Mick Avory had some bespoke equipment produced to save having to lug a full drum set around. 'I had some pads made up, the beginnings of the fold-away drum kit,' he explained. '[It had a] wooden base, foam and skins on top. I had three of them and some cymbals with tape on and that was my practice kit. We'd have a little jam and [Ray] used to record everything on a little cassette and he'd say, "Try this and join in" and we'd develop it a little bit.'

These rehearsals at Ray's were generally very productive but there was sometimes tension in the air, and Dave has written, with evident pain, about one particular incident. It began when Pete asked Ray to listen to an idea which Dave had come up with. 'I started to play and sing, with Pete accompanying me,' recalled Dave. 'After the first verse Ray abruptly turned his head and said, "I don't like it, it's silly."' Pete jumped in and said he thought it was great, but Ray brushed aside his views, and said that he had a better idea for a song. At this point, Pete stormed out. 'I was very upset,' said Dave. 'Ray had always been difficult but this was the first time he had been so hurtful from a creative standpoint. I had always supported Ray's musical ideas but now he was discounting mine as worthless.'

When things went well, though, they went very well. '"Sunny Afternoon" was made very quickly,' said Ray. 'It was one of our most atmospheric sessions. I still like to keep tapes of the few minutes before the final take, things that happen before the session. Maybe it's superstitious, but I believe if I had done things differently – if I had walked around the studio or gone out – it wouldn't have turned out that way. The bass player went off and started playing funny little classical things on the bass, more like a lead guitar, and Nicky Hopkins, who was playing piano on that session, was playing 'Liza' – we always used to play that song – little things like that helped us get into the feeling of the song.'

The descending guitar which begins 'Sunny Afternoon' has become one of the most memorable introductions in pop history and Ray's opening couplet paints a picture with a skill few songwriters can equal. In just thirteen words, the listener understands that the singer's world has been turned upside down and, after another line, we know that he is past caring. Ray sings in a voice that is his most 'English' yet, with a plummy, upper-class lilt, helped along by a bout of hay fever at the time of recording. It's an ironic blues song, in a sense, telling a story not of back-breaking work and poverty, but of unimaginable wealth and laziness. Few people could have much sympathy for someone rich enough to own a yacht, and guilty of 'drunkenness and cruelty', too. It's a sophisticated tale, but nonetheless infectious and charming. The song demonstrated that Ray was at the peak of his powers as far as delivering a fully-formed character study within the confines of a pop song.

For the first time, the band made a promotional film, originally for Belgian television, to accompany the song. Filmed in February, the band are shown miming along in a snowy woodland park. Their breath is visible before their faces, Mick Avory is wearing gloves and Ray keeps blowing on his hands to keep them warm. This humorous juxtaposition of lyrics and setting was pure Kinks.

Back in the studio, the band had an album to finish. 'A lot of the time Shel wasn't too fussy and if there was something I wanted to do again he'd say, "Oh no, no one will notice that",' recalls Mick. 'It was all a little rough and they tended to sound like demos to me. The ones that mattered we'd spend time on and they still sound good, but album tracks, and B-sides, we weren't worried about too much.'

In the first week of June, just as 'Sunny Afternoon' was released, the band played at Morecambe in the north-west of England. They travelled home from the seaside town via the M6 motorway and, as was normal, Pete Quaife and roadie Jonah Jones travelled separately in the equipment van. Quaife wanted to avoid the aggression and hostility that could surface after a gig, but he also wanted to make sure Jones stayed awake during the long drive. This time, though, Quaife nodded off and, unfortunately, so did Jones. The van hit a truck and the driver was thrown through the windscreen, suffering serious head injuries and a fractured pelvis. Quaife was hurt but got off relatively lightly, though he needed stitches in a head wound and broke his foot.

'The accident was the crescendo because at that time Pete was feeling left out of everything,' said David Quaife. 'He used to ask, "How are we doing with the money?" and he'd be told, "Ah, well, we'll tell you later." He had a nervous breakdown because of it all when he was living in Lynton Grange. He'd come back with the demos and he'd play them at 78 rpm so he could hear what the bass lines were, but then when the actual record would come out they'd cut everything out or changed it. I remember Dave complaining about it at our house one day.'

With Quaife in hospital, the three remaining Kinks went back in to Pye to add some overdubs and tinker with a few recordings. With Ray, and to a lesser extent Dave, increasingly running things in the studio, Pete Quaife's absence was hardly felt. 'Pete often used to change his mind about things,' said Avory. 'He sometimes used to do things that I thought were off the wall or to aggravate, just to be different. I got on with him alright and I think he liked the business enough but he realised he was never going to be on an equal terms because Ray and Dave were brothers. Ray was the controlling one, the clever one.'

Some gigs were cancelled, but they did go to the BBC to lip-synch 'Sunny Afternoon' for the TV show *Whole Scene Going*. Ray wore a black polo neck under his jacket and a carnation in his lapel, while the band struggled to give any sense of reality to the performance.

With more shows fast approaching and the need to promote the new single, The Kinks needed a temporary bassist. They found John Dalton via their booking agent.

I went to the same school as Cliff Richard and I always point out that he's three years older than me . . . I always get told he doesn't look it! He was my prefect, and apart from me we didn't get any rock and roll at the school. I used to take in a little wind-up gramophone which got me in a lot of trouble. I remember Cliff reciting things like *The Owl and the Pussycat* and our English teacher would tape it . . . I used to dislike Cliff because I was jealous of him. He'd made a record, 'Move It', and I wanted to be that person making the records. I was a really big Elvis fan and I just thought he was copying Elvis. He was making the records and I was still standing in front of the mirror with a hairdryer.

It was American rock rather than the more homely English variety that Dalton aspired to. 'I remember a film coming out called *The Girl Can't Help It*,' said Dalton. 'All the American stars did a little cameo. I'd heard of Elvis but I hadn't really seen him and when I first saw Eddie Cochran I said to my mate, "Is that Elvis?"'

Dalton was so consumed by the music scene that he bought a guitar. Local bands didn't really have bass players but, at school, they had a tea-chest bass, and he managed to learn a song called 'Jet Black'.

'I was at a party and a band called The Bluejacks were there, minus a bass player,' said Dalton. 'I started playing "Jet Black" and they loved that, so they said, "Do you want to join the band?" I said, "I can't play anything", so they said, "We'll teach you, and we've got a gig on Thursday." It was at a dog track, it was nerve wracking It was November, it was foggy, I didn't know a word and I was a fairly shy 15-year-old.'

On leaving school, Dalton thought about being a carpenter and was involved in making sidecars for motorbikes. An amiable sort, with a passing resemblance to Paul McCartney, he would still play gigs at the weekend with The Bluejacks, who travelled in two cars to shows up to an hour away. The personnel changed over the years, with Danny King and the Bluejacks becoming Jimmy Virgo and the Bluejacks, and, after Jimmy left in 1962, a complete change in name to Kenny Lee and the Mark Four. Nonetheless, his time with the group gave Dalton some valuable experience of recording and touring. As The Bluejacks, playing rock and roll and rockabilly tunes, they had recorded a demo of Gene Vincent's 'Say Mama' and 'Brand New Cadillac', which they paid for themselves, and as The Mark Four 'Rock Around the Clock', which became their first record.

'We had a road manager,' said Dalton. 'Bill Fowler, a really nice guy. He just drove us to the gigs, but it was status. He left us to go with The Merseys, then we went to the Arthur Howes agency.' By the time The Kinks came calling, via Arthur Howes, Dalton had actually stopped playing and was working full time as a coalman. 'I said I can't play with a band like that,' recalled Dalton. 'The way it was put to me was, "It's only for a couple of weeks you've got nothing to lose."'

Before meeting The Kinks, Dalton obtained a picture of the band so he knew what they looked like. The problem was, he didn't know which band member was which.

When Dalton walked in to the audition he was immediately christened 'Pull My Cock Off', previously the band's nickname for Paul McCartney, though he would later be known simply as 'Nobby'. 'I just went to the audition and it was awful,' Dalton recalled. 'No one was really interested in me. Dave was lying flat out on the floor playing his guitar, Mick was bashing away at his drums, Ray wasn't even there for a while and then he walked in. We just played a couple of songs, they looked at me, at my face, and I think they thought, "Well he looks OK". I think Ray was more concerned because this was lunch time and they were being filmed for *Top of the Pops* that evening. I think he thought I'd look OK on TV and it wasn't going to be for long. This was the Thursday, I think we had a rehearsing session on the Friday and then a double concert booking that weekend, then we were off to play in Spain.'

'Wace and Collins were very very funny, very upper class and as The Kinks were big mickey-takers [the banter] just never stopped,' recalled Dalton. 'Robert would buy anything as long as it was expensive. He tried to get me to buy a coat once to wear on stage, I said, "But it doesn't fit." He said, "But it doesn't matter, it's £150."' He also remembered how the band's management briefed him: 'When I joined the band Grenville got a stack of records from the office, stuffed them in my hand and said, "Learn those!" I thought, "Well I'm not going to need all these album tracks."'

After the disastrous American tour, Grenville Collins had made sure that The Kinks were always accompanied overseas. They would certainly need help in Spain. The band were booked to play half a dozen shows but, after the first one was poorly attended, the promoters started to complain about the absence of Pete Quaife. 'I think it was the get-out,' said Dalton. 'I mean, what was the difference between me and Pete Quaife being there? We did one show, but at the second they wanted to keep the money. I read that I was put in jail, I think I might have remembered that! It just made a better story.'

It wasn't easy for foreigners working in a fascist country and, while Dalton had a work permit, the promoter argued that it had been acquired under false pretences. Mick Avory was harassed by the Spanish police for stepping on the grass in a square during a photo shoot in Madrid. The band had had enough, and headed home early.

The Kinks returned to an England gearing up for the World Cup, which was due to kick off on 11 July 1966. As well as being a good summer for football, the charts were also filled with songs that have since become classics: 'Sunny Afternoon' was ahead of The Beatles' 'Paperback Writer' and Tina Turner's 'River Deep, Mountain High', while Frank Sinatra was at number five with 'Strangers in the Night'. During that summer, Lisbet Thorkil-Petersen, who Dave had met in Copenhagen, came over from Denmark, took a flat in London and enrolled on an English course. 'Much to my delight and surprise,' said Dave in *Kink*.

The Kinks, with John Dalton, played shows in Northern Ireland and Scotland throughout July and met up at Ray's house to watch the World Cup Final on 30 July, before a long drive to Devon for a show that night. The match went into extra time and The Kinks set off late – very late. They eventually arrived shortly before the midnight curfew and played for just a few minutes before being closed down, amid boos and jeers from a large crowd.

By late summer, things were on hold. At the request of Grenville Collins, Allen Klein arrived in London to talk about The Kinks' US deal with Pye. Klein was an accountant from New Jersey who had negotiated substantial payouts for Sam Cooke and then The Rolling Stones. Soon, he was in place as The Kinks' US business manager. He spent three days in London and negotiations meant that the new album was delayed from August until October, when new agreements were signed off. In the UK, a new five-year contract was agreed with Pye, while in the US, Klein arranged a new deal with Reprise, also for five years.

During the contract talks, Pye assembled a 'best of', *Well Respected Kinks*, which went to number five in the UK album chart. Dave Davies went to visit Pete Quaife, who was convalescing in Denmark with Beden Paustian, but was greeted with some surprising news:

Quaife wasn't coming back. He resigned and signed his way out of the band in September.

'He didn't like it, having time off,' said David Quaife. 'It gave him too much time to think and then he got pretty morose, he just said, "I can't do it anymore." Ray turned up at Mum and Dad's and he said, "Come on we've got to get your son back in the groove." They said yes, because he was getting £40 a week or whatever, but that wasn't very much for what The Kinks were achieving. But Pete had a real breakdown and smashed loads of stuff in the house.'

John Dalton was told that he would be in the band full time from now on, and the *New Musical Express* of 16 September announced that QUAIFE QUITS KINKS – OFFICIAL and quoted Robert Wace: 'I feel that Pete may have made the wrong decision to leave, but it is his decision. It could be at least six months before he was well enough to rejoin the group and he has decided instead to make his career in other fields.'

'Pete was a bit of a strange character,' said Mick Avory. 'It seemed a strange time to leave, when you're having success. I couldn't get close to him because he had these weird things he used to do [musically], sort of a different wavelength to me.' The *Record Mirror* chart of September 1966 had The Kinks at the head of the table. This list was based on a compilation of the placings of a band's albums, EPs and singles during the year. By the end of the year, the final table showed The Kinks in third place behind The Beach Boys, in first, and Dave Dee, Dozy, Beaky, Mick and Tich. This success was largely down to the album that The Kinks released in October 1966.

After numerous delays while a new deal with Pye was agreed, the album finally went on sale at the end of the month, under the title *Face to Face*. This name immediately conjures up ideas of confrontation, but whether it referred to problems between the brothers or in the band is unknown. Ray later called *Face to Face* a collection of songs rather than an album. At the time, in an attempt to unify the record, he pushed for sound effects to introduce each track, but this was dismissed by Pye. Three did make it on to the album, though, and the first sound on the record is a ringing telephone, which is answered by Grenville Collins, introducing

Dave Davies singing 'Party Line', a Davies brothers co-composition. Dave added lyrics about he and Pete Quaife trying to call girlfriends in Denmark from their hotel and getting crossed lines. Elsewhere, the record offers the sound of waves lapping on a beach ('Holiday in Waikiki') and thunderstorms ('Rainy Day in June').

'Dandy' could be a follow-up to 'Dedicated Follower of Fashion', or a message to Dave Davies himself: 'Dandy, you know you're moving much too fast/ And Dandy, you know you can't escape the past'. 'Making good music was the supreme feeling and objective,' said Shel Talmy. 'They weren't going to be my new best friends. Ray was at the height of his powers, the music was great fun, everything else, the politics with the managers and record company was less than fun.' Appropriately, then, the album had a more serious side: 'Too Much on My Mind' was an admission of Ray's fragile mental state, and 'Rosie Won't You Please Come Home' was a straightforward plea to the Davies sister in Australia. 'Session Man' could have been about any one of the musicians hired to work on Kinks albums over the years, or it could have been about all of them, though Ray named one in particular.

> [It was] inspired partly by Nicky [Hopkins] . . . Shel Talmy asked Nicky to throw in 'something classy' at the beginning of the track. Nicky responded by playing a classical-style harpsichord part. When we recorded 'Sunny Afternoon', Shel insisted that Nicky copy my plodding piano style. Other musicians would have been insulted but Nicky seemed to get inside my style, and he played exactly as I would have. No ego. Perhaps that was his secret. Session players are, for the most part, anonymous shadows behind the stars. They do their job for a fee and then leave, rarely seeing their names on the records. Their playing never stands out, but if you take them out of the mix, the track doesn't sound the same. You only miss them when they are not there.

The musical evolution on display on *Face to Face* was not solely Ray's. Mick Avory made his most telling contributions to a Kinks album to date, and the outro to 'Holiday in Waikiki' and 'Little Miss Queen of Darkness' are among his career highlights. 'I liked *Face to*

Face because I was making a debut [on an album] and getting into the music and trying to do my best to fit around the songs,' said Avory. 'I could drum songs because I listened to the music. I didn't just listen to the bass player. A lot of drummers and bass players work together. I listen to the vocal as well.' The problem was, Ray often kept the vocal back until the very end and the band didn't know what he'd be signing, or how. 'You had to surmise what the vocal was,' added Avory, 'because we didn't always get a guide vocal. Ray was a bit secretive about it, but when he loosened up a bit, he gave us a bit better idea.'

The album contained harpsichords and drones, further examples of the band pushing new boundaries. 'We allowed ourselves to experiment sonically with overtones and ambience,' said Ray in 2012. 'It was a lovely time. "Too Much on My Mind", I can relate to it as much now as I did then. There are some solid songs that came out of my own personality. "Too Much on My Mind" is straight from my soul, if you like.'

Face to Face was well received on both sides of the Atlantic. In *Crawdaddy!*, the first US rock magazine to sell itself on serious rock criticism, Paul Williams wrote that, 'There's a lot of depth to this album . . . A work of beauty. If "Too Much on My Mind" is his statement of policy, then "Sunny Afternoon", following, as it does, a nervous breakdown, is Ray's State of the Union Address to the world.' The *New Musical Express* called it a 'remarkable achievement' and awarded it four stars.

In its design, too, the album was a departure for the band. Instead of the generic portraits that had featured on most of their albums and singles to date, *Face to Face* showed a proto-psychedelic, pre-*Yellow Submarine* or Monty Python illustration of a cloud of colourful butterflies exiting from a man's head, the top of which appears to have been sliced off. 'I didn't like that sleeve,' said Ray. 'I wanted the cover to be black and strong like the sound of the LP, instead of all of those fancy colours. I was starting to let things go and accepting things that I shouldn't have.'

Things were relatively quiet that autumn for The Kinks. Mick

Avory was the polar opposite of the stereotypical mad drummer and spent much of this period attending art classes, learning oil painting every Thursday night he had free.

By mid-November, Pete Quaife had moved back to London and returned to the fold, and John Dalton went back to delivering coal. 'I'd got on very well with the band,' he said. 'There were only four of us and we travelled everywhere by car with the road manager Stan, a lovely man, we were always having fun. Then I got a phone call and was called in to the office, and they explained it nicely to me that Pete wanted to come back and there wasn't a lot they could do about it because he was still a quarter of the company. None of the band got in touch with me, it was only the management.'

'That accident had smashed me up quite badly,' said Pete Quaife. 'I thought that I was able to continue playing and touring but, after a few trips here and there, I realised that I needed to recuperate properly, I was in a lot of pain and unable to concentrate. So I went to Denmark to stay with my girlfriend for a long-awaited holiday. It worked and when I felt better I rejoined the band.'

Dave Davies coaxed Quaife back into The Kinks by inviting him to a session in November to play on a new song called 'Dead End Street'. Quaife was reluctant, but Dave played along on bass with him and they were both happy with the outcome. 'I've been away all this time and suddenly people are again asking me what toothpaste I use and what my hobbies are,' said Pete Quaife of his return to the media circus. He also talked about the way The Kinks were now working on new material together, rather than deferring to Ray and Shel Talmy. This gave him the opportunity to leave his own creative mark on the songs. 'We go in and make a demo of the basic tune,' he explained. '[We] take a copy home to work on then we come back a few days later, pool all our ideas and record the tracks. Saves a lot of time and money.'

Not content with having just finished *Face to Face*, the band released 'Dead End Street' as a single, just three weeks later. This time, there was nothing ironic or oblique about the social commentary. 'I don't like it when people are out of work and hungry, obviously,' said Ray Davies. 'That's why I wrote "Dead End Street". I even made a film to go with that song on *Top of the Pops*, but it showed slums and poverty, and so they wouldn't run it. I guess they prefer films about running around in parks, jumping over chairs. I was upset by the refusal but was pleased to see that when *Panorama* showed a film about the slums they used "Dead End Street" as the accompanying music!'

The promotional short, filmed in gritty black and white, was shot in north London's Kentish Town, the resulting footage intercut with atmospheric stills of working-class life. The film tells a brief story about a team of undertakers arriving to take a body from a terraced house. Despite the feeling of gloom that overhangs the film and the song, as in the 'Sunny Afternoon' promotional footage, The Kinks were determined to add their own brand of humour. In one shot, a solemn-looking Ray knocks on the front door of the house in full undertaker garb and it is opened by Dave in drag. Later, when the undertakers stop with the coffin for a cigarette break, the 'corpse' jumps up and a Keystone Kops-style chase ensues.

'Dead End Street' was Shel Talmy's last job as producer with the band. In fact, the final mix was not his work. Talmy hurt his shoulder and was away from the studio when Ray Davies reworked the track. '"Dead End Street" was produced by [Talmy] but he wasn't there,' Davies told *Goldmine* magazine in 1996. 'But that was the contract. Sometimes a producer is good as a catalyst to get people to do things. I think he was effective for the time. I wouldn't listen to him now although I'd respect his opinion. It was a different thing producing then; now you've got to be part of the band.' There was never any discussion about retaining Talmy once his contract was over. Ray had long wanted to be the producer and now he would have the chance.

'I wasn't overly impressed with him,' said Ray Davies. 'But I liked the fact that he used reverb in a sensible way. I liked him. He had good insight into what I wanted to do, or at least I felt he did. He seemed a nice, personable guy.' Other bands' members got on well with Talmy too. 'I liked Shel and I remember we had a lot of problems with him,' said Dave Davies. 'I think he fancied himself as the new Phil Spector. There was a learning curve for Shel and us. I think once he realised we wanted a bit smaller and grittier, in-your-face sound, it started to work well.'

Talmy may not have added an amazing array of studio trickery to The Kinks recordings, but in a subtle, understated way he was able to coerce them to record the songs as Ray Davies had envisaged. Not only could he direct them towards the best 'sound' but he also helped to choose and shape hit singles, something which the band very rarely managed in the decades after his departure. 'I'm very proud of the fact that the recordings still stand up,' said Talmy in 2009. '[The music] has not dated, it has not aged, and it's as good as – if not better than – anything that's around today.'

'Dead End Street' reached number six in the UK chart. The Kinks played only two shows between the release of *Face to Face* and the end of the year, and didn't spend much time in the studio either. A quick stop at Pye in late November yielded four new demos – early versions of 'Two Sisters', 'Tin Soldier Man' and 'Afternoon Tea', and a new song called 'Village Green'. This final track was to provide the catalyst for a further evolution that would dominate the band for years to come: the concept album.

Part 3

When I first met Paul Weller he had a badge on that said, 'Who the fuck is David Watts?' He had to be my friend after that.

Ray Davies

Hamburgers and Tomato Sauce

Ray Davies had ended 1966 in good spirits: he was over the worst of his health problems and depression, Pete Quaife was back in the band and *Face to Face* had been well received. He spent New Year's Eve celebrating with his family at the Queen Alexandra pub in Fortis Green. The year ahead, however, was to be one of big changes in the music industry, and for The Kinks.

By 1967, The Beatles had fallen out of love with America, especially after the 'Bigger than Jesus' controversy had seen their records burned by crowds whipped up by conservative religious radio stations. After a series of huge stadium shows, they finally retired from touring altogether, fed up with the constant battle to be heard above screaming fans. Their US rivals, The Beach Boys, had also given up on performing live, Brian Wilson preferring to concentrate on songwriting and studio work, the fruits of which were released on *Pet Sounds*. Meanwhile, The Doors were tearing up the west coast and The Monkees, manufactured to fill a slot in the television schedules, had claimed instant fame. More avant-garde, counter-cultural bands, such as The Velvet Underground and The Grateful Dead, were also emerging, while the new concept of the 'pop festival' began to gain popularity.

Closer to home, as he revealed in *Kink*, Dave Davies was beginning to feel jaded with the party scene: 'The false talk, the false smiles, the superficiality. The hangers-on. I felt that I had no real friends.' He found out that Lisbet was pregnant and decided they should marry, which they did in April 1967, at the Fredericksberg town hall in Denmark. None of his family were present. Lisbet was four months into her pregnancy and the marriage was kept out of the press. 'She insisted it would be alright if we didn't marry,' recalled Dave in *Kink*. 'I took a long hard look at her and inside my own feelings. Maybe it would be nice to get married, have kids and buy a house.' It seemed Dave's days of casual promiscuity were over, but his public image as young, free and single remained.

That same spring, Pete Quaife married Annette 'Beden' Paustian, Lisbet's cousin, who was also pregnant. Their wedding took place at the Finsbury Park Registry Office in London and was also kept quiet. Beden suffered childbirth complications in May and several Kinks shows were cancelled due to Pete's absence. Pete then moved back to his mother's house in Muswell Hill so he could continue with the band while Beden stayed with her family.

For Ray, this was an especially positive time. He was working fast on new material, in between tours, and, by early 1967, had twelve songs in various stages of completion. As usual, these fought shy any of the current trends or fashions, and included amongst them was perhaps the defining work of Ray's songwriting career. But before he could take it into the studio there was a rather more conventional project to complete.

On Saturday, 1 April, the band and associated engineers set off for Scotland where they planned to record a live album, at the Kelvin Hall in Glasgow. '*Live at Kelvin Hall* was done three-track and we drove up in a VW van and all the kit was in the back . . . we used less than ten microphones,' said Alan O'Duffy. 'Alan Mackenzie organised for some girls to come and dance on stage with the band. What a reaction and what a great record. Today it would all be forty-eight track and maybe forty-eight microphones. They just miked up a kick drum and a drum, and a guitar and another guitar, and a bass, and a vocal and another vocal, and one for the crowd, and that's it folks, extraordinary.' The post-production, if it could be called that, was minimal: they adjusted the sound levels and that was about it.

Though a commercial flop, released at different times in the UK and US, and lost in their mid-sixties catalogue, it is an important document of what a Kinks show of that era was really like. The screaming goes on throughout, not just between songs, and the band is at its sweaty, powerful best. Ray does manage to get the crowd's attention at one point and conducts them through a rowdy sing-along of 'Sunny Afternoon' in the kind of mass pub shanty that he always envisaged for it.

After *Live at Kelvin Hall*, the band went straight back to the studio and began work on a new song of Ray's – 'Waterloo Sunset'.

'I got so upset about not going to America that I got really depressed,' said Ray Davies. 'I moved to a house up in Elstree, which was a nice big manorial mansion.' It was here that he would write some of his best work. Perhaps as a response to 'exile' from the US, his writing, which was already consciously English, came to focus even more precisely on London, the city of his birth. The career highpoints of 'Sunny Afternoon' and 'Waterloo Sunset' made plain Davies' remarkable ability to observe aspects of British life, but also to cut through stereotypes, bearing down on the day-to-day realities of the common people, without resorting to cockney or pastoral clichés. These were paths that he would follow for the next three years, and it was a creative seam he would mine with great success.

In the newfound sexual freedom of the sixties, The Kinks played around with the notion of sexuality more freely and bravely than their peers. The very nature of their band name led people to connect them with the idea of 'kinky sex', something that, initially at least, they played up to in photo shoots with thigh-high boots and whips. Dave Davies was also quite open about his promiscuity, though he didn't disclose until much later that he was sleeping with both men and women. The band liked to challenge the status quo. Anyone could be taken aim at and any social nicety was a potential target. The aforementioned world of fashion ('Dedicated Follower of Fashion'), fellow musicians ('Session Man'), promiscuous party-goers ('Dandy') and upper-class twits ('House in the Country') were all addressed, and dressed down. Even when it came to music The Kinks were happy to go into battle. First they went up against the Liverpool sound with the Merseybeat-destroying 'You Really Got Me', and then, with 'Waterloo Sunset', made a deliberate attempt to put London, not Liverpool, at the centre of the musical map.

'Waterloo Sunset' is perhaps the quintessential London song. With it, Ray perfectly married melody with simple yet evocative lyrics to paint a memorable panorama. If Davies had achieved his teenage ambition to become a filmmaker, he could not have hoped to capture the scene more vividly. The narrator is close to the real Ray Davies at that time – withdrawn, observing others living their lives. He had walked over Waterloo Bridge often when he went to art school and he knew the area intimately. Though the singer was a character, Ray drew upon his time as a child in a hospital bed surveying the very same scene. Though he hadn't had them in mind when he wrote the song, Ray told Keith Altham that if 'Waterloo Sunset' were a film then 'Terry' and 'Julie' would be the much-talked-about acting couple Terence Stamp and Julie Christie, who starred that year in a film adaptation of *Far From the Madding Crowd*.

The recording of 'Waterloo Sunset' was perfected over a number of sessions. 'One of my memories is the Wimpy bar,' said Alan O'Duffy of life in the studio with The Kinks. 'It was all hamburgers and tomato sauce and chips, this dreadful diet that those guys put up with from across the street. The Stones would go up the road to this Chinese restaurant the Lotus House on Edgware Road, but The Kinks were all about the Wimpy bar. I remember a combination of the sweat of the guitar amps and the smell of the Wimpy bar, there was nothing glamorous about it at all.' Seedy as it might have seemed at times, the music more than made up for it. 'I was only 17 or something but I remember recording "Waterloo Sunset" thinking this is a really nice song and liking the storytelling aspects of it.'

Ray, now producing, had a completely formed lyric, but didn't tell anyone what he was going to sing, only which chords they needed to play. Under his direction, with the final sound mapped out in his head, Ray, Dave, Rasa and Pete provided harmony backing vocals. Then, at last, Ray sang the lead, letting the rest of the band in on his secret.

'It painted a picture of a scene that everyone's seen,' said Mick Avory. 'Lots of people have said they always think of that song when they cross Waterloo Bridge.'

When it came to mixing, Alan MacKenzie let Ray work the faders to end the song, it was as close as he ever got to perfection. 'I had achieved everything I set out to do creatively and I was 22 years old,' wrote Ray Davies in *X-Ray*.

The effects of the US ban continued to be felt, as the song failed to even chart in America after its 26 July release there. How the record-buying public of North America would have responded had The Kinks toured with it remains a matter for alternative historians. It's a London folk song, a hymn to the city to be passed down from one generation to the next. In the UK it was held at number two by The Tremeloes' 'Silence is Golden', but was nonetheless an indisputable hit, and a clear expression of the peculiarly English idiom The Kinks were now developing. 'I became almost grotesquely English,' said Ray Davies in the film *Imaginary Man*.

When 'Waterloo Sunset' began slipping down the charts, it was passed on the way up by 'Death of a Clown', which went to number three in July, and was credited to Dave Davies. Dave had first thought about a solo single early in the year while messing around on the old piano at his parents' house. The false friendships and empty relationships of the 'swinging' London scene had made him feel like an unloved jester, great for getting a party going, but not a figure to be taken seriously. 'Suddenly the whole roller-coaster ride of the past three years seemed wearisome,' he wrote in *Kink*. 'Disconsolate, I felt like a cheerless clown.' The new song was slated for inclusion on the next Kinks LP, and Ray worked on it with his brother in the studio. 'Ray helped arrange the middle,' said Dave. 'I wrote a couple more verses and there we had it.'

The band pulled out all the stops on the recording. Ray leaned in and picked the grand piano strings by hand during the intro, and Nicky Hopkins played piano throughout. 'They had a tack piano,' explained Alan O'Duffy. 'That's a piano with something like drawing pins on the hammers so it made a "tack" sound.' They also employed an echo delay to give more depth as Dave sang of his innermost heartaches, about false friends and his real feelings about fame: 'So lets all drink to the death of a clown/ Won't somebody help me to break up this crown.'

When Wace and Collins heard the result, they suggested it should be released as a solo single. Ray was in agreement and Dave was happy with this arrangement. Ray thought that the band could concentrate on more serious, album-oriented work, and Dave could go off and do the wild, single work instead. It would be a burden off Ray's back.

'Slightly wailing in concept, but a good song with a haunting quality,' reported *Record Mirror* approvingly. The *New Musical Express* added that 'It's kinda folksy in a way, with a steady beat and a tune you can really get your teeth into.' The single did very well, leading to plans for a Dave Davies solo album, and he quickly lined up a few songs. 'Susannah's Still Alive' went to number thirteen in the autumn, while another, 'Funny Face', was about his lost love Sue. 'Many times during my life thoughts and feelings about her would rise to the surface,' wrote Dave in *Kink*. When plans for the solo album fell through, Dave found that the next Kinks album allowed him the greatest creative input he had enjoyed to date.

In the August 1967 issue of *Disc and Music Echo* magazine, Ray Davies was asked to review the new Beatles album, *Revolver*. True to character, he wasn't short of opinions. REALLY, IT'S A LOAD OF RUBBISH blared the headline. Davies went through the album track by track and hardly had a good word to say about any of it.

'Taxman' – It sounds like a cross between The Who and Batman.
'Eleanor Rigby' – It sounds like they're out to please music teachers in primary schools.
'Love You Too' – George wrote this – he must have quite a big influence on the group now. I was doing this sort of song two

years ago – now I'm doing what The Beatles were doing two years ago . . .

'Yellow Submarine' – This is a load of rubbish, really. I take the mickey out of myself on the piano and play stuff like this. I think they know it's not that good.

'And Your Bird Can Sing' – Don't like this. The song's too predictable. It's not a Beatles song at all.

'Got to Get You into My Life' – Paul sounds like Little Richard.

'Tomorrow Never Knows' – Listen to all those crazy sounds! It'll be popular in discotheques.

Perhaps he was lucky that John Lennon and Paul McCartney weren't asked to review the next Kinks album, *Something Else*, which was issued just over a month later. It opened with a snippet of studio chatter, 'Nice and smooth,' said Dave, before the band set off at breakneck speed.

The first track, 'David Watts', was one in a long line of songs in which Ray travelled back to his school days, singing of a fictional head boy who he admired and wanted to ape. 'There was a boy called Denton at school who was head of football,' said Ray. 'I was always fascinated by any structure of school society. I only went to a secondary school but the system was there.' But the song's origins weren't quite as simple as that explanation suggests: a retired army officer called David Watts, had recently promoted their show at the Rutland Showground, after which the band had gone back to his country house where, having had a few drinks, he had propositioned Dave. Ray threw in the lines about being 'so gay and fancy free' after this party. 'I suppose I tend to be rather cruel to my friends,' he said. 'I'm really getting at myself as well. I seldom exaggerate characters, like David Watts, I deliberately underplay them and that is why the lyric tends to sound sarcastic. People are seldom offended by what I do or write about them. Either they fail to recognise themselves or they have enough intelligence to laugh at it.' Musically the song is a pounding rocker, and became a touchstone for future generations of mod musicians.

The third song on the album, which follows 'Death of a Clown', was 'Two Sisters' and appears to be a thinly veiled account of Ray's resentment of Dave's relatively carefree lifestyle, though Alan O'Duffy doesn't recall any friction between the brothers in the studio at that time. This track was also notable as the first time strings were pushed to the fore in a Kinks recording.

'Two Sisters' wasn't the only musical experiment on the album: 'No Return' was infused with bossa nova rhythms and 'Tin Soldier Man' added a brass section. 'Harry Rag' (slang for fag or cigarette) and 'Situation Vacant', meanwhile, were typical Davies domestic vignettes. 'End of the Season' and 'Waterloo Sunset' provided a strong close to the album, the former cementing Ray's continuing fascination with the autumn.

Following on from *Face to Face*, *Something Else* was, overall, another consistently strong offering. *Melody Maker* called it 'One of the albums of the year', while *Record Mirror* concluded that 'It's destined to be another big hit for the boys.' Despite these glowing recommendations, it became the first Kinks album not to chart.

That autumn, the band did play some live dates, unlike the period after *Face to Face*, and also made TV and radio appearances, a trial of which Pete Quaife had long grown bored. '[You] have to arrive at 9 a.m. but then sit around while things are being set up,' he said of appearing on *Ready, Steady, Go!* '[You] go to the canteen but are told you can't get anything to eat until 12 noon, "union rules". Then the microphones aren't plugged in, then the amps don't work, then you can't hear what the hosts are saying and suddenly you have to play.'

Not more than a month after *Something Else* was released in September, The Kinks had already moved on and were busy promoting a completely new single, 'Autumn Almanac', a sublime example of Ray Davies' growing maturity as a writer and arranger. From the opening line, 'From the dew-soaked hedge creeps a crawly caterpillar', it was evident that it was something special. The tongue-twisting words were hard enough to say, never mind sing, but the song was a delight both musically and lyrically, and gave more clues about where the band would soon be heading. It revels in the simple things in life – sweeping up leaves, having Sunday dinner, toasted currant buns, going to the football – and is also heavily dosed with both nostalgia for a simpler past and a longing for things to stay unchanged. 'I like autumn things,' said Ray. 'After I wrote it, for a whole month I was thinking about it. I wasted a lot time, because I was sweeping up dead leaves and putting them in the sack. I'm susceptible to that sort of thing – to walls and flowers. You can probably get something more from a wall than a person sometimes. It's just put somewhere. It's in line, in order. Ah, ridiculous. What I try to do probably doesn't come out.'

The song is easy to hum or sing along to but was a challenge to play, and the middle section was actually a verse played backwards. They used a Mellotron, a keyboard instrument built around banks of tapes of instruments playing individual notes – a kind of primitive sampler which takes some practice to master. The song also contains timing changes, so what, on the face of it, seemed to be a straightforward piece about nature and the changing of the seasons, was rich with trickery and new technology. It's often said that a definition of genius is being able to make the complicated seem simple, and this song, perhaps, proves that point.

'It's a miniature movie, basically, that unravels itself as you are listening to it, and it has all these little movements or scenes,' said Andy Partridge of XTC, a band that continued The Kinks' songwriting tradition of sharp character studies during the late 1970s and early eighties. 'And they all seem to take place in the kind of mythical cosy London that the Ealing studios always had in their films, like *The Lavender Hill Mob*. The song just keeps turning and changing; you see a new facet every few seconds. But there's nothing unsettling about the fact that there are so many parts. Normally that would just be the death of a song, it would just scramble people's brains. The lyrics are very everyday. There's no "calling occupants of interplanetary craft" in it. All the language in it is what you'd say over a cup of tea.'

'Autumn Almanac' made it to number five in the UK chart, and it would end up being the band's highest-placed single position for the next three years. 'There are few groups more capable of painting vivid and descriptive verbal pictures than The Kinks,' claimed the *New Musical Express*. The single was backed by another high-calibre B-side, 'Mr Pleasant', another of Ray Davies' great character studies.

With Larry Page ousted and Shel Talmy's contract expired, Ray was happy to be able to take as long as he wanted over new material. Moreover, he was under less pressure to produce the same volume of songs as in the early days. Neither was he was in a rush to tour: between December 1967 and April 1968, the band played only five known shows, a far cry from the dozens in any four-month period during their early career. This inactivity had allowed Dave Davies to explore a solo career, but neither Pete Quaife or Mick Avory were able to do the same.

Quaife, in particular, was fed up with being ignored, openly complaining that, although he wasn't another Ray Davies, he was creative and life with The Kinks was stifling his creativity out of him. 'Pete was outgoing like me and he was always up for trying different things,' said Dave Davies. 'He was never scared to give it a go. Him being an accomplished musician was also a great help when we started recording in the studio because if we needed something he would suggest parts for guitars and bass, and he'd help with arrangements and he was a great backing singer too. It was Pete who came up with the "Sha la la's" on "Waterloo Sunset".' These frustrations would carry over into the new year but, before then, there was talk of a planned US press visit, recording sessions in Burbank and television spots. Once again, though, the fallout from the 1965 visit prevented the band obtaining visas and their plans fell through. Instead, the next couple of years would be spent pursuing decidedly English dreams.

CHAPTER 11: 1968

The Village Green Preservation Society

A year of social upheaval, political strife and violence followed in 1968. The Americans were struggling in Vietnam and protests against the war were held around the world. Riots broke out across the US after the assassination of civil rights leader Martin Luther King Jr in April while, at home in Britain, sixteen days later, Enoch Powell gave his 'rivers of blood' speech in Birmingham. Bobby Kennedy was shot and killed in June and Soviet tanks rolled into Prague during August. The list of death and destruction seemed to be unending. In Paris, the streets were littered with burnt-out cars as demonstrators battled with the police. Even Ray Davies' old stamping ground, the Hornsey College of Art, saw a student sit-in.

Ray and Dave Davies were more concerned about what was going on closer to home. They had young families, and enjoyed Sunday lunch and a spot of football. Both had turned out for the 'Showbiz Eleven' football team which had been playing charity games since 1957, and had, at various times, included the likes of Billy Wright, John Charles and Bobby Moore. When his back wasn't bothering him, Ray would play in numerous teams, often alongside journalist Keith Altham. 'I played football with him a few times for Ed Stewart's All-Star Eleven, a show business team and a BBC DJ team which occasionally trotted out,' said Altham. 'He was a very good footballer, excellent balance. I played every week so I was fit. I was supposed to lay on the balls so they could score all the goals – the only ones I found that could play were Ray, Rod Stewart and Leapy Lee, the one-hit wonder was a good footballer.' When Ray and Dave played in the same team, they often played on opposite sides of the pitch and yet seemed to have a telepathic understanding of where the other would be at any moment, and what they were likely to do when they got the ball. Whether they were generous in sharing the ball with each other is unknown.

Despite their youth (Dave was just about to turn 21 and Ray was 23), both brothers were starting to worry about Britain's threatened heritage – the old England that was being pulled down and built over around them. Ray was fascinated by old photographs and Dave was upset about post-war reconstruction, the demolition of Victorian terraces, and roads built across fields leading to faceless concrete office towers. As usual, what was worrying them and making them angry became the focus for their songwriting.

While the band hid themselves away in the studio, *Live at Kelvin Hall* was released to general apathy in the UK, and *Something Else* finally came out in the USA. The latter, at least, was well received, with positive write-ups in influential publications such as *Rolling Stone* and *Crawdaddy!*, but, despite a spirited press campaign, it failed to reach the US top 100. The musical landscape was changing in the wake of The Beatles' album *Sgt. Pepper's Lonely Hearts Club Band*, which had been released in June 1967. Formerly singles-led groups were increasingly putting effort into recording a cohesive album rather than padding out the singles with hastily recorded filler. During 1968, American group The Band responded to *Sgt. Pepper* with *Music From the Big Pink*, Jimi Hendrix released *Electric Ladyland* and ex-Them lead singer Van Morrison presented his second LP, *Astral Weeks*, which failed to chart at all, but was hailed by *Rolling Stone* as the record of the year. How would The Kinks, still best known for their singles, react to this sea change?

January and February 1968 were quiet months for The Kinks. Ray had a commission from the BBC to write a weekly song for the TV show *At the Eleventh Hour* and contributed nine. Of those, eight were to be sung by 27-year-old Jeannie Lamb, who was married to jazz saxophonist Danny Moss and appeared on shows such as *That Was the Week That Was* and *Secret Army*. Of the songs Ray provided – 'You Can't Give Me More Than What You Have' (broadcast 30/12/67), 'If Christmas Day Could Last Forever' (broadcast 6/1/68), 'We're Backing Britain' (broadcast 13/1/68), 'Poor Old Intellectual Sadie' (broadcast 20/1/68), 'Just a Poor Country Girl' (broadcast 10/2/68), 'The Man Who Conned Dinner From The Ritz' (broadcast 17/2/68), 'Did You See His name?' (broadcast 24/2/68), 'This is What the World is All About' (broadcast 2/3/68) – The Kinks attempted to record only 'Did You See His name?'

In March, The Kinks returned to Pye for work on their sixth album, about which Ray had big ideas. The first song to be heard from these sessions was 'Wonderboy', which was released as a single. Peter Jones, reviewing it in the 6 April 1968 issue of *Record Mirror* wrote, 'Not necessarily their best, but they set exceptionally high standards. Philosophy-pop is the phrase I've just created for them.' It was in the charts alongside Louis Armstrong's 'Bare Necessities' from *The Jungle Book* and other 'novelty' songs.

This was the first time that the direction Ray Davies wanted to take was *really* alienating some of his own band. Dave Davies thought the song was 'beautifully haunting' but Pete Quaife did not agree. '"Wonderboy" was horrible,' said Quaife. 'It sounded like Herman's Hermits wanking. Jesus it was bad. I hated it. I remember recording it and doing the la-la-las and just thinking, "What kind of prissy sissy nonsense are we doing? We're the guys that made 'You Really Got Me', for Chrissakes!"' The song was slathered in harpsichords and 'la-la-la' backing vocals. This *was* the same band that had recorded 'You Really Got Me', but they had grown up: Ray Davies had a mortgage and was anticipating the birth of his second child. 'In that song is all the layers,' he said. 'The cathartic feelings, the problems, the images, my thoughts on my position in the world, why I should be a parent.'

'Wonderboy' failed to sell, not charting at all in the US and failing to make the top twenty in the UK – the first Kinks single to miss out since 'You Still Want Me' in April 1964. It ended a run of twelve singles getting to at least number eleven in the UK charts. This relative failure signalled the start of a difficult year, as The Beatles and the Stones cashed in on the American market while The Kinks could only watch from the sidelines.

With around fifteen fresh songs put on tape, the band set off on a UK tour with newly installed road manager Ken Jones – a calming influence. They played a headline slot on the dying package tour circuit with The Tremeloes, The Herd and others, performing twenty-one shows in twenty-three nights during April. By that time, most bands preferred to tour on their own, and crowds were getting smaller for multi-band shows, as were the venues, and The Kinks found themselves performing, more often than not, in cinemas.

A return to the studio in May produced more album material and another future single, 'Days'. Ray Davies had sensed that the band weren't fully behind him on his recent songs and he began to wonder if The Kinks might be reaching the end of the road. He attempted to document this feeling on 'Days'. The result is a glorious if emotionally draining three minutes of pop music. It is both anthemic and eulogistic, so perhaps an unsurprisingly popular choice for funerals: the lyrics provide one of the most eloquent goodbyes imaginable. It appears some members of the band didn't like 'Days', however. A much-repeated story tells of Ray's fury when, during a lengthy recording session, Pete Quaife wrote 'Daze' on one of the tape boxes. 'I said, "Don't be an arsehole",' explained Ray. '"This means a lot to me, this song."'

In the early twenty-first century, Quaife addressed the long-running tale during an online question-and-answer session with fans. His account of the incident relives the frustration he felt at the time, but differs from Ray's version of events in a number of details:

> I did not refer to 'Days' as 'Daze' . . . I do not know how he came to think of it . . . I remember the time and the place . . . We were in Studio 2 recording. We had been there for EVER! As usual we, the

musicians, had nothing to do. All of the instrumental recordings had been done and we were 'required' to sit there and observe the 'Master' at work. Hours and hours had gone by and we were all very bored with listening to Ray go over and over and over the same bloody piece. It wasn't necessary and made absolutely no difference to the recording. Meanwhile I was doodling on a tape box — a little man wearing a working man's hat, long coat and rough shoes. Ray saw it and had one of his screaming fits, 'Why was I drawing funny little men whilst he was creating a masterpiece?' I thought it was a complete overreaction to the situation and sodded off out of the studio.

As well as a new tour manager, the band had a new booking agent, Barry Dickens, who got them a number of shows in Sweden. Rather than a tour of fashionable rock festivals, however, they were presented with a series of amusement parks to play in. The band were disappointed that they seemed to have fallen so low, performing to disinterested families milling around fairground attractions. There were also numerous problems with poor sound equipment and the performances met with bad reviews. The experience hardly helped raise their spirits.

During all of the recording and touring, a steady stream of legal papers was being served and acted upon. By June 1966, the trail had reached the court of appeal and, at the end of the month, a ruling was finally handed down: the courts decided that the contract between Boscobel and Denmark Productions was void, partly because Dave Davies had been underage when it was signed, and largely because Larry Page had 'abandoned' the band during the 1965 tour of the USA. In the initial court ruling in May 1967, the judge had said: 'Mr Page knew the group intimately and could have foreseen their reaction. By his action he destroyed the trust that was vital for the continuance of a relationship between them.' Page put in a further appeal to the House of Lords, but this was finally dismissed, once and for all, in October 1968. Kassner Music still claimed to be Ray's publisher, though, and that dispute was eventually settled out of court.

Ray continued to write. During July and August the band were still putting down new tracks for consideration on the upcoming album, even though they had more than enough material. The album would turn out to be the most collaborative Kinks record of their career and one of their best, although Ray would re-appraise his view of the record in later years. 'I wrote it to be a flop,' he said. 'I'd moved to a bigger house, and wanted to write about England and imaginary people and myths and legends that I made up. I was away with the fairies.'

'It's where I set my imaginary world,' said Ray Davies. 'It's a series of dreamscapes. It's to do with innocence and lost youth. The village green is beyond fashions, news, war, the media.' In this period, Ray wrote of an idealised England, with helpings of English poet A.E. Housman, and a procession of fictional characters inhabiting the village of his mind. He succeeded in conveying a feeling, rather than a distinct narrative, through some memorable songs, given great arrangements, and performed brilliantly by the band. 'I wanted it to be *Under Milk Wood*, something like that,' said Ray, referring to Dylan Thomas' radio play about the day in the life of a small Welsh town. In particular, he emulated the way Thomas drops in on different characters throughout the piece.

'Making that album was the high point of my career,' said Pete Quaife. 'It is something of which I am very proud. For me it represents the only real album made by The Kinks. It is probably the only album made by us in which we all contributed something.' One of his contributions was a bassline from Bach in the song 'Wicked Annabella'. 'I felt a little bit guilty . . . at the time. I had visions of an irate Johann visiting me late at night ready to clobber me with music stand.'

Mick Avory confirmed that this was more of a 'band' effort than ever before. 'It was more collaborative, rather than going in like session men and just doing it.'

Barrie Wentzell first met The Kinks, or at least Ray Davies, in 1965. 'I was freelance. *Melody Maker* had a photographer, John Hopkins, but he left and I ended up being a contributing photographer,' he said. 'I ended up going to Bob Houston, the assistant editor's, place in Hampstead and Ray Davies was there. I knew that Ray and Dave used to play on the *Melody Maker* football team. Bob was playing all this jazz stuff and Ray was saying, "Oh, I hate that. I hate that and I hate that." I thought, "This is really good, what a wanker," but when I ran into him a few days later he said, "Oh no, I couldn't say anything because it was really good." So I thought you have to watch what he says because he's quite cantankerous, he was just sending us up.'

Durham-born Wentzell shot, among others, Diana Ross, Johnny Cash, Jimi Hendrix and Count Basie for *Melody Maker* between 1965 and 1975. The Kinks did about ten photo shoots with him over the years, most of which started out in a pub. In the summer of 1968, he was told by Pye Records that the band wanted to do a photo shoot on Hampstead Heath, and went along with staff from the record company. 'I didn't know at the time that it was for an album or anything,' said Wentzell. 'Afterwards Ray gave me a call and said, "Have you got colour pictures from the shoot?" and could I drop round to Pye to show him because he wanted something for this album called *The Kinks are the Village Green Preservation Society*. That area of Highgate, Hampstead Heath, looked like . . . well it was a big village green so it was perfect for that album.'

Relations were always very friendly between Wentzell and The Kinks, perhaps because, in some ways, they were both learning their respective trades at the same time. 'There was no wall or distance like there is now,' said Wentzell. 'Back then everyone just turned up in what they were wearing, met in a pub and then took a stroll around. Mick was always dressed like anyone in the street, Dave would go through various costume changes, Ray was always a natty dresser. We went off to Kenwood House and had tea, we were wandering around for a couple of hours.' In fact, the relationship was so informal that Wentzell never got paid for his work on the album sleeve (at least not before it was re-issued) and, for a while, he didn't even realise one of his pictures was on the back cover until he bought a copy for himself. Sadly he never got his colour pictures back from Pye and that material is now lost forever. This didn't stop him working with The Kinks again, however.

Others would look back on their contribution to the album less happily. Nicky Hopkins claimed he had performed the vast majority of keyboard parts on the album, although the only credit for keyboards on the album goes to Ray Davies. And Pete Quaife became even more disaffected when band payments changed from an equal four-way split to an arrangement which saw the bass player and Mick Avory each receive £40 a week. Quaife's step-father earned more running a grocer's shop.

On 21 September, the *New Musical Express* ran Keith Altham's review of the album. 'The priceless antique mind of Ray Davies warns us not to forget those little things which mean a lot in our bygone days,' he wrote. 'This is Mr D's personal musical museum – it's worth more than just a thought.'

The twelve-song album had been finished in August and pressed in September for the European market but, after it reached the shops in certain countries, and after Keith Altham wrote his review, Ray had second thoughts and changed it substantially. 'I was doing an interview with them for the *NME* and someone sent me an early acetate, which I reviewed, and it had a track, a cover, that never made the final album,' recalled Altham. In fact two of the original twelve songs, 'Days' and 'Mr Songbird', were cut. Ray had wanted to expand the album to two records, but Pye refused, hence a compromise: two new songs replaced the tracks that had been removed, and three further songs were added, to take the final album up to fifteen tracks, which could fit on a single LP.

The resulting cut of *The Kinks are the Village Green Preservation Society* was finally released in the UK on 22 November. It didn't even have a name until very late in the summer. The title was Ray Davies' admission that the past few years had left him disconnected from the things that had really mattered while he was growing up. The new-look album got some critical praise but achieved only poor sales. The airwaves were then ruled by the double-LP popularly known as The Beatles' *The White Album,* along with The Rolling Stones' *Beggars Banquet,* Jimi Hendrix's *Electric Ladyland* and the *Sound of Music* soundtrack. The Kinks had been left behind.

Ray was a chronicler of the 1960s, but not just of that version of the decade which acknowledges only Carnaby Street, *Alfie* and the miniskirt. The world around him may have been swinging into a multi-coloured, psychedelic future, but Davies was retreating to black and white. The album failed to chart on either side of the Atlantic and it took many years for it to gain a reputation as a masterpiece. Meanwhile, Ray would stay out of step with the times for most of the rest of his career.

He set out his manifesto clearly in the opening track 'The Village Green Preservation Society'. Everything he stood for was listed plain and simple: vaudeville, strawberry jam and Desperate Dan, draught beer and custard pies – things he really did love, despite the song's ironic tone. More than forty years ago, Ray Davies was singing about saving 'little shops', which seems a strikingly modern sentiment. The closing refrain of 'God save the village green!' would be cannibalised as a promotional byline for the band in years to come.

Change of another kind was addressed in 'Do You Remember Walter?' – the process of growing up, and what happens when people drift apart and then meet up again years later, to find they no longer have anything in common. Driven by energetic acoustic guitar, 'Picture Book' jauntily concerned itself with the way people record their own lives. 'Johnny Thunder' was an acoustically tinged rewrite of 'David Watts' and was about a boy from Ray's school, whom he had admired while growing up.

With a genesis in Howlin' Wolf's 'Smokestack Lightning', 'Last of the Steam Powered Trains' was a metaphor for the band themselves, forging their own lonely way through life. 'I live in a museum,' sang Davies, who played the wailing harmonica on the track too. Musically the song was a triumph, starting like an engine slowly pulling away from a station and slowly accelerating before ending at high speed many miles down the track.

'Big Sky' addressed philosophical, spiritual issues: 'People lift up their hands and they look up to the big sky/ But big sky is too big to sympathise'. Ray was asked whether 'Big Sky' was actually God, but avoided a direct answer.

'Sitting by the Riverside', 'Animal Farm' and 'Village Green' were the literal and figurative centrepieces of the album. All invoked images of simple village life. 'I wrote for the way something should sound,' said Ray. '"The sky is wide" is a line [in "Animal Farm"] I knew I could just about reach that note and, to me, the whole record is the way I sing that line. I knew that before it was recorded. I must've been so confident, so sure of myself.' In 'Village Green', the singer is looking at how things had changed after he left the village. Not many twenty-somethings would look around and notice for themselves what was being lost and measure it against what was being gained. This was the first song that Ray wrote for the album. 'I had the whole idea of the record in my head,' said Ray. 'There was a village feel to Fortis Green where we grew up. I went to a church school, it was a tidy neighbourhood; the world existed in a square mile.' 'Village Green' featured Nicky Hopkins on harpsichord and gave Ray the opportunity to use greater orchestration. 'I stood around the piano with Lew Wharburton,' said Ray. 'Basically, I "da-dee-dahed" it through a microphone, he'd take it home and notate it. A man called David Whitaker did the string parts on "Village Green".'

'Phenomenal Cat' is a weird children's fantasy, the best example of Ray being 'away with the fairies', as he put it. Musically, it flits here and there on a 'flute' (actually a Mellotron) and is one of the trippiest songs The Kinks ever put to tape.

More strange village characters appear in the shape of 'Wicked Annabella' and the Latin-tinged 'Monica'. Mick Avory was taking the opportunity to experiment where he could on these recordings. 'On "Wicked Annabella" and "Picture Book" I took the snare off just to get a different sound,' he said. 'I put newspaper over a floor tom-tom in "Phenomenal Cat". I just got a deader sound, but it sounded right. When you're in a band like The Kinks, there's so many different styles of songs and things you can do. It takes a bit of experimentation.'

The album ends with a return to the theme of 'Picture Book' in 'People Take Pictures of Each Other', inspired by Ray Davies attending a country wedding, and offering a commentary on what Ray Davies had just done with fourteen exquisite songs: he had documented people's existence by capturing them in a portrait.

As a whole, it was unlike anything the band had done before, and Pye didn't know what to do with it. None of the songs were obvious single-material, though 'Picture Book' and the title track might have been worth trying in that market. It was reported that the combined sales of *Something Else* and *The Kinks are the Village Green Preservation Society* totalled only 25,000 copies. The Beatles' *The White Album*, issued on the same day, by comparison sold two million in its first week. This confirmed that The Kinks were simply no longer commercial, a shocking development for a band that usually shifted over two million copies of each single it released. 'I was upset because people didn't get a chance to hear it,' said Ray. 'I know when I write a good song and I really thought there were good numbers on it. It just had to be thought of in modern terms and presented in a proper way.'

'It was so Ray,' said Keith Altham. 'He was the Noel Coward of rock and roll for me. He had that wit and that ability to conjure up a particular kind of Englishness that was very marked because most people in those bands started with an R&B thing, started with a transatlantic accent and they started with songs that were embedded in the deep south of America. Those songs had nothing to do with their own roots. Ray was really the first person to come along and write from *his* own cultural experience, being English and being born in London, and writing from his own life. They started with something which belonged to somebody else and made it their own as time went by.'

It really was a case of right album, wrong time. It would later be viewed as a masterpiece but, at the time, nobody cared. 'For me, *Village Green Preservation Society* is Ray's masterwork,' said Pete Townshend. 'It's his *Sgt. Pepper*, it's what makes him the definitive pop poet laureate.'

In the aftermath of the original album's release, The Kinks were booked on to the cabaret circuit in northern England – much to Dave Davies' dismay – but the final two months of the year were fairly quiet. On Christmas Day 1968, Rasa and Ray, now living in a Borehamwood mansion, had a second daughter, Victoria. At the same time, Pete Quaife made a decision: he had really had enough of the sitting around, having played few shows during the second half of the year, and was also feeling claustrophobic in the studio. At the start of 1969, he gave notice of his intentions and, by March, was gone, this time for good.

Decline and Fall

'I think the record is the best of the year.' So wrote Robert Christgau in the 10 April 1969 issue of New York's *Village Voice*. The subject of his outspoken praise was *The Kinks are the Village Green Preservation Society* which had recently been released in the USA, several months after the UK version. After years of drifting away from the public eye in North America, The Kinks were being talked about again. Paul Williams, in the 14 June 1969 issue of *Rolling Stone*, added, 'I'm frustrated now. I was okay, trying to make you feel how good The Kinks make me feel, but I can't pass on greatness. I can't sit here and come up with phrases to argue genius, I can only shout, as modestly as possible, about how deeply I'm affected. I've never had much luck turning people on to The Kinks. I can only hope you are onto them already. If you are brother, I love you. We've got to stick together.' This was the start of a cult following in America. The Kinks would have to start at the bottom again, they didn't have any big new singles to promote, but America was at least willing to listen again to what they had to say.

Pete Quaife had informed the band of his decision to quit but, at first, the rest of The Kinks failed to take him seriously. He was known to change his mind and, sure enough, they persuaded him to stay on for a short while to help out on some new recordings and promotional work.

All of The Kinks played on a new Dave Davies single, 'Hold My Hand', in January, although it failed to chart and is probably best remembered for its rocking B-side, 'Creeping Jean'. The next Kinks single was the humorous 'Plastic Man'. 'Ray always had that strange, wry, English way of looking at things, that ironical inbuilt almost-sneer, but it was cleverer than that,' said Keith Altham. 'Nothing would have pleased Ray more than that video of "Sunny Afternoon" that they did in the snow and the undertakers thing that got banned [the promo clip for "Dead End Street"]. I found Ray's sense of humour really funny but some people didn't because I don't think they understood that he was being funny.' The BBC weren't amused by 'Plastic Man' and banned it because Ray sang the word 'bum'.

As 'Plastic Man' struggled to reach the top thirty, Pete reiterated his desire to leave the band. 'Pete and I never sat down and discussed why he left,' said Dave. 'We had this mutual thing of, like, if the other one says this or does that, then that's OK. I didn't even question him on it. If he wanted to leave then that's what he wanted to do. I look back and I realise how lucky we were to have that closeness and understanding.'

'I know from our discussions that Pete felt he was sometimes undermined and underestimated,' said Pete's friend Jeff Bailey. 'There were issues as with all businesses, some he churned over. I remember the scooter he bought and customised, and how everyone worried about his safety in case he came off it and got hurt. The worry being that he may not be able to play for the band and could have led to lost gigs and money.'

A few months before he left, in late 1968, Pete Quaife had been out for the night in Soho with Bill Fowler from the Arthur Howes Agency. At one club, Pete watched the house band play with a guest guitarist, a Canadian by the name of Stan Endersby, who caught Pete's eye. 'I'd been looking around for a couple of months for someone who would fit into my conception of a group,' said Pete to the *Toronto Telegram*. 'I was really getting nowhere until one night I saw Stan gigging on guitar with this terrible band. What he was doing really knocked me out, so I introduced myself and we started talking and found that we had a lot of the same ideas.'

'[Endersby] had played with several other bands and obviously knew his stuff,' said Pete. 'He said he knew of two Canadians that were great musicians. So we flew them over and started rehearsals. We travelled around the country for about six months, playing in bars and such.'

While he was winding up his involvement with The Kinks, Pete's new band took shape, under the name Mapleoak (marrying the Canadian maple and the English oak). They unexpectedly found themselves pictured in the *New Musical Express* on 5 April. The photo was taken on Hampstead Heath, just where The Kinks had previously been pictured for the *The Kinks are the Village Green Preservation Society*, and the headline read KINKS SPLIT. This was the first that any of the other Kinks had heard about Pete's new group. 'I definitely felt that [Quaife] had lost all his love for the band," said Ray Davies in *X-Ray*. 'And that hurt me.' A week after the KINKS SPLIT headline, the *New Musicale Express* quietly announced that the band would be carrying on with a new bass player, without further comment from the band or Pete.

'Pete did enjoy the band, its members, the worldwide travelling, and the fame and all the contacts he made,' said Jeff Bailey. 'You have to be of a certain mentality. You get very little time to be yourself or make your own decisions. Others make them and expect you to honour those decisions, which is fine for a while. However, with Pete he just became deflated. When he left The Kinks he was a bit like a coiled spring. Pete and I and our partners went to West Sussex in a caravan, not a pop star retreat, so he could unwind.'

When he did return to London, Pete and his new band began rehearsing at the Marquee. His links to Denmark led to a series of gigs there, playing a mixture of covers and original material. On their return to England, Mapleoak got a record deal with Decca.

'Peter liked his Scotch and we liked our "recreational tobacco",' said Stan Endersby. 'Peter had a tendency to be both hot and cold, but that was his nature and with friends you sometimes put up with things. I always considered him a friend.'

'I used to drive a little bit for them,' said David Quaife. 'Mapleoak had a manager from Billericay who provided a van and they'd be up in the church hall to practise not far from the Clissold Arms. Then after just one or two gigs it was straight into the recording studio. Up at Pete's place he was still a nervous wreck in those days so it didn't last long.'

A year after their formation, in April 1970, the debut Mapleoak single, 'Son of a Gun', was released by Decca. When it failed to sell, Pete began to lose interest and left the group soon afterwards. The remaining trio completed an album which could loosely be called country-rock, but, when that bombed too, the group broke up in May 1970.

In later years, Quaife seemed quite bitter about his Mapleoak experience and he seemed to shift the blame for their failure onto Stan Endersby. After The Kinks, perhaps his expectations were just too high. 'As *Village Green Preservation Society* was my high point, so is Mapleoak my low point,' he said with the benefit of thirty-five years' hindsight. 'It was at the suggestion of Stan Endersby that we should find some musicians and just gig around for a while. Nothing more. Consequently it was all a big embarrassment. I did my bit and then got out of it quickly.'

In the aftermath of Mapleoak, Quaife moved to Denmark with Beden, but adjusting to life as an *ex*-pop star proved difficult. Her father got him a job working in a restaurant – a world away from adoring crowds and *Top of the Pops* – and things started to go wrong between the couple. Pete and Beden soon separated and he did his disappearing act, vanishing to who knows where for a couple of months.

'Beden's family was paying for everything,' said David Quaife. 'They were expecting [Pete] to have a lot of money. He ended up living in Denmark, then he had a bed sitter.' Pete later met a new girl, Hannah, and, in the late 1970s, David went to visit them in Denmark. 'I stayed in his bedsit for a couple of nights over Christmas and everything was OK,' he said. 'Then we had a long chat about things and he told me why he'd left, he wasn't forced out but he felt left out, and it left a bad taste in his mouth.' Pete would never return to the music industry.

With Quaife gone from The Kinks, the band dynamic changed somewhat. Mick Avory became more of a buffer between Ray and Dave, and he was soon asked to help recruit a new bass player. There was one obvious candidate.

'Ray asked me if I could get John Dalton,' said Mick Avory. 'Pete was quite adventurous and had a good understanding of music, he just naturally seemed to play the right thing. John was a good rock and roll bass guitarist. He played with a plectrum which gave a different sound, he had spot-on timing and was easy to play with.'

Dalton's willingness to return to The Kinks wasn't a given, as Ray Davies might have expected. After his treatment the first time round – dropped suddenly, without a word from the band – Dalton took a little convincing. 'I never had a contract and that is where I fell down,' he said. 'When I went back after Pete quit for the second time I was happy in my life, I had a job that gave me a comfortable wage and when Mick called me up I said "Well, I'm quite happy" and I think they expected me drop everything and jump at it. Mick phoned me back the next day and said, "I've had a word with Ray and we can make you a quarter of the company, and all that." But I never signed anything. One day we even cancelled a rehearsal so we could think of a name for the new company but it never happened, which was a shame.' Avory confirmed that discussions about Dalton becoming a full member of the band did take place: 'John loved the business and the band and the music, but he stayed a hired musician. He was supposed to be part of the group and part of the company but that never happened.'

Dalton was immediately thrown into sessions for the next Kinks album. They still weren't playing many concerts, so he had time to learn the material that they'd recorded between 1966 and 1969. His first show after rejoining the band was a bizarre one-off trip to the Lebanon. Fewer than ten other shows were played during that summer. Ray Davies did some production work in the USA with The Turtles, and then The Kinks readied the follow-up to *The Kinks are the*

Village Green Preservation Society. While recording, they heard that the US ban had finally been lifted, which gave them renewed impetus.

The Kinks' seventh studio album was called *Arthur or the Decline and Fall of the British Empire*. Its genesis was a meeting between Ray and representatives of Granada Television at the end of 1968. They asked if Ray would write a musical drama which they could film and broadcast, and introduced him to Julian Mitchell, who later wrote ten episodes of television crime drama *Inspector Morse* and the play *Another Country*. They worked together on a script during the early part of 1969. 'He was a brilliant writer,' said Ray. 'We used to have script meetings at his house in Chelsea. I really thought we were on the same wavelength and the final script was wonderful.'

Ray was inspired by his sister Rose, husband Arthur Anning and son Terry going to live in Australia. He wanted to use Arthur as the central everyman character and show the emotional trauma caused by families uprooting and moving across the world. He embroidered Arthur's back story with, for example, a fictional account of his service in the Great War. 'I decided to make it about one person, someone who didn't really count, that's all,' said Davies. '[I] mixed it with a few people I knew, put them into one. I told Julian Mitchell a story about someone I knew. He liked it and worked on it and it came from there. He was easy to work with.' Ray continued to play the new songs he was writing to Mitchell and the writer crafted dialogue around them.

Despite the obvious family connections, Ray Davies also pointed out that he liked to invent characters and that the songs weren't based solely on fact. 'That gave us the opportunity to write about subjects that really interested me,' he said. 'Britain's recent history, how it had survived the war, how its class system operated and the way it treated the ordinary people who made Britain great.'

Throughout the summer, The Kinks worked in the studio to build up a stock of new material. The plan was to release the album that autumn, while Granada filmed the television drama. Then, when the film was broadcast in January 1970, it would give the album a sales boost.

Arthur represented yet another bold creative step forward: unlike the concept of the Village Green, it was to be a fully formed 'rock opera', and where *The Kinks are the Village Green Preservation Society* had addressed what Davies saw as the decline of England, he expanded the scope of the new album to address the decline of the Empire. It was only five short years since The Kinks had topped the charts with 'You Really Got Me', but the hard-rocking singles band was long gone.

The album opens with one of The Kinks' best-loved songs, 'Victoria' (written soon after the birth of Ray's daughter who bears the same name) – a stomping, affirmation of their Englishness, but set in a time long gone, with another mention for the village green. Ray decided to use an English music staple, the brass band, on this track. 'I liked the idea of brass,' said Ray. 'I've always liked big band and soul music. But on Kinks records I give the trombone the lead part. A lot of orchestrators shy away from that because the trumpet's got to be the right voicing. So the voicing is kind of different on Kinks records, because it's a reflection of the way I hear it.' At first listen it might seem to be a rousing song in honour of the eponymous monarch, but the song is actually a stinging rebuttal of how her subjects were treated. 'When I grow I shall fight/ For this land I shall die' sang Ray. The cost of preserving the Empire was a high one.

'Yes Sir, No Sir' is another of the war-related songs on the album. The drum and bass march is overlaid with some subtle guitar noodling. Ray is cast as an army pawn, forced to ask even for permission to breathe. Authority must be maintained and if the soldier dies 'we'll send the medal home to his wife' laugh the officers. This theme continues into 'Some Mother's Son', which follows the story from the schoolyard to fighting in the First World War. Ray had used this title as part of the lyric in 'Wonderboy' and still found it provocative enough to build a whole song around. The line 'All dead soldiers look the same' is deeply moving.

'Drivin' had been released as an advance single in the summer but had failed to chart. While the fighting goes on overseas, its narrator goes for a country drive, looking forward to a picnic. It was inspired by memories of the fifties of his father Fred taking the Davies family to Southend in the car, an old black Vauxhall 12 that Fred called 'Betsy'.

'Brainwashed' featured both Dave Davies' loudest guitar parts for quite a while on a Kinks record and more brass. Indeed, Lew Warburton arranged brass and string sections for several songs, following on from the orchestral arrangements that had been used on *The Kinks are the Village Green Preservation Society* album.

'Australia' was the centre of the album and again showed how much the emigration of his sister had affected Ray. The song itself sounds like an advert with Beach Boys harmonies. Dave later said that he'd had tears in his eyes when singing it. 'Australia, no drug addiction/ Australia, no class distinction/ We'll surf like they do in the USA' – a paradise where 'everyone walks around with a perpetual smile on their face'.

Ray turned his attentions from physical migration to class mobility on 'Shangri-La'. When working with Julian Mitchell, it had been suggested that Ray write about the main character's 'pebble dash nirvana' in suburbia. The character had undergone a shift in class by moving out of a tenement to a suburban semi-detached house. However, having swapped outside loos for the comfort of wearing slippers by the fire, Ray again points out that Arthur can't reach any higher: he has once more been put in his place. After a very subtle opening, the song explodes into an almost baroque chorus. 'I played 'Shangri-La' to somebody, an old friend of mine,' said Ray. 'I knew, halfway through it he was embarrassed by it because it was about him, and he realised it, and I can never talk to him again. I wanted him to hear it and then I realised: there he is.' In fact, the song appears more universal in its depiction of modern middle-class life, with lines such as, 'The little man who gets on the train/ Got a mortgage hanging over him/ But he's too scared to complain.'

The theme of war returned with 'Mr Churchill Says', Ray taking the bold decision of using the great war leader's 'fight them on the beaches' speech. A harpsichord-laden 'She's Bought a Hat Like Princess Marina' is, again, about social class and the lower echelons getting ideas above their station, before the album closes with the almost celebratory 'Arthur', one of the great forgotten Kinks tracks. The eponymous rocker features some hypnotically swirling guitar work by Dave Davies and the whole band clicks into gear as they declare that Arthur was right all along. 'Now we know and we sympathise,' go the gang vocals. 'We'd like to help you and understand you.'

The original sleeve for *Arthur* featured a long section of text addressing the band's fans. 'Where have you been this last five years?' it asked before offering a summary of The Kinks' activities.

Arthur was The Kinks' last album recorded at Pye and, but for a matter of months, might have laid claim to being the first 'rock opera'. The Who's *Tommy* was being recorded at the same time, but came out first, in May 1969. *Arthur* followed in October and failed to chart at all in the UK, and reached only number 105 in the US, despite a positive critical response. The *New Musical Express* said: 'Still the Kinks' recognisable sound but occasionally with an added toughness that lends more appeal.' They were sadly over-optimistic when they added, 'Should do well.'

Once the album was completed, the accompanying script was submitted to Granada and they began casting and designing sets. Twenty-seven-year-old Jo Derden-Smith, who had filmed documentaries on The Doors, The Rolling Stones and, most famously, Johnny Cash at San Quentin prison, would produce; Leslie Woodhead, who had made his name on the *World in Action* current affairs show, was to direct; and Frank Finlay, who had been nominated for an Academy Award as Best Supporting Actor in 1965 for his part in *Othello*, was given the part of Arthur. But the whole project fell apart abruptly. At a pre-production meeting, there was a dispute about whether Derden-Smith could take over the director's role and, when his request was turned down, he walked out. Granada promptly closed it down. There was nothing The Kinks could do. Ray was philosophical about these set-backs. 'I was disappointed, but not devastated the way I would be if that happened now,' he said in 2011. 'I think that I felt there was always something else to do . . . and so life would go on.'

The Kinks' records were being issued in the USA by Warner-Reprise, who had recently bought Atlantic Records, and had a roster which included Randy Newman and The Grateful Dead. With the lifting of the American tour ban, The Kinks had great hopes of re-establishing themselves in the USA.

Just as it was never ascertained who had actually banned The

Kinks, no one really knew why the bar was suddenly lifted. When asked, Ted Dreber, assistant to the President of the American Federation of Musicians, couldn't find any paperwork relating to any ban. He could only offer that the union had the power to 'withhold permits for a group if they behave badly on stage or fail to show up for scheduled performances without good reason'. 'Our ban ended as mysteriously as it began,' wrote Dave Davies in *Kink*. 'Fortunately, it hadn't completely ruined our careers.'

The Kinks were back in the USA as soon as *Arthur* was released, in a reversal of the apathy towards touring that had followed their past few albums. They flew into New York on Friday, 16 October, and opened at the Fillmore East with two shows on both evenings of that weekend. *Variety* reported that the band were 'somewhat unsure of themselves, but regained their performing composure after a couple of sets'. For the first time, The Kinks had the luxury of monitors on stage so they could actually hear what they were playing. 'Not really knowing what to expect, we were under-rehearsed and nervous,' wrote Dave in *Kink*. 'It was apparent that this tour was going to be hard work.' Dave tried to make it a little easier by drinking and experimenting with as many new drugs as possible during the trip. It was here, in his New York hotel room, that he tried Angel Dust, a hallucinogenic drug sometimes known as PCP, for the first time.

The band played around twenty shows between mid-October and Christmas 1969, and discovered that the American touring circuit had changed radically since their experience back in 1965. Gone were the package tours and the screaming teenage girls: this was the Age of Aquarius, when the hippie movement and 'Flower Power' were at the height of their visibility. Pop concerts had been replaced by 'rock events'. American acts such as The Byrds, Jefferson Airplane, The Doors and Crosby, Stills & Nash, had retaken the music market and, while some British bands were welcomed, the 'invasion' was now a distant memory.

'Being a fan of American rock and roll, it was great,' remembered John Dalton. 'With the Mark Four we'd played a lot of American air bases and I was dying to go over and see it for myself. We had to work ourselves up a bit at first, they'd lost four years and we started

The newly-named Kinks, resplendent in their hunting jackets, behind the stage curtain at a gig in May 1964. Left to right: Mick, Dave, Pete and Ray. *Getty Images*

top to bottom: Ray and future wife Rasa, August 1964, Dave and friend Ivy, Pete Quaife, Mick Avory at the Starlite Club, October 1965.

Marianne Spellman Collection

the KINKS

the KINKS

NOW ON RELEASE

**YOU
REALLY
GOT
ME** (KASSNER MUSIC)

SOLE BOOKING:
THE ARTHUR HOWES AGENCY

the KINKS

the KINKS

the KINKS

The Kinks backstage, recovering from their set, in 1964.
Left to right: Mick, Pete, Dave and Ray. *Mirrorpix*

top: Performing on *Ready Steady Go!* in 1966.

WireImage/Getty Images

above: Robert Wace and Grenville Collins plot The Kinks'
next move from their shared office.

Phillip Jackson/Associated Newspapers/Rex Features

opposite: Relaxing on Hampstead Heath during the
Village Green Preservation Society photo shoot, 1968.

© *Barrie Wentzell*

Growing their hair for RCA in 1972.
Outside The Flask pub in Highgate, left to right:
John Dalton, Dave, John Gosling, Ray and Mick.
© Barrie Wentzell

opposite: Ray preparing for an interview in a pub.

right: Ray indulging in the demon drink before his dramatic appearance at the Great Western Express Festival, Summer 1973.

below: On stage, later the same day, at the White City Stadium. It was at this concert that Ray announced the retirement of The Kinks. A very short retirement – Debi Doss, who took this photograph, was hired in 1974 as one of the backing singers for The Kinks' US *Preservation Act* tour.

above: Ray relaxes at Konk Studios with a game of snooker.

© *Barrie Wentzell*

left: John Gosling on tour.

Courtesy of John Gosling

right: Ray performs as the common man, Norman, during the tour for the *Soap Opera* album at the Spectrum Arena, Philadelphia 1975.
© *Roger Barone Archives*

below: Ray as Mr Flash, 1975.
© *Roger Barone Archives*

Ready for more fun and games. Checking into the Hyatt, aka 'The Riot House', left to right: John Dalton, John Gosling and Mick.

Courtesy of John Gosling

below: Saturday Night Live: The Kinks performing on 10 October 1981.

NBCU Photo Bank via Getty Images

Stadium star: Ray on stage in Dallas, May 1983.

Marianne Spellman

At the video shoot for 'Come Dancing'. Left to right: Ian Gibbons, Ray, Dave, Jim Rodford and Mick. *Redferns/Getty Images*

Passing the torch: Damon Albarn and Ray performing together on Channel 4's *The White Room* in 1995. *Redferns/Getty Images*

Mick, Dave, Pete and Ray Davies pose backstage with the award for their induction into the UK Music Hall of Fame, 2005. *Getty Images*

Left to right: Ronnie Spector, Dave Berry, Ray, Sandie Shaw, Paloma Faith, Carl Barat and Nona Hendryx perform on stage during a recreation of the 1960s British TV pop show *Ready Steady Go!* as part of the Meltdown Festival 2011, curated by Ray. *Redferns/Getty Images*

Ray takes the applause at
the closing ceremony of the
2012 London Olympic Games.
Getty Images

supporting people again. At the start we only played at weekends and had to kill time during the week. We saw a lot of bars and enjoyed ourselves.'

The Kinks were welcomed wherever they went. *Cash Box* magazine called the band 'newly discovered cult heroes' and an almost-underground movement began to coalesce around them. To prepare the ground for The Kinks' US return, Warner-Reprise hired press agent and journalist John Mendelssohn to compile an eighteen-track promotional LP to be sent around the country reminding radio stations and journalists of the group's weighty back catalogue. Mendelssohn wrote the accompanying press release and signed it off with 'God Save The Kinks!', a slogan which became a rallying cry for their fans and stuck with the band through to the early 1970s.

The Kinks played in major cities across the country (Boston, Chicago, Detroit) and, while these shows all sold out, they were held at small venues: the band were starting at the bottom again. In Chicago, they played as support to The Who, who had once warmed up for them. While The Kinks had been stuck in the UK, their fellow Londoners had spent two years touring the US, and had become superstars. After this show, Dave, in a fit of rage, punched a glass door at the hotel, cutting his hand.

After landing in Los Angeles for a mini-residency at the legendary Whisky a Go Go, The Kinks played eight shows to great reviews. 'Their acceptance here and not in other places is because The Kinks are a group's group,' said *Rock* magazine. It was the smallest venue of the tour and *Rolling Stone* reported that queues four-deep stretched down Sunset Strip. Mick Jagger was seen in the audience on two of the nights.

Things were going so well that the next tour was already being planned. 'We're presently planning our next album and we hope to have it finished by the time we return,' said Dave. 'The way things look, we may record most of it here. Things are looking brighter now.' Ray, too, was upbeat. 'I've been overwhelmed with the response we've had,' he said. 'I expected people not to know what we've done in the past three years.'

Leaving Los Angeles, The Kinks travelled north to play at the

Fillmore West in San Francisco and at Reed College in Portland, Oregon, before heading back east. The band were getting back into touring mode, and a show in Philadelphia was warmly reviewed by *Billboard*: 'The music came out clear and sharp. Vocals alternated between composer Ray Davies and lead guitarist Dave Davies. Dave's natural ease and showmanship contrasted his brother's penetrating intensity.'

This sharing of frontman duties showed that The Kinks had reached a new level of confidence and maturity. There was a bond between the band members on and off stage. 'I was bringing up a family at exactly the same time as Dave; we seemed to have children the same age,' said John Dalton. 'When we went away, my wife and all the kids went over and stayed with his wife.' Ray had ceased to be precious about sharing centre stage with Dave; John Dalton and Mick Avory were happy to be on the road; and the band were playing at places where people had longed to see them and appreciated them. It looked as though the seventies would be good for The Kinks.

A Few Well-Known Tube Stations

he Kinks ended the 1960s on BBC 1. They mimed to 'Days' for the show *Pop Go the Sixties*, a seventy-five-minute colour special broadcast on New Year's Eve 1969, celebrating the major hits of the previous ten years. With studio performances from Cliff Richard, Adam Faith, The Rolling Stones, Sandie Shaw, Dusty Springfield and The Who, the show itself was a testament to a decade of phenomenal musical achievement in which British acts had played a leading role. It was also a telling sonic and visual representation of how far the country had moved on from the austere world of the immediate post-war era. The Kinks all had long, centre-parted hair; John Dalton was heavily bearded; and Ray Davies wore large, round, rose-tinted spectacles. Perhaps, however, those glasses were an ironic affectation, because the times were once again a-changing, the optimism of the sixties slumping and giving way to the pessimism of the seventies.

One of the decade's greatest musical forces, The Beatles, were nearing the end of their career. September 1969 had seen the release of *Abbey Road*, the Fab Four's eleventh studio album and the last one they recorded together. Although one more album, Phil Spector's production of *Let it Be*, would eventually emerge in May 1970, by that point The Beatles had already announced their break-up and begun their descent into legal acrimony.

In the US, in May 1970, four student protestors were shot dead at Kent State University in Ohio, during an anti-war demonstration as the Vietnam conflict dragged on. In the UK general election in June, Harold Wilson's reforming Labour government, which had presided over the country's shift to a more liberal society, was ejected from office and Edward Heath's Conservatives ushered in, to the surprise of many commentators.

The 1970s would be an era of oil shocks, inflation and unrest with the trade unions, during which power-cuts and large-scale strikes would become the norm.

As the new decade rolled around, The Kinks moved distinctly outside of the mainstream. They shunned the burgeoning heavy metal crowd, which they had helped to create with the distorted guitars of 'You Really Got Me'; resisted 'going glam'; and drifted away from the grass-smoking, hallucinogenic fantasy world of progressive rock with its fifteen-minute guitar solos. Instead, they drifted into skits about school days, and produced more concept albums – a delayed outpouring of Ray Davies' art school instincts, which had largely been suppressed during the band's hit-making heyday. 'I just wanted to experiment,' said Ray. 'It was almost like fringe theatre. There was nobody like The Kinks at that time.'

Along with the stubborn desire to do his own thing, Ray also suffered a growing reputation as a difficult man to work with. 'He was great to me when I was doing interviews with him, I never had any trouble, or later as a PR,' said Keith Altham. 'But I heard about the problems and I witnessed one little onslaught that took place on *Top of the Pops* with [Slade's] Dave Hill when he decided to find out if he was wearing a wig or not. I think [Slade manager] Chas Chandler backed him off.'

Part of Ray's 'difficult' reputation stemmed from his exercise of almost total control in the studio. He was now intent upon pursuing his singular vision for the band. Moreover, he was also determined to make it big in America.

After the relatively successful US dates in the autumn of 1969, the band were keen to make a quick return, and flew back in January 1970. This tour, however, was a more typical Kinks-style disaster. The tour started in Philadelphia and took in north-eastern venues as far up as Montreal. But, by the middle of February, and only four concerts into the tour, Mick Avory was ill with hepatitis and the rest of the shows had to be cancelled.

All band activities were put on hold and Ray took the chance to appear in a BBC TV play *The Long Distance Piano Player*. Part of the BBC's *Play For Today* series, the film was named in deliberate reference to Alan Sillitoe's *The Loneliness of the Long Distance Runner*. In Sillitoe's original, the protagonist is a young borstal inmate who deliberately loses a cross-country race to disobey the authorities and demonstrate his own independence – a story which had always resonated with Ray. In *The Long Distance Piano Player*, Ray Davies plays the part of a Yorkshireman due to play a piano marathon. Ray's character is pulled from side to side by a wife who wants him to stop playing, and a friend who urges him to carry on. Ray's participation ensured front-page coverage on the *Radio Times*. He gathered favourable, if guarded reviews, with *The Times* saying the play had 'a remarkable atmosphere, helped by the damp, respectable squalor of the church hall' and that Ray's portrayal was 'more than passable'.

Recording sessions in London were postponed until April when the band convened at Morgan Studios. *Arthur* had been the last Kinks' album to be recorded at Pye, and Ray Davies had been thinking of changing studios even before then, due to a combination of factors. '"Plastic Man" was my death knell for Pye,' he said. 'The sounds were not spreading and evolving in a way that I wanted. [Then] I think there was a dispute over the rates we were being charged. I did a try-out at Morgan and I liked the bass sound.'

Situated on the corner of Maybury Gardens and High Road, in the unglamorous suburb of Willesden, Morgan Studios had been founded in 1967 with a single room, but soon expanded. By the time The Kinks arrived, in April 1970, there was a second studio and an upstairs control room, of which Ray was fond. As usual, Ray came with a clutch of new songs. Grenville Collins suggested that it would be good to augment the new material with an extra player when they went back on tour, and the band agreed. 'We used the piano so much on the records and we were getting live work back in America, so it made sense,' said Mick Avory.

'We found a keyboard player in a church playing organ,' recalled John Dalton. 'His name was John and he had a big long beard, and this duffle coat with a hood and we just named him "John the Baptist" and it stayed.'

'John the Baptist' was John Gosling, a church organist from Stoke Newington, north London. An old school friend, Pete Frame, then the editor of *Zigzag* magazine who later famously compiled a series of *Rock Family Trees*, called Gosling and told him that someone had sent in a wanted ad to be printed in his magazine. The ad didn't say who the band was, only that they wanted a keyboard player to tour the USA.

The 22-year-old Gosling was born in Paignton, Devon, and had been playing the piano since the age of 6. 'I was taught by a vicious old crone who used to whack my hands with her walking stick if I got something wrong,' he said. 'I really wanted to play the church organ, but I wasn't allowed lessons on that until I passed Grade 5 piano so I had to endure a few more bruises.' By his early teens, he was proficient enough to be his school's organist, had taught himself the timpani to a level where he played it in the school orchestra, and sang in the church choir: 'My parents were not musical but my Dad loved listening to his old classical 78 rpm records on a gramophone he built himself. He was a clever man, he went around the British Isles wiring a lot of cinemas for sound when it was first introduced, then he became a projectionist and some weekends would show films to the family projected from an upstairs window onto the garden wall.' The music in his blood might have come from his paternal grandparents: his father's mother had been a cellist, and his father's father had been the organist and choirmaster at St Andrew's Willesden Green.

His first attempt at being in a rock band was when he made his own bass guitar out of chunks of wood and formed The Challengers with a friend. He would travel to rehearsals at the local school on a motorbike with his bass and amp in a sidecar. 'We were inspired to do that after hearing The Kinks perform "Long Tall Sally" on

Saturday Club, a popular radio show at the time,' he said. Gosling also played bass in a couple more local bands, then formed a further one of his own, in which he played piano, before discovering Bob Dylan and moving into the folk scene as a singer-songwriter. His last endeavour before joining The Kinks had been a Dylan-inspired blues group he called Hard Rain. 'I also played a few well-known Tube stations,' he admitted.

Answering the advertisement, Gosling was told to report to Morgan Studios, where it was revealed to him that the band in question was The Kinks. He was familiar with their hits but didn't own any of their records. 'Grenville Collins and Robert Wace were like The Thompson Twins from *Tin Tin*,' said Gosling. 'Grenville was the man I spoke to on the phone about the audition. Two posh gentlemen, too posh for their own good.'

It could have been intimidating for a newcomer to walk into The Kinks' camp, but Gosling was easily welcomed. 'Ray was friendly but guarded,' he said. 'Instantly recognisable and obviously very talented. Dave was the same. When I walked into the studio for my audition he handed me a beer, the first of many over the years. It was a nice gesture and it put me at ease. Mick was a very funny bloke, but was on the point of leaving the band when we met and I couldn't understand why. He was a major part of The Kinks' overall sound. Mick and I later spent a lot of time together in some very dubious establishments.'

The audition was more like a recording session in which Gosling had to get himself up to speed fairly quickly. 'We put down several backing tracks but Ray's guide vocals gave little indication as to what the songs were about,' he said. Songs attempted that day were 'Powerman', 'This Time Tomorrow', 'A Long Way From Home' and a brand new one called 'Lola'. 'It was certainly an education, but I wasn't made to feel as if I was under any kind of scrutiny. There was no starry behaviour. I remember feeling completely at home – almost as if I'd always been there.'

Gosling seemed to be the perfect fit. In May, he was asked to join the band, and was soon called upon to help promote the new single. His TV debut saw him wearing a gorilla mask as the band mimed along to the song. The clip wouldn't be broadcast until the single, 'Lola', was released several weeks later, on 12 June.

'I wore the whole [gorilla] suit in a promo film,' recalled Gosling, 'then just the head for TV. I've also been a caveman, a Viking, a pioneer of flight, the Phantom of the Opera, a vicar, a schoolmaster, the list is endless. Someone had to do it, usually me.'

Gosling's initiation into The Kinks' live show was short and informal – a couple of brief rehearsals at Ray's house, and one in a room above a pub. Grenville Collins took him to the Tate Gallery one afternoon and filled him in on a few touring details in the cab on the way. Gosling made his live debut with The Kinks on 22 May, at The Depot, Minneapolis, USA. With such short preparation time, it could easily have been a daunting prospect. 'I've always been a great believer in making live performances sound as close to the recorded versions that everybody knows and loves,' said Gosling. 'For that first gig, I jotted down the chord progressions and arrangements to "Shangri-La" and a couple of other tricky ones on a scrap of paper which kept falling off the keyboard. My gear broke down halfway through the set, and Nobby [Dalton] has never forgotten me for walking up behind him and tapping him on the shoulder for assistance while he was strutting his stuff. I remember there was a girl backstage with a small handgun in her purse, my introduction to the USA!'

It was John Dalton to whom Gosling became closest. Together, they always felt like the two outsiders, not being founder members of the band. 'John is a great bass player, a true rock and roller,' said Gosling. 'He's kind, unpretentious and uncomplicated. With him came a great set of mates, of whom he is still the greatest. Nobby looked out for me and saved my life.'

The US tour was to last seven weeks and stretch from coast to coast, even though they started in the middle of the country. 'We'd always used keyboards on the records and not on tour, which left a hole in the sound,' said John Gosling of his hiring. 'It was the same with brass later. To start off we had a set list and later we did these silly tours where we'd just play the records. It's nice to play your new stuff but people want to hear your hit records, the ones they know best.'

Grenville Collins travelled with the band to the US during on three trips Stateside during 1970. He saw first-hand how crazy things could get at the after show-parties, which usually carried on back at the hotel until the very early hours. Gosling and Dalton tried to keep up, drinking so heavily they were nicknamed the Juicers. Mick Avory needed little or no encouragement to join in, and Dave Davies was as wild as ever, even though he sometimes shared a room with Collins as the band sought to keep costs down. Ray kept his own counsel for the most part. Eventually Collins had seen enough and early one morning called a band meeting. Mick Avory recounted Collins' speech to the assembled crew: 'This has got to stop. It can't go on like this. It's all going around the town that you're imbeciles. You're supposed to be a serious band.' It was at this point that Gosling walked through the door: 'He'd just been down the joke shop and appeared [wearing] a Viking helmet with a Viking horn.' Gosling announced his arrival with a long blast on said horn and Collins lost the band's attention.

In the summer of 1970, The Kinks made a significant dent in the pop charts around the world, for the last time in many years, with 'Lola'. Ray Davies recognised that many classic hit singles had truly memorable introductions. Now a veteran writer of chart hits, he understood the need to get the listener to recognise a song instantly and he set out to find a memorable start to 'Lola'. He had bought two new guitars to use on the record, a Martin and a vintage Dobro resonating guitar. The combination gave the single its distinctive heavily strummed acoustic guitars mixed with searing electric tones, producing a slightly ominous-sounding introduction. Mick Avory provided an almost sloppy, rolling, backing to the track which pushed it along.

The lyric is, of course, the most memorable part of the song. Over the years there have been several versions of the story behind it. The tale recounted most frequently involves an encounter between Robert Wace and a beautiful 'girl' in a Paris nightclub. The story goes that, after dancing for hours, they walked out into the early morning Paris daylight, at which point Wace noticed that the 'girl' had a good growth of stubble.

The story has an appealing simplicity but Mick Avory, for one, has offered an alternative explanation, suggesting that Ray took inspiration from the transvestite bars of west London that Avory visited at the invitation of the publicist for John Stephen's shop in Carnaby Street, Michael McGrath. Certainly Ray remembered these clubs when writing his book *X-Ray*. But perhaps there was also something in the air? A year later the sleeve of the UK release of David Bowie's third album, *The Man Who Sold The World*, would feature its star in a dress and the arrival of Ziggy Stardust was just two years away. Arguably 'Lola' was glam before glam.

But even after the sexual advances of the 1960s, the subject matter of the song proved troublesome for some radio stations. There was talk of bans and, in some places, they faded the song out before the twist at the end could be revealed. On 25 July, when covering the single, *Record Mirror* gave the entire front cover to a colour photograph of the band and the headline, 'SEX CHANGE' RECORD: KINK SPEAKS. Ray was questioned about whether Lola was a man or a woman, but he avoided giving a straight answer, concluding with 'It really doesn't matter what sex Lola is, I think she's alright.'

Just as the song was about to be released, and in what now seems an almost unbelievable turn of events, Ray was forced to make a 6,000-mile round trip back to London, after just two nights of a US tour: the BBC wouldn't play the record. Their decision was not, as it happened, because of the song's transvestite subject, but because Ray had sung the line 'Tastes just like Coca-Cola', which went against the BBC's strict no-advertising regulations. Ray replaced the offending word – 'Tastes just like cherry cola' – and returned to the tour. The *New Musical Express* liked the single, calling it 'an engaging and sparkling piece with a gay Latin flavour and a catchy hook chorus'.

For many Americans hearing 'Lola' on the radio, it was a surprise to discover that The Kinks were still going. As the single soared high in the chart around the world (reaching the top ten in the UK, US, Australia, Sweden, Canada and Germany, among others), the band spent the summer in a series of Holiday Inns across the US, drinking and being chased by groupies, as if it were the 1960s again.

For most of the early autumn, The Kinks were holed up at Morgan Studios, where Jethro Tull, Supertramp and, most recently, Paul McCartney had been working. The band were at the studio in September when Ken Jones broke the news of Jimi Hendrix's death. 'Ken was king of the roadies but unfortunately had aspirations of eventually becoming our manager,' said John Gosling. 'He'd previously worked for Jimi Hendrix. We were mean to him at every opportunity. He could play the harmonica and also the drums. His was not the easiest of jobs but he remained faithful.' Hendrix's death was another blow to a music scene that had lost the Stones' Brian Jones in July 1969.

Like John Gosling, John Dalton was pretty much allowed to work by himself. 'In the studio I was left to do my own parts,' he said. 'We'd start at Ray's house – he'd be at the piano and we'd jot the chords down. We didn't have a great idea about how the song would end up.'

The Kinks continued to record for a new studio album of their own, and also fitted in a few weeks of work on music for a movie soundtrack. 'Somebody came up to us and asked us to do a film,' said Ray Davies. 'I'm sure that they looked down the charts and thought, "Well, who's in the charts this week?" I don't know if these people ever heard my work. I doubt it.' The film was *Percy*, a comedy based on the novel by Raymond Hitchcock, father of English singer and songwriter Robyn Hitchcock, which told the story of the first penis transplant. It featured a very respected and famous cast, including the likes of Hywel Bennett, Denholm Elliott, Elke Sommer, Britt Ekland, Patrick Mower and Arthur English. Promo posters for the film explained the story pretty well, with the image of a naked man's body, a carefully placed leaf, and the following text:

Edwin Anthony had a very nasty accident.
And lost something very vital.
So they gave him Percy.
Now Edwin wants to know
where Percy's been before.

Though the soundtrack wouldn't be issued until the film was ready in the spring of 1971, sessions were completed in November 1970. Importantly for The Kinks, *Percy* would count as the final album in their contractual obligation to Pye. All thirteen tracks were Ray Davies originals. The opening, 'God's Children', was used as the lead track on an EP from the film, but sank without trace. The song itself is a gentle piano-based tune, which, like the other music in the film, Ray Davies had carefully timed to fit the visuals.

An instrumental version of 'Lola' was far from just a version of the backing track with the vocals removed: in fact, it sounded more like an unfortunate outtake from the Larry Page Orchestra. Worse, it lasted for almost five minutes. Another gentle, piano-led song, 'The Way Love Used To Be', was altogether more appealing, with swooning strings which never become overly sentimental. Further instrumentals include the bluesy 'Completely', harmonica-led 'Running Round Town', the piano tinkering of 'Whip Lady', and the Latin-flavoured 'Helga'. One of the album's highlights is 'Moments', which closed side one on the LP. Showing Ray Davies at his poignant and nostalgic best, it uses strings as well as any Kinks song ever did.

'Animals in the Zoo', 'Just Friends' and 'Dreams' are the weakest Kinks songs on the record, but things improve with 'Willesden Green', a slow, bluesy rocker that saw John Dalton doing his best Elvis Presley impression — a pretty good one — complete with a spoken interlude. This was the only time that a Kinks song was sung by a Kink without the surname Davies.

No sooner had the *Percy* tapes been given to Pye than the label released their last 'real' Kinks album: *Kinks Part One — Lola Versus Powerman and the Moneygoround*. This, The Kinks' eighth album, was more varied than the band's recent efforts, though it did continue their recent tradition of a long and almost unwieldy title. It was also a loosely assembled concept album, it's vague theme being scorn for the record industry at the end of two years that had seen The Kinks' popularity wane. 'The LP was the struggle of a band really deciding to fight back,' said Ray Davies in the liner notes to the 2004 CD reissue of the album.

Two Dave Davies songs were included, the plaintive 'Strangers' and the claustrophobic 'Rats', about the 'pin stripes' of the music business. 'Denmark Street', with barrel-house piano, recalled the base of their early operations with barely disguised bile. 'Get Back in Line' remains one of the better Kinks songs put to tape, confronting the working-class struggles that characterised their upbringing and suffocated the lives of their extended family. 'Top of the Pops' and 'The Moneygoround' continued the attack on their own industry in completely different styles, one approaching heavy rock, the other sounding like Leo Sayer, and very much of its time. 'This Time Tomorrow' opened with the sound of a jet plane flying off into the sunset as the song dreams of escape. 'Lola' and the other single, 'Apeman', round out a solid collection.

It went some way to putting The Kinks back into the public eye, especially in the USA, where the album got to number thirty-five in the album charts after its distribution on 2 December 1970. It sold fewer copies closer to home, however, failing to chart after its 27 November release, despite positive reviews. 'The music's pure Kinks simplicity,' read the *Melody Maker*, 'but it works.' The *New Musical Express* led with RAY DAVIES IS PURE BRITTANINA [sic] and added that 'Ray is an extraordinary artist and one who should be given the greatest amount of critical acclaim and respect'.

While much of the album was tongue in cheek, there was an underlying and undeniable sense of injustice in Ray Davies' writing. Robert Wace and Grenville Collins both felt his barbs and later spoke out against the sentiment behind some of the songs. 'I didn't see the funny side of that at all,' said Wace. 'Grenville and I were very upset by some of the lyrics on the album because, by and large, they were untrue. The fact was that Grenville and I never earned a dime from his songwriting.' It wouldn't be long before Wace and Collins, like so many others before them, would part ways with Ray Davies.

Everybody's a Star
in Hillbilly Country

After almost a decade in the music business, The Kinks' capacity to attract bad luck remained intact. In January 1971, the band was due to play a series of shows in Australia, the first such gigs in several years. When the time came to travel, they found they hadn't been paid their advance by the promoters and, worse, even as the band arrived at the airport, they were still without plane tickets. The tickets had not been collected and a postal strike further delayed their arrival, so the group were left in the farcical situation of waiting around at Heathrow until the plane took off, on the off-chance that the paperwork might turn up at the last second. It didn't, and they had to bundle their equipment back into taxis and head home. Instead of enjoying an Australian summer, the weekends of February and March, saw them playing university and polytechnic gigs around Britain.

Soon afterwards, a handful of German dates were cancelled for a reason that only became known years later: Dave Davies was suffering from depression. He was also becoming paranoid and had lost confidence in his ability to play before an audience. He later admitted that he refused to get professional help because he was scared of the diagnosis. 'I felt stranded,' he said. 'There are things that are more important than smashing away on a guitar on stage. My world was becoming a lot bigger, broader, deeper and I was searching for a means to connect with it. I felt like there were very few people I could communicate these ideas to. I was 24 in 1971. Pretty young.'

The Kinks' next big trip was a month-long visit to the US at the end of March. It was a big deal and Dave was under pressure not to pull out of these dates. *Percy* was about to be released and the band also had new songs to play live from the *Lola* album.

Brian Wilcock would later work with The Kinks, but, in 1971, was with Savoy Brown, a blues band formed in south London which had become well known in the US. 'I'd always been into The Kinks, bought several albums, knew most of the catalogue, but had never seen them live,' said Wilcock. 'I had set out to see them a couple of times and they didn't appear, including one time around 1966 when they were billed to co-headline with a bunch of groups at an all-night festival at Wembley but didn't show up. They did have a reputation for missing shows, for whatever reason. One time when I was with Savoy Brown, The Kinks were due to support them at the Fillmore East in New York, in about March 1971, but they pulled out.' As Wilcock himself put it, Savoy Brown 'were a nonentity in the UK' and he heard a rumour that this may have been a factor in The Kinks' non-appearance.

Most of the shows on that tour were played at college gymnasiums, starting in New York, working up and down the east coast, then jumping to California via Detroit. In the first week they played a memorable show at the prestigious Philharmonic Hall, which is part of New York's Lincoln Center. Few rock bands had been allowed to play there and it remains a mystery why The Kinks were booked. Backstage before the show, the band began to appreciate the grandeur of the venue when they discovered a grand piano in their dressing room. Ray was not his usual composed self and, according to Dave Davies, was staggering around drunk on tequila before the show even began.

THE KINKS DRAW AN UNRULY CROWD reported *The New York*

Times. Journalist Mike Jahn wrote that the audience was 'somewhat aggressive' and that the few dozen people who ran forwards to stand up at the front during the show turned around and shouted obscenities to anyone asking them to sit down. 'By the end of the show, several dozen people had crept on stage,' Jahn observed, 'a few of them playing with the vocal amplification speakers. At the concert's end, several hundred crowded on stage and forced the group off.'

'That was one of the most chaotic gigs ever,' said John Gosling. 'We were banned from playing the place ever again. Half the audience got up on the stage during the encore, encouraged by Dave. Ray had slipped, because the floor was wet with all the beer sprayed onto it, and he went staggering back towards the amps.' As Ray stumbled backwards across the stage still singing 'Lola', Dave saw him coming and stepped neatly aside, at which point Ray crashed into the stack of amplifiers, bashed his head and had to be taken off stage. People in the front row were shouting at the band, asking if Ray was dead. Dave and John Gosling took it in turns to play solos until a bandaged Ray returned.

'The following night in Providence was just as outrageous and the audience again joined us onstage for the encore,' recalled Gosling. 'Our encores were often quite eventful, and at times more memorable than the preceding show. Ray did one in his underpants, and on another occasion rode across the stage on my shoulders for some reason. We even did a tribute to Le Pétomane, I mimed a fart solo while Ray made the noises backstage into a microphone. Very tasteful.'

After a show in Santa Monica on 7 April, Dave was taken to hospital, and the final half a dozen shows and recording sessions in the US were cancelled. He was again diagnosed with depression, another in a series of psychological problems. In New York, he complained of hearing a thousand voices in his head, like several radio stations broadcasting at the same time. As had been the case with Ray in the 1960s, Dave was not really in any state to be on the road. 'Internally and spiritually, I was going through an immense transformation,' said Davies. 'I was getting into mystical things. And yet I was still in the world of "get up there and play the hot riffs". Playing every night, drinking, sex, the rock'n'roll life, the usual. And I found it really difficult to cope with these two worlds.'

The band returned to England in time for Ray and Dave to see Arsenal win the FA Cup at Wembley, and then began preparing for the rearranged Australian tour, scheduled for the end of May.

The Kinks were a wreck while touring during the early 1970s, as a result of paranoia, depression, heavy drinking and living life on the edge. Ray could be a social drinker when he wanted, but often kept to himself, preferring to watch a film in his hotel room rather than join the party. Dave, Mick and the two Johns were the hardcore party animals, ably assisted by a childhood friend of Mick Avory's, Colin the Scrap. 'The Scrap came on the road with us as a sort of personal assistant,' said John Gosling. 'He was stage barman and court jester. He could be one of the funniest people on the planet, especially when he was tired and hungover, which was often.' Colin chose the bars they visited and whose hotel room would be trashed on a given night.

Whether supporting or headlining, The Kinks were fortunate to be paired with good bands who they enjoyed seeing. Lindisfarne and Fairport Convention were favourites of John Gosling's. 'What a great bunch of blokes they turned out to be,' he said. 'They were quite fond of beer too, so we shared an occasional post-gig nightcap. Jim Cregan, the guitarist with Cockney Rebel, used to join us in the bar too. We had some terrific American supports: Little Feat, Tom Petty, Cheap Trick, and quite often Dave and I would get to the gig early to catch their sets. An early support was Elton John, but we thought he looked too silly to ever make it.'

The Kinks' antics continued down under, now in the midst of the wet Australian winter. After landing in Sydney, the band took a flight to Brisbane for the opening show, and succeeded in making their way into the papers after a drunken scene on the plane. Using hired equipment, most of the shows involved some sort of technical problem, leading to another riotous concluding performance. 'At the end of our Australian tour we played a gig at an open-air swimming pool in Perth during a rainstorm,' said John Gosling. 'The stage had blown over in the wind and we were forced to play standing on some stone steps, soaking wet, while members of the audience threw themselves into the pool. It was surreal. We left for England the following day.'

During the summer, The Kinks were in negotiations with RCA over a new record deal. They were a big label: they had David Bowie and Alice Cooper – and Lou Reed was about to sign too. The Kinks wanted more exposure in the USA and RCA could provide that. They also wanted funding for various side projects and film tie-ins, but that request was turned down. They signed anyway.

'We just signed a deal with RCA,' said Ray Davies in 1988. 'They had even given me a box of cigars. I thought I shouldn't get carried away with it, so I made the most working-class album I could. It's about the urban redevelopment of inner London and how it's really become an urban wasteland. There are places where people just can't go anymore. They built cheap housing and packed people in like rats. The kids there have no jobs and no future. It's everything the smart-asses like Johnny Rotten described, I think he used to be quite visionary in that way.' Vast swathes of Victorian housing was demolished, often with ugly tower blocks of flats being erected in their place, destroying any sense of community that might have lingered before. The album he was talking about was *Muswell Hillbillies*, the name being a reference to the TV show *The Beverly Hillbillies* in which a family of country hicks strikes it rich and moves to Los Angeles.

'Recording sessions in the early part of the seventies were more concise,' said John Gosling. 'We would convene at Morgan Studios in Willesden, and Ray might start strumming a chord sequence and maybe try out fragments of vocal. We would gradually join in once we got the "feel". Dave would usually have his songs complete by the time we eventually recorded them. It was a fun and creative time for all of us.' Ray and Dave were collaborating better than they had in years, and probably better than they ever would again. Often they would head back to Dave's house after a session to continue working. It was also the last period in which the entire Davies clan spent a lot of time together. Ray, Dave, Fred and various sisters and brothers-in-law would head to the Archway Tavern at the bottom of Highgate Hill, just over a mile from Fortis Green. At weekends, they could hear live music and have a sing-along. The pub made such an impression on the Davies' that the album cover photograph was shot there.

John Dalton and John Gosling enjoyed an unusual amount of creative input into the album. 'I would come up with the odd intro or ending and maybe a little run here and there that Ray would give his approval to,' said Gosling. 'Generally he knew what he wanted and was usually able to convey that to us in some way. There was always some room for improvisation.'

Even though The Kinks were expert at documenting their own time and place, many of their songs sound as fresh and relevant now as they did forty years ago, and Ray Davies' '20th Century Man' has almost *more* significance today than when he wrote it. Through six minutes, the song builds slowly to epic proportions, expressing frustration with modern life. The lyrics have a timeless quality, perhaps signalling how little certain aspects of British life have changed in the four decades since: 'Ruled by bureaucracy/ Controlled by civil servants/ And people dressed in grey/ Got no privacy got no liberty'.

Ray found that, though his new songs were about what was happening right around him in a small area of north London, the sentiments had global resonance. He recently recalled receiving an award in Amsterdam because he had written about urban renewal and development. The original gatefold sleeve of the LP opened to show the band in front of some corrugated fencing, which encircled a block of houses ready for demolition, and that image captured the whole mood of the album perfectly. Having sung out about what was being lost on *Village Green Preservation Society*, The Kinks were now worried about what the replacement might be.

The title of 'Oklahoma USA' references America, as do bonus tracks on later CD versions of the album – 'Mountain Woman' and 'Kentucky Moon'. That carries through into a country feel on some tracks but, overall, the album evokes a jazzy, pre-war England, as exemplified on 'Have a Cuppa Tea' (based on Davies' grandmother) and 'Uncle Son' (who was also taken from a real-life character). 'Holiday' was more Southend-on-Sea than Santa Monica, but the title track, 'Muswell Hillbilly', contained lyrics about the Black Hills and old West Virginia – undercut by the singer's admission at the end of the song that he's never seen either. The song is actually about his parents' move to Muswell Hill before he was born.

Overall, the album is one of The Kinks' finest, even though it produced no hit singles. In fact, the lack of obvious singles was deliberate: having grown frustrated with Pye's focus on chart hits and reluctance to push albums, Ray wanted RCA to treat *Muswell Hillbillies* as valuable in its entirety.

John Gosling was all over the album, playing baby grand piano, harmonium, Hammond organ and even accordion. 'It is as difficult as it looks,' he said. 'The left-hand buttons produce chords so you have to memorise the right ones for the song. It's easy to forget to keep the air going in and out when you're concentrating on the music. I had dear old Ken Jones, our tour manager, helping me with that. He'd also had to lay on the studio floor during the bass drum overdubs for "Lola", holding the drum still while Mick kicked it a hard as he could. A real trouper. If you look at the *Muswell Hillbillies* album cover he's the guy on the right standing by the door keeping a watchful eye on us.'

'Muswell Hillbillies [was] a very special record to me,' wrote Dave Davies in *Kink*. 'It was an affectionate recollection of characters from our past.'

In early November, The Kinks formally signed to RCA and, on the 18, were flown to New York to celebrate. The band received a big enough advance that their thoughts turned to opening their own recording studio. The New York party was high profile and the guest list impressive, including Andy Warhol, Alice Cooper and Keith Moon, to name but three. While in the city, the band played a handful of gigs to promote the new album, which was issued on both sides of the Atlantic during the last week of the month.

British critics liked the album. 'As one has come to expect from writer Ray Davies,' said *Melody Maker*, 'the lyrics reflect the life he sees around him.' This is exactly what Ray had wanted to convey. It was 'about trying to live', he told *Melody Maker* in 1971, 'getting up every day, and problems like writing letters and paying bills. These are real problems to me, actually getting them done. I just don't know how other people get on with these problems.' In the

US, reviewers were not overwhelmed. 'It's such a drag to hear the routine 1971 country slide guitar rot turn up on a Kinks album,' commented *Rolling Stone*. Despite RCA's backing, the album only peaked at number 100 in the US chart, while in the UK it failed to place at all.

Signing to RCA was the last major management undertaking by Grenville Collins: he left soon afterwards. Once he was gone, Ray tried to renegotiate a smaller percentage for Robert Wace, but, rather than be marginalised, Wace decided to walk away as well. The official termination of the contract between band and management was made on 30 December. Asked by John Mendelssohn why he stopped managing The Kinks in his book *Kink Kronikles*, Robert Wace replied: 'You're asking me something that could take me two hours to answer. I just basically resigned.' He discussed his departure further in Rolling Stones' manager Andrew Loog Oldham's autobiography, *Stoned*, in 2001. 'The problem [of leaving],' he said, 'is that you create these people and then, sooner or later, you get fed up with them or they get fed up with you, and then the bugger of it is that you can't go on stage and play the guitar. I mean, they've got the residual.'

These comments arguably overstate the contribution of management to a band's success: while Wace had helped get the group started, he had hardly 'created' them. It is undeniable, however, that the backing he and Collins, with Larry Page, provided during The Kinks' crucial battle with Pye over 'You Really Got Me' ensured a necessary right turn in the band's career that had set them on a course to fame, and it is far from clear that their departure, and the concentration of even greater creative responsibility in Ray's hands, was a positive development. To some, the change in management was a mixed blessing. 'I was saddened by their [Wace and Collins'] departure,' wrote Dave Davies in *Kink*. 'Ray was becoming increasingly more difficult to handle. While I was retreating into myself . . . he wanted more control. I felt this only made him meaner and more selfish.'

Whatever the underlying reasons for the split, or its implications for the bands' future, it was apparent that The Kinks had finally shed the last vestiges of the 1960s and, as they were wined and dined in the Big Apple, so Talmy, Wace, Collins, Page and Pye became distant memories.

> I wake up reasonably early and have bread and jam until twelve,' said Ray Davies. 'Today I got up and started dancing and singing around the room, writing a song at the same time. I have to work all of the time, if I don't work I have nothing. You have to live each moment as fully as possible. I wrote most of the day and by six I was exhausted. Maybe I have something wrong physically, I'm always tired by about six. Maybe I need more protein, because I don't eat meat. I have respect for meat and that's why I don't eat it.

Davies was speaking in January 1972 as a new era dawned for The Kinks. He was in complete control and could do anything he wanted, whenever he wanted.

Most of the first month of the year was spent working on another BBC project, a television special to air in June, based around a live show but with additional interviews and footage of the band filmed in north London. A crowd of around 2,000 witnessed the filming of the concert portion at the Rainbow Theatre, which had originally been the Astoria Cinema, in Finsbury Park, London. The stage had a large projection screen behind it onto which were beamed colourful, semi-psychedelic images. The Kinks were bolstered for the show by the addition of ex-members of The Mike Cotton Sound, a group which had formed in the 1950s, and had backed the likes of Gene Pitney and Stevie Wonder, while also playing their own brand of jazz and blues. John Beecham (trombone), Alan Holmes (clarinet) and Mike Cotton (trumpet) would be amongst a group of brass players who would continue to play with The Kinks on and off for the next few years.

At the Rainbow, The Kinks failed to follow through on Ray's plans to build a structured event around *The Kinks are the Village Green Preservation Society*, *Arthur* and *Muswell Hillbillies*. Instead they pleased the crowd with hits like 'Lola', 'Sunny Afternoon' and 'You Really Got Me'. By the following month, however, the band's live act had undergone a radical transformation, and the opening show of their

US tour, in Tampa, Florida, on 25 February, would set the tone for the next few years.

From a basic, four-piece rock band with drums, bass and guitars, they had expanded to include keyboards, a horn section and stage effects, such as slides and films. The growth of their fan base, built by continually touring in the US, was even more remarkable because of the band's constant changes in style and delivery: from their early straight-ahead rock, through the storytelling and grand narrative themes of *Arthur*, and the country tinged *Muswell Hillbillies*, they were now exploring a music hall-flavoured production. Accordingly, the band had expanded further, becoming an eight-piece ensemble with the addition of the three horn players.

It was The Kinks' easiest US tour to date. No one got banned, no one fell ill, and they were greeted with enthusiastic crowds raving to a mix of old hits, often played as a medley, and more recent material. 'The three-man brass line-up has made a big difference,' said Mick Avory. 'We've got a much fuller sound. Rather than just going out to do a gig for the sake of it, we thought a music hall thing would be much more interesting.'

When the band reached the west coast, RCA put on another grand reception party for them, this time at the Continental Hyatt House Hotel in Los Angeles. The Continental became a regular haunt for The Kinks during the seventies, and many other bands stayed there too, which led to it gaining the nickname 'the Riot House'. The bands certainly made the most of any free time they had in California, as John Gosling remembered. 'We all went to see Elvis courtesy of RCA,' he said. 'We sat next to Black Sabbath, who we'd been heckling at the Whisky a Go Go the night before. We went to see Zeppelin in LA as well. They were staying at the same hotel, the Riot House. The following evening was a night off for all of us and the opportunity to celebrate. Mick had a wrestling match with John Bonham in the corridor, and there were all sorts of unspeakable things going on in various rooms. Somebody nicked my bed and put it in the lift. Worst night's sleep I ever had. After we left an entire floor had to be redecorated.'

*

In May, the first Kinks single in eighteen months was released, after a hiatus that would have been unthinkable in the sixties, and which was a further sign that Ray was now firmly in control. Using the Dobro guitar, Dave Davies achieved a memorable sound for 'Supersonic Rocket Ship', while Ray sang about the class divide reflected in the introduction of trans-Atlantic Concorde flights: 'Nobody needs to be out of sight, out of sight/ Nobody's gonna travel second class/ There'll be equality/ And no suppression of minorities'.

A short promo clip was filmed by Laurie Lewis, who had previously shot footage for the band in the USA. The clip features the band prancing around Ray Davies' back garden in astronaut outfits, with John Gosling, dressed as an early aviator in leather helmet, goggles and oversized fairy wings, trying to take off. This was all mixed in with stock footage of objects floating through space and early attempts at aircraft crashing into wooden buildings, calling to mind Buster Keaton.

The single was received reasonably well, provoking some anticipation for the next album. 'A colourful mid-tempo goodie,' said the *New Musical Express*. 'It's got that magic Kinky touch to it,' added *Record Mirror*, before declaring it a 'chart cert'. And they were right: it reached number sixteen in the UK.

The band spent the next two months in and out of Morgan Studios working on the next album. Having given RCA the unexpected *Muswell Hillbillies* as their first album, The Kinks came up with another unusual idea for their next record. *Everybody's in Show-Biz* was to be a double-disc set, the first of which would feature new songs, the second a live album taken from the Carnegie Hall recordings.

The studio half of the album opens with 'Here Comes Yet Another Day', which could easily be read as a diary of The Kinks on the road, as could 'Maximum Consumption' ('Life keeps using me, keeps on abusing me, mentally and physically'); 'Sitting in My Hotel Room' ('If my friends could see me now they would try to understand me/ They would ask me what on earth I'm trying to prove'); and 'Motorway' ('Motorway food is the worst in the world/ You'll never eat food like you've eaten on the motorway'). None of those four songs paint an appealing picture of life on tour. Only 'Look a Little on the Sunnyside', a vaudeville romp, was an attempt to lift the spirits but, musically, even that is little removed from a New Orleans funeral march.

The live material, however, was energetic, and full of brassy brightness and audience participation, though perhaps too much room was given over to songs from the band's recent history, with seven of the eleven songs being from either *Muswell Hillbillies* or *Lola Versus Powerman and the Moneygoround*. As a result, it is little more than a mildly interesting snapshot of the Kinks' 1970s material. Moreover, the studio songs seemed to cast a glum shadow over the live set: was the verve of that Carnegie Hall performance little more than act?

Critics were less than impressed, including The Kinks themselves. In the *Record Mirror*, Ray Davies actually admitted that the album was 'nothing new', while Nancy Erlich, writing in *The New York Times*, went further: 'The new material is desperately grim . . . and consistently depressing.' The listening public seemed to be of the same opinion, clearly unconvinced by the front cover and its cartoon representations of comics like Laurel and Hardy, Harpo Marx, W. C. Fields and George Burns. In a year which saw the release of classic albums such as Deep Purple's *Machine Head*, T. Rex's *Bolan Boogie* and The Rolling Stones' *Exile on Main St.*, it is perhaps not surprising that The Kinks' album reached only the modest height of number seventy in the US top 100, and failed to chart at all in the UK.

Increasingly, Ray Davies was being pushed by RCA as the band's main attraction. This was especially noticeable when, at the end of a three-page spread in the *Record Mirror* in October 1972, a half-page advert proclaimed 'RAY DAVIES AND THE KINKS ARE ON RCA' as though they were now his personal backing band. The label had no illusion about who the 'talent' was. As the decade wore on, it was an assumption that the rest of the band started to take to heart.

They continued to tour through the rest of the year. They supported The Beach Boys for a series of high-profile shows, which ended in New York, to some great reviews and exuberant crowd reaction. *Melody Maker* reported that The Kinks had to play half an hour of encores to keep the crowd happy, while *Disc* said: 'They managed to entertain us in a way that no one, and I mean no one, has managed to all this season.'

Back at the Holiday Inn on Eighth Avenue that night, the crowd reaction and adulation was lost on Dave Davies. He was hearing voices in his head and was thinking about jumping from his high-rise bedroom window. In *Kink*, he revealed that he thought he might be suffering some sort of brain damage from all of his drinking and drug taking. He'd had his first bad acid trip on the US tour in 1969 and, on that occasion, had found Ray totally unsympathetic, as he disclosed in *Kink*: 'I went to Ray's room to talk, to find some comfort in my misery. He seemed like a total stranger to me, unemotional, uncaring.' This time, he felt helpless and totally alone. Luckily for Dave, an old girlfriend just happened to knock on his door while the suicidal thoughts were going through his mind. 'That was a big, big turning point,' he said. 'I came very close to jumping out of that window in New York. I know it sounds really corny but I was helped spiritually at that point. Someone came to the door at the right moment, and I believe in that now.' Dave decided that he would stop taking acid from that moment on and, in a bid to cleanse his body, he became a vegetarian, too. It was an opportune moment to get clean: he only had three weeks to prepare himself for the next tour.

The Kinks would be headlining their own series of shows into the autumn. For the US leg, they hired Dawson Sound with their 'revolutionary acoustic suspension sound system'. Steely Dan, then an unknown band, were the opening support act and running the new sound system was British-born Dinky Dawson. Before the first show in San Antonio, Dawson was pulled into a conversation with Ken Jones, the tour manager, during which he formed the impression that the opening act were not to be allowed a sound check. Dawson couldn't believe what he was hearing, he wanted his new system to be used properly and he argued his case with Jones. 'Ken and I went at it for a few minutes before he threw up his hands and left. Steely Dan got their sound check.' Apart from Dawson's recollection, there is no evidence of any such edict having come from The Kinks, or anyone around them, although the sound engineer regards an incident from later in the tour as illustrative of a certain disregard for support bands: 'Before Steely Dan's last show as opener in Chicago, Ray insisted on a full rehearsal, taking up the stage until it was time for the doors to open. There was barely enough time to set up the Dan's equipment, but by this time, I knew the Dan's set and could have mixed them blindfolded.'

When the tour reached the Felt Forum in New York, Dawson found himself up against a whole new set of problems. 'Just before the sound check, the union sound engineer decided he would mix the show,' he explained. 'I wanted to burst into laughter but knew better. I wasn't even angry. I had learned about teamsters and stagehands on my first visit to America in 1969, when Fleetwood Mac opened for Sly and the Family Stone at the Garden. Back then, a union soundman pulled a gun on me to make his point that this was a union house. More specifically, it was *his* union house. I quickly learned not to mess with them.'

Back in the UK, The Kinks played a dozen shows to promote their new single, 'Celluloid Heroes', the album-closer from *Everybody's In Show-Biz*. Like most of the band's post-sixties singles, it failed to make much impression in the charts, but slowly became a crowd favourite, and is now regarded as one of The Kinks' best songs.

At almost six-and-a-half minutes long, it is certainly a slow burner. 'There are stars in every city/ In every house and on every street,' sang Ray, dismissively, contrasting such naive yearnings with a list of true Hollywood greats who had been immortalised in concrete on Hollywood Boulevard: Greta Garbo, Bette Davis and Rudolf Valentino, to name but three. Unfortunately even constant live performances – the grind of touring in the US was now Ray's very single-minded preoccupation – couldn't get 'Celluloid Heroes' into the American charts. The single's failure was a frustrating end to the year.

In 1972, Ray and Dave had taken steps to establish their own recording studio in north London. They chose a decaying factory building on Tottenham Lane in Hornsey, near the corner of Church Lane, and decided to call it Konk. It was the natural next step in gaining full control of their music. In their own studio they could do what they wanted and take as long to as they liked to do it. They also hired Marion Rainford as a full-time publicist and assistant at the studio.

Dave was the driving force behind Konk. 'I'd always been the one that was into the equipment,' he said. 'I had a little set up at home and was always trying to get Ray [interested]. He ended up borrowing mine, so I didn't have any! Rather than spend tens of thousands in Morgan [Studios], I thought it was easy, you just lash out and buy the same and do it yourselves. I couldn't get Ray to sign the bloody cheque!'

'It used to be a tobacco warehouse and everything's on different levels and different nooks and crannies,' explained Mick Avory. 'So we picked the biggest space at the studio and built it from there.'

In January 1973, Ray turned his attentions back half a decade to 1968, and *The Kinks are the Village Green Preservation Society*. He had long felt he had unfinished business with the project and, after the critical and commercial apathy with which The Kinks' recent material had been greeted, wanted to present his *Village Green* vision more completely. Great Britain had officially joined the European Economic Community on New Year's Day and a series of cultural events were planned to celebrate this. One of these was the *Fanfare For Europe* concert, a perfect setting for The Kinks to present their vision of England, even if it was an England past. Although it wasn't fully functional, The Kinks began convening at Konk to rehearse Ray's Village Green concept show.

When it came to the concert, they employed a full brass band and six-piece choir to give a fuller sound. The Kinks wore costumes, there were elaborate and atmospheric lighting rigs, and photo and movie projections. This was the first clear indication of where Ray Davies intended to take the band's live shows. During 'Where Are They Now', the audience saw pictures of incarcerated gangsters the Kray twins, sixties fashion designer Mary Quant and, cheekily, The Rolling Stones. Songs from *The Kinks are the Village Green Preservation Society* era were sprinkled between medleys of the band's big hits, and the show was reviewed by all as a great success. Days later, a slightly scaled-down performance of the show was filmed at the BBC for their *In Concert* series.

By March, Konk had been equipped to a standard that allowed some recording, and The Kinks moved in. It is where they recorded almost everything until the end of the band. For a perfectionist like Ray Davies, Konk allowed him the largesse he'd always craved in the studio. Having time to work in their own studio didn't suit everyone though. 'Once Konk was operational things seemed to change,' said John Gosling. 'Ray rarely seemed happy with anything. We took forever over every track until we eventually ran out of ideas. Sitting through endless overdubs and remixing sessions became terminally boring. I still think we should have had an independent producer.'

'Inevitably things took more time because we had our own studio,' said Mick Avory. 'You could experiment more. Things took too long sometimes, but then again we did have a bar, so it wasn't that bad.' Having a place to drink and relax proved invaluable for the band members. 'We spent a lot of time in there,' recalled John Dalton. 'We put a bar in there, and a snooker table and a dartboard. So when Ray was just mixing, we'd play snooker and darts and drink.'

The experience of making music at Konk was very different to the fast recording techniques they had used in the 1960s, when they had been in and out of studios very quickly. They'd do take one, which the band thought was really good, but Ray would ask for another one, and then another. 'Then, forty takes later,' explained Dalton, 'Ray [would] say, "Will you play back the first one again? That's the one." Because you've got a lot of nervous tension there when you [first] record. It's got that little bit of magic. It happened many times.' People left hanging around were liable to get restless. The band was not overly keen about the live shows being more theatrical, either, and it was only really Ray who carried affection for the days of music hall, vaudeville and radio stars like Max Miller. 'I didn't think it was necessary,' said Mick Avory. 'It was what Ray wanted to do, his writing took him there and he was always into the theatre. The band just got taken along with it and we also had to do the other work of playing the old hits every night, so there were really two shows. It was a challenge, so I enjoyed it from that respect, but we knew it wouldn't be a commercial success.'

The first thing to be released from the band's sessions at Konk was the double A-sided single 'Sitting in the Midday Sun'/ 'One of the Survivors'. The former was a perfect summertime melody about a happily unemployed character, the latter a return to Johnny Thunder on his motorcycle, a character last heard of on *The Kinks are the Village Green Preservation Society*.

In May, a small article in *Record Mirror* announced that Konk was complete and ready for business, and that The Kinks were looking for an engineer to man the studio. The set-up costs for Konk were around £70,000 and came from the advance paid by RCA. While the band would save on paying for the use of other studios, they also wanted to earn back some of their investment by hiring Konk out to other bands while they were away on tour. A little later, they set up their own Konk label and band members got involved with production work. Dave Davies and John Gosling formed their own company for this, Dazling. 'It was an exciting idea put forward by Dave over a particularly good curry,' said Gosling.

> He knew all the best places in London. We had been finishing off the production of Café Society's album at Konk for Ray, and were talking about getting involved with other artists on the label, including my old friend Andy Desmond. We made a lovely album with him, Dave sang some backing vocals on it and on one song did a blistering guitar play out plugged straight into the mixer. It was an afterthought and sometimes the best things happen that way. We got Mick in on one track, and backing singers Shirlie Roden and Pam Travis doing harmonies. Touring musician Al Holmes did some lovely stuff, too, with his woodwind. I wrote the string arrangements and conducted them, so there was quite a lot of Kinks involvement on that one. Dazling, like Konk Records, was full of promise. Dave and I worked so well together in the studio, but ultimately we were dependant on the success of the label and the influx of more artists.

Unfortunately for Dazling, this influx was slow to arrive and came only when the company was long gone.

Preservation

The Kinks' biggest show of summer 1973 was set for the White City stadium on 15 July, but, as is so often the case with summer events in Britain, the weather was miserable. Along with the six other acts, The Kinks were to be part of a ten-hour live show. Ray arrived at the last moment, in a rough state. No one in the crowd was aware of the drama unfolding in Ray's personal life and so his announcement that he was going to leave the industry after the show was a shock to everyone.

'I was there with Roy Hollingsworth,' recalled photographer Barrie Wentzell. 'Standing right at the front of the stage, Ray Davies said he was going to retire and we looked at each other and said, "What?" So afterwards we went backstage and chatted to Mick Avory and asked what was going on, he said, "I don't know it's just Ray". [The Kinks' press secretary] Marion Rainford was there, she was like a character out of *Poirot*.' Rainford tried to tidy up the mess Ray had left, glossing over his pronouncement while worrying about his welfare.

'UPSET' DAVIES QUITS ON STAGE reported the *New Musical Express* on 21 July, in a piece which quoted Marion Rainford: 'One has to understand that Ray is in a very emotional, confused state,' she said. 'Rasa left, with Ray's two children, and she hasn't been heard from since. Ray is naturally a very worried man. He hasn't eaten since she left, he hasn't slept, it's a miracle he got through the gig. But I must say that neither The Kinks nor I believe for one moment that Ray will really quit the business. He's a grieving man and he made an emotional statement.'

Another photographer at White City that day was Debi Doss, an American from St Louis, Missouri. 'I came to London in 1972, ostensibly to undertake a year's independent study,' she said. 'I was tracing the history of folk music in England, but what I did was blag a photographer's pass to shoot my favourite bands from the orchestra pit. One of the gigs I shot was The Kinks at White City in 1973. During the song "Alcohol" Ray was notorious for shaking his beer can and then spraying the demon beer over the audience. As I was in the pit taking photographs I got soaked. I have a photograph to mark the moment Ray announced the retirement of The Kinks.'

None of the other band members made any public comments. They didn't know how serious Ray was, but they did know he would need time to recover both physically and emotionally.

After an overdose of 'uppers', and having his stomach pumped in hospital, he was allowed out under the care of his brother. Dave helped Ray in the weeks following White City and the pair managed to put previous arguments behind them. For a while, at least, they were close again. Talking about his relationship with Dave, Ray acknowledged the effect that illness had on it. 'It was a bad time, of course,' he explained. 'But [it was] good from a different point of view. It did bring us much closer together. Emotionally and creatively, we were up against the wall. And that blood bond came back into play. But after a few months it got back to normal again.'

'The three weeks that followed were awful,' said Dave. 'But in a way, because he was so fucked up, it gave me strength.' As time passed Ray's determination to give up the music business waned and he managed to regain some of the old fire. 'I went on holiday with my brother to Denmark to see a bunch of shows in the clubs,' said Ray. 'We were like a couple of punk-rock "punters" wanting to get back on stage again. The experience washed away all my tedium. That White City concert did give The Kinks a new life in a way. After that holiday, we started with records like *Preservation* and *Soap Opera*. It was the turning point I was looking for to happen.'

While Ray and Dave were away, the rest of the band were in limbo, not knowing what, if anything, was going to happen next. Roy Hollingsworth wrote a long open-letter to Ray in the pages of the *Melody Maker*. It's title was 'Thank You for the Days, Ray': 'If you are going to go, Ray, and if you really want to, then thank you for the days. Nobody will press you to stay. Those who love you will let you make whatever decision you wish to make. But you must believe that if you leave, then there's precious little left. Think again, Ray. Think again.'

Ray was convinced that his marriage to Rasa was falling apart because he was touring so much – and he was right. He also thought that if he retired from music, Rasa would come home to him, but it wasn't that simple. She divorced him later that same year. 'I really felt I was getting nowhere with my own life,' said Rasa in 1984. 'Ray was very busy working. It's something that I could cope with today, I'm sure, but I couldn't cope with it then. I had two very small children and I was always alone. I was seeing less and less of Ray. When he was at home, he was very into himself and working, writing a lot. He makes himself busy all the time. It's as if he's got this thirst; he's got to be busy. He's unable to relax. He's a loner. I think he needs somebody there in the background. The marriage just crumbled.'

By September, Ray Davies was ready to release a statement:

> Several weeks ago I wrote a letter to the world. It turned out to be a letter to me. But I do feel that I made a decision, whether emotionally motivated or not, to change the format of the band. White City was not a good place to say goodbye. The sun wasn't shining, my shirt was not clean . . . The Kinks are close enough now to be able to work as a team in whatever they do and anyone who thinks that it is only my back-up band is very much mistaken.

He ended with a comment about what had happened since his breakdown. 'I spent a couple of weeks with brother Dave. At first we didn't talk about music but then we started singing and playing guitars and before we knew it we were trying to play some Chuck Berry riffs.' The statement coincided with the announcement of some autumn concert dates and news of a trip to the US. God had saved The Kinks once more.

Britain was struggling through social and political troubles. The continuing violence in Northern Ireland escalated and spread, as the IRA detonated bombs in London. The rising price of oil pushed up fuel prices and petrol rationing was introduced, while a three-day working week would soon be instigated as disputes with miners, power station workers and railway workers rumbled on.

In the shadow of these difficult times, sessions for the new Kinks album, *Preservation Act I*, started in September. Echoing what was happening in the news, the album picked up the 'sleepy old England' baton from *The Kinks are the Village Green Preservation Society*, but, this time, told a story of the green and pleasant land under threat of a battle between the evil capitalism of Mr Flash and socialist leader Mr Black.

In the studio, relationships were a little awkward at first. 'We all had to pretend like nothing had happened,' said John Gosling. 'Ray was doing weird things like walking around [wearing] glasses with no lenses in.' For some, Ray's denial that the group were simply his 'back-up band' rang hollow during the recordings. 'That's when it almost became Ray Davies and The Kinks,' said Mick Avory. 'He was virtually doing everything – writing the songs, singing them, producing the albums.'

From the conceptual pieces that started with *Village Green Preservation Society* through *Arthur* and *Muswell Hillbillies,* Ray had been heading in the direction of an epic for some time, and decided that *Preservation Act* was too big for one record: it would fill two volumes, *Act 1* and *Act 2*, to be released eight months apart.

'On *Preservation*, Mr Black overthrows corrupt Mr Flash and the first speech after he takes power is that everything's gonna be just the same but worse,' said Ray Davies to *Mojo* in 2006. 'I miss the Cold War because it focused us on the realities of what's happening in the world . . . it represented a boundary and there are no boundaries anymore.'

Preservation Act 1, in which Flash rises to power, begins with the song 'Preservation', built around a sub-Hendrix guitar, that sets the scene with a lyric about corrupt politicians lying to the nation. 'Morning Song' threatens to morph into a 1930s romantic musical score and, while useful on stage, adds little to the album. 'Sweet Lady Genevieve', with its gentle harmonica and folk-rock feel, was tailor made for the *Old Grey Whistle Test* generation, and stills stands up forty years later. Much of the material is mid-tempo rock, the only exception being 'One Of The Survivors', which sounds like a mid-seventies Lou Reed track, and 'Sitting In The Midday Sun', which could be the theme tune to a family television sitcom.

The album struggled on both sides of the Atlantic, failing to chart in the UK and stumbling to only number 177 in the US. *Sounds* called it 'strangely disjointed', while *Rolling Stone* judged it 'too diffuse and inconsistent'.

As 1974 arrived, The Kinks were back at Konk working on *Act 2*, and bringing in new people for what was planned to be a busy year of touring. Back in April 1973, when The Kinks had played at the Winter Ballroom in San Francisco, they had been supported by local band Dan Hicks & His Hot Licks, who were performing some of their final shows, and then included singer Maryann Price. 'I loved The Kinks, from "You Really Got Me" and those big riffs,' said Price. 'I wasn't aware that Ray had also written "Waterloo Sunset", I wasn't aware that he was that versatile.' Price had studied at the Peabody conservatory in Baltimore and then in New York, 'Just to get out of Baltimore'. Her recording career began with work on radio commercials at the age of 17. There she met her mentor, Hank Levy, a baritone sax player. 'I did demos for songwriters in the Brill Building in 1965 and then I moved to Las Vegas in 1966 for three years,' she said. 'That's where I was performing. I was recording before I was performing because I was terrified of performing.' Price joined the Hot Licks, a jazz-swing-country band, in 1969.

Of supporting The Kinks at Winterland, her memories are hazy. 'I saw a little bit of the show but I was high – you can write that,' she said. 'I did our show and [Ray] heard me, but I don't recall much of their show. By then I was out in a limo with my foot hanging out of the door!'

Davies did, indeed, take note of Price's performance and, when he needed a backing singer, tried to track her down. 'He knew the Hot Licks were about to break up and then he found out about it and wrote to me,' Price explains. By 1974 she was newly married and living in Sausalito, just north of San Francisco, and Davies obviously wasn't sure of her address. 'He addressed it to Maryann Price, South Alito, no zip code,' recalled Price. 'Somehow it got to me and I saw the London postmark. I'm paraphrasing, but it said, "Dear Maryann, would you like to join my band and tour and record with us?" It was signed Ray Davies, and I looked at my husband and said, "Who is Ray Davies?" He looked back at me with complete pity in his eyes and said, "Maryann, Ray Davies is the leader of The Kinks". I went, "Woo, woah, ok then!"'

Price was keen not to let the opportunity pass. 'I called the number as far as I can remember, because I wanted to respond immediately,' she said. 'Before I knew it I was on an airplane and I went over three or four times before we toured back in the States. I remember landing at Heathrow and getting a cab to this little hotel where Ray had booked us in. Later Ray came over and greeted me and my husband, and we went into Konk and we played a gig. I didn't know the complete repertoire and we hadn't rehearsed the old songs, we'd just worked on the new material and I was on stage a day or two after I arrived. Bill Haley and the Comets opened, which was a dream come true for me.'

The show with Haley, at the University of Leeds, was the third of a spring tour. Price's introduction to the band's back catalogue was a swift one, but, as the shows progressed, she realised that she already knew lots of the songs, without being aware that they were by The Kinks. 'I was on stage as window dressing,' she said, 'only knowing the hits and then Ray started pulling out these songs. I was turning to people off stage and saying, "Oh my God, he wrote that?!" I spent most of that first show just going, "Oh my God" on stage. I was absolutely astounded at the depth and breadth of his abilities. What a way to find out, standing on stage with the band.'

While the band worked on *Preservation* in the studio, they played lots of weekend shows and Price learned more about their history. She found the studio environment much more comfortable. 'I was an old hand,' she said. 'I'd been on three or four albums with the Hot Licks, and I'd started out when I was 17 and now I was almost 30. Ray gave me a couple of leads, which was nice, and for the harmonies I just ran at it and made up my own parts.'

Set free to explore the album to its full extent by their new Konk studios, the band took their time to truly master the new material. As the new show was to have a narrative, the normal ad-libbing of a live performance was reined in so that certain effects and films could tie in with the music they were playing. The new ensemble – the five core Kinks, the three-piece brass section and two female singers – also presented a new dynamic to which they needed to adjust. The other backing singer was Pam Travis. 'Pam was easy as pie,' recalled Maryann Price. 'She had a good sense of humour, was about a foot and a half taller than me, and had "big ears" as we say in the business – that's a compliment [she had a keen ear]. She was a little tamer than I was. I considered myself one of the boys and was a little wilder. At one of the RCA parties they had this big deli tray and I just threw myself onto this table.'

Despite the Davies brothers' reconciliation in Denmark during the summer of 1973, once back in the studio, the interaction between them again shrank to a tense minimum. Dave wasn't overly happy about the theatrical route the band was taking and still felt uneasy about touring. His attempts to co-write with Ray were also rebuffed. When he asked his older brother, the response was dismissive. 'No, I don't think so,' he replied. 'Anyway, anyone can write songs.'

'They communicated in the studio only through headphones and talkback between the control room and studio,' said Price. 'On tour if we stopped off for food, one would go one way and the other would go the other way. I never saw them sit at the same table.' Dave had been willing to follow Ray's lead into dramatic performance, but, by the end of the *Preservation Act 2* sessions, was fed up. 'I thought that surely Ray had had enough of this self-indulgence by now,' said Dave. 'Our albums weren't selling that well, although we had a tremendously loyal following in the States. Frankly, I was concerned about our direction.'

Once they had endured three months at Konk, working on *Preservation Act 2* and rehearsing, The Kinks plus entourage set off for the US in early April. Touring with The Kinks at this time was still a riotous and alcohol-soaked experience. 'John Gosling was a loveable drunk,' said Price. 'As was I. We'd get bored on the road and things could get crazy, that's what we did.' The tours could also be long and draining, and Ray's on-stage demeanour erratic: he'd stop and start songs without telling the band and he also suffered problems with his back, causing some shows to be cancelled.

On the whole, Maryann Price has happy memories of her time with The Kinks and her anecdotes about Ray make clear both her respect and affection for the sometimes difficult frontman. 'He was the only person I ever met who could keep a twelve-string guitar in tune,' she said of his dedicated, professional side. But he was also capable of playfulness. 'You know those plastic banana harmonicas that you buy at tourist places? At one show Ray said, "You go centre stage with one of these plastic banana harmonicas and act like you're playing and I'll crouch down behind one of the amps and play a solo." So I did it and we pulled it off. *Rolling Stone* reviewed it and said, "Who was that woman on the plastic banana harmonica?"'

Price only lasted six months with the band before heading home for good. 'My husband was in California and I didn't really want to leave,' she said. 'I told people it was because I was newly married, but the real reason was that I missed good old California and all the Mexican heroin. Fortunately I am clean now!'

The *Preservation Act 2* album was released in the USA during May 1974, three months earlier than in the UK, while the band was touring North America. Perhaps unsurprisingly, *Act 2* offered more of the same, and, unlike the *Village Green* album, which had been the genesis of the current project, the songs simply failed to live up to their concept's promise. Spoken-word interludes sprinkled throughout kept the narrative flowing, but the music itself was less than inspired. The press was less than impressed. The *New Musical Express* criticised the 'thin excuse for a storyline' and writer

Ian McDonald weighed in with further criticism: 'Ray Davies has merely created a drawn-out sequence of socio-political platitudes.'

In interviews at the time, Ray Davies talked about how he viewed the whole *Preservation* concept as a personal one. '*Preservation* is about what a mass of people will do, how masses react,' he explained. 'The character I'm going to play in the musical can do that to people. I'm not saying that *I* can, but people, when they want to enjoy themselves, will show it. I think what I do in the musical is break down any of the barriers I've got as a person. I think what I do is, I put barriers up so I won't get hurt. I'm not sure I'm sensitive, but I have to put up little barriers or else I get bruised.'

Any goodwill that the band members had towards Ray and his continual pushing of the theatrical was beginning to dissipate quickly. Touring as a large ensemble was not what they thought The Kinks should be about. The core of Dalton-Gosling-Avory found it hardest to adjust, missing the spontaneity of a rock show, and now required to play to cues and put on an act. 'We'd have a load of strangers on stage,' said John Gosling. 'When we did *Preservation* I thought it was quite interesting. I had to bring in "Demolition" when it came up on screen. You couldn't get drunk and fall over. Ray wanted to try these things and I agreed but it went on for too long.'

After Price's departure in July 1974, a replacement was needed urgently for an *In Concert* recording for BBC Radio. Claire Hammill had been recording at Konk and stepped in for a couple of shows. She was introduced to Ray Davies in 1973 by her manager Tony Dimitriades. 'Tony brought Ray round to the flat we shared in Marble Arch,' she said. 'I lived there with Alan White of Yes and Rory Flynn, Errol Flynn's daughter. I was in awe of Ray when I met him. Everyone is a fan of The Kinks – they were the voice of our generation and spoke a different language to The Beatles or the Stones.'

Hammill was very happy at Island Records where she had released two albums, 1971's *One House Left Standing* and 1973's *October*. As a teenager, she toured these records in the US with the likes of Procol Harum, Jethro Tull and King Crimson, but then found out that Island wanted to issue a single to boost her popularity instead of funding another album. 'I had no intention of moving but Tony persuaded me to sign with Ray's company,' she said. 'I wanted Ray to produce me for sure but wasn't too happy about leaving Island to whom I had a great loyalty. I think Tony played on my ego, and so I signed.'

Hammill had been signed by Ray Davies in the hopes of Konk Records becoming a conveyor belt of talented artists who would be able to release two or three albums a year between them, with the aim of selling 5,000 LPs each. 'I thought I could get these little bands, almost like having a football team,' said Ray. 'That's what I really intended it to be.' The whole concept soon fell apart. Andy Desmond and Café Society were signed but singer-songwriter Desmond's album *Living on a Shoestring* would be his only effort for Konk, while Café Society's Tom Robinson famously fell out with Ray over delays in getting their album completed. Davies wrote The Kinks' B-side 'Prince of Punks' about Robinson, a song which accused its subject of being a 'middle-class phony'.

At Konk, Claire Hammill went on to record two albums, *Stage Door Johnnies* and *Abracadabra*. The first of these was Ray Davies-produced and included Clem Cattini on drums, as well as contributions from Kinks' touring musicians Laurie Brown and Alan Holmes. 'Ray sang backing vocals on some stuff, that was fun. He also got me to record "Come On-A My House" and a version of "Cocktails For Two". He made me pause after the "cock" part of the word and he thought it was hilarious, so it was "cock . . . tails for two". I can remember him laughing, I wonder what happened to those tapes. He was charismatic and wonderful and gorgeous. Of course I was in love with him, everyone is!' Despite efforts by all concerned, her two Konk albums failed to make any headway in the charts, and her career stalled, at least for the next few years.

Hammill sang with The Kinks for the BBC and then travelled to Manchester for the filming of TV special *Starmaker* on ITV. The show featured The Kinks playing new songs which would soon form their next album, *A Soap Opera*. Ray sang and played out scenes to the songs with other actors. After a couple of days spent rehearsing in London, filming took place on 25 July at the Granada studios in Manchester. It was an experience which drove a wedge further between Ray and the others. Dave Davies felt he and the rest of The Kinks were treated worse than a house band and were literally pushed into a corner while Ray took centre stage.

Dougie Squires had been a fan of the band from the early days. 'Like the whole of my generation I knew The Kinks and danced to "Dedicated Follower of Fashion" on TV.' As the leader of The Dougie Squires Dancers, he had appeared on various music programmes throughout the sixties, livening up performances by famous bands. The *Starmaker* director, Peter Plummer, called in Squires and asked him to choreograph the show. 'I was given the tape and met up with Ray and Peter to discuss the approach,' said Squires. 'There wasn't a lot of staging to do but I was thrilled to be part of it. Ray was thrilled with the idea of starting with him on the camera dolly and performed it well.'

The titles only listed Ray Davies and female lead June Ritchie as actors, with Ray also credited as the writer. The band weren't even mentioned, and were placed were behind scaffolding as Ray sang the opening 'Everybody's A Star' dressed in a shiny Elvis suit and platform heels, his collar up above wide lapels and his bare chest showing below. The dancing girls wore gold boots and hot pants with afro wigs – all rather 'glam', and very much of its time.

'June Ritchie was a joy to work with and there was no tension on the set as Ray and the boys were equally co-operative,' said Dougie Squires. 'If there were any problems we never saw them. I thought it was a little gem in its way and, as with most of their work, quite original. They were very dedicated to what we were doing and quietly professional. I think it meant a lot to Ray that it was being produced.'

The rest of The Kinks were hardly seen and, even when he was singing, Dave was shown long range from across the studio. They were at least mentioned in the end credits. 'I hated the whole experience and it practically broke up the band, the way we were treated on that show,' said John Gosling. 'We were like second-class citizens stuck in a corner of the studio. We weren't even given a chance to get a decent sound balance. *Soap Opera* [which came out of this television special] is the only CD by the band which I don't have and don't want. It was load of bollocks and possibly the lowest point of our career.'

The reviews of *Starmaker* were not kind. Roy Hill from *Record Mirror* attended the preview showing: '[Ray's] music these days seems to have taken a turn for the worse and he croaks his way through the songs.' With Ray playing an ageing rock star who swapped places with ordinary Norman, an accountant, Hill thought it 'too much like pure autobiography for comfort'. A major problem seemed to be the attempt to cram too much into just half an hour.

After the TV show, The Kinks returned to promoting *Preservation Act 2*. The full-page mid-summer press adverts that appeared were unlike anything used to promote The Kinks before. 'THE KINKS *Preservation Act II*/ A SCATHING ROCK COMEDY FOR TODAY'S BLACK TIMES' read the text, above a group picture of the touring cast. Ray Davies sat at the centre of the assembly in full stage gear, stocking-clad backing singers draped around him. Dave Davies and Mick Avory were dressed as sinister-looking spiv characters; John Gosling was a bearded vicar; while an uncomfortable looking John Dalton posed as a Che Guevara figure, complete with beret and rifle.

Lyndsey Moore was brought in as another short-term replacement for Maryann Price as the band headed to Scandinavia for half a dozen shows in September, but more substantial changes were being lined up for shows in the US which were due to begin in November.

Brian Wilcock, who had been with Savoy Brown when The Kinks had missed a show with them in New York in 1971, was approached by Tony Dimitriades in mid-1974 to work with Lindisfarne, who he managed. Dimitriades was also involved with Konk Studios and so, when The Kinks needed a sound engineer for the US *Preservation* tour, Wilcock got the call. Wilcock had been working with bands since 1967, when he was 22, and had a keen interest in R&B and blues music: 'I hung around with some guys who started Savoy Brown, who went from London pubs to American tours in less than three years, and as soon as they could afford a full-time roadie I gave up my office job in the civil service.' He moved on to Lindisfarne but only when they needed him. 'Tony was keen on me, but didn't want to have to pay me a wages retainer while Lindisfarne weren't working,' said Wilcock.

He accepted the job with The Kinks and reported for duty shortly before the tour commenced. 'I was just there for the last few days of rehearsals,' he said. 'The show was almost a theatre show, with props, video screen with recorded sound effects and speech, and lots of spoken word.' Wilcock only met Ray Davies for the first time at the initial rehearsal and said he always got on well with him, 'despite the odd emergence of his demons!' He also got on well with the rest of the band. 'The brass section, girl singers, the crew – in fact, possibly the best vibe of any group I ever worked with. There were a few on-stage shenanigans which tended to be forgotten very quickly. In those days, the business was a lot more relaxed; if somebody recommended you for a job, it was taken that person's word meant they thought you would be good for that position. I just went along, met everybody, took over the sound desk at a rehearsal, sorted out the money agreement with Ken Jones and a few days later was on the plane to New York.'

Wilcock stayed with The Kinks for five years and worked as sound engineer and roadie. Because he lived near to Konk, he also got more involved there, working as a tape operator and as personal assistant to both Ray and Dave. It was a full-time occupation.

Just before the band set off on tour in November, Ray married Yvonne Gunner, a London school teacher he had been seeing secretly. Rasa and Ray had divorced in late 1973 and Ray hadn't seen his daughters since. No one outside the band even knew Ray and Yvonne were dating and the marriage didn't become public knowledge until they divorced in 1981. Neither Ray nor Yvonne has ever spoken about the marriage. The only insight into the relationship to leak into the public domain came when Dave Davies wrote in *Kink* of his first meeting with Ray's second wife: 'We had a stinking row and I stormed out of the restaurant. I thought she was just some stuck-up, spoilt middle-class kid from the suburbs.' Eventually Dave and Yvonne managed to get along on better terms, or, in Dave's words they 'tolerated' each other. Getting on well with his new sister-in-law would prove to be a good idea, because, as he was about to find out, Ray had learnt from his mistakes of the past with Rasa and would be taking Yvonne on every tour thereafter.

A Pint of Guinness and a Cheese Sandwich

The preparations for the full *Preservation Act* tour of the US were lengthy and detailed, which was to become quite usual for The Kinks over the next few years. The touring cast was bigger than ever, with the five permanent band members joined by a four-piece horn section and six backing singers. Two male vocalists, Lewis Rich and Trevor White, were joined by the returning Pam Travis, and newcomers Anna Peacock, Debi Doss and Shirlie Roden.

Roden was brought up in Wales, in a musical family, with two older brothers who had been in bands. She had classical piano training and her voice coach was a member of the Welsh National Opera. Eventually, she moved to London and turned professional. 'I answered ads in *Melody Maker*, one of which turned out to be for Robin Le Mesurier's band Reign,' said Roden. 'They really had more money than music. Two managers financing the band. I remember we once did a gig with 10CC, who were huge at the time, and we had a bigger PA than them! The audition I went for was at Manticore, a hugely expensive rehearsal place in Fulham. I immediately bonded with the band, which already had Debi Doss in as singer.'

Roden hooked up with Andy Desmond through a university friend. Desmond was signed to the Konk label and Roden was recommended when he needed a backing singer. 'John Gosling and Dave Davies were producing the album,' said Roden. "Baptist and Dave, who were both good guys, or so it seemed then. I saw a different side of them when I was employed to be in the concept musicals, as it seems they didn't really want a load of singers, actors and dancers fronting the band and there was underlying resentment.'

First Desmond and then John Gosling mentioned that The Kinks needed new backing singers and she agreed to an audition. 'I was nervous, because Ray was a pretty big star really,' said Roden. 'But he was charming. It was just him and me, and as I walked down the wooden stairs into the studio, he said "Are you a star? I'm looking for a star!" I sat at the grand piano in the Konk studio and played and sang a Laura Nyro song, "Poverty Train". He must have liked it because he offered me the job. Then the office asked me if I could recommend any other girls, so as Debi and I had worked together well in Reign, I mentioned her. And of course, she got the job too.'

Debi Doss had been in contact with The Kinks' office since she started taking pictures of the band prior to the White City show, and had corresponded with Marion Rainford, but she hadn't met any of the band. She, too, auditioned. 'Konk Studios seemed very dark and labyrinthine,' said Doss. 'The audition took place in the studio in the bowels of Konk and Shirlie and I were in the studio with Ray listening and observing from the control room above. I remember what I wore, skinny blue jeans and a checked shirt, my hair was quite short at that time and cut in a boy's style. I was quite nervous but, with the bravado of youth, had decided to perform an Aretha Franklin song a cappella, "Sweet Lover", and one of my own, "Stay". As I wasn't an accomplished piano player, Shirlie kindly played piano for me on my song as I'm sure my hands would have gone all over the keyboard.'

Along with Pam Travis and 26-year-old New Zealander Anna Peacock, the quartet of female singers for the tour was soon complete. While the band worked in the Konk studio, the four girls were often left to devise their parts, in the front room of the Konk office, where they had a large bay window to sit in and work things through. 'There was no written music for anything and sometimes not even lyrics printed out,' said Shirlie Roden. 'Coming from a rock background, I was used to picking things up quickly, although with four girls, working out four-part harmonies was sometimes tricky. It was all very exciting because we were preparing to go to America to tour and I'd never worked over there before.'

The idea was that, each night, the first part of the show would be a more traditional Kinks set, and the second act the *Preservation* show. As time ticked on, the girls and band started practising together, and in came the male singers, lighting and sound crew, projectionists, and so on. Konk's studio was crammed to capacity, which meant things could become disorganised. 'It was great fun,' said Roden. 'Especially when it came to creating the stage clothes we were to wear for *Preservation*. Us girls all stockings and suspenders and split skirts, and the boys in their gangster outfits. Konk at that time had a billiards room and bar and it was all art deco, with silk lampshades and fringes. Quite plush really.'

After rehearsals had been completed, it was finally time to get out and play to an audience. 'It was terribly exciting when we finally got picked up by the car to take us to the airport,' said Debi Doss. 'It meant that we were really touring! We met up in the bar at the airport, now there's a surprise, the lads liked to have a few beers before the flight.' Tour manager Ken Jones had a good deal with Air India and so The Kinks always flew with them to New York, which is where the *Preservation* tour of the US was due to start in late November 1974.

The core band of Ray and Dave, Mick Avory, John Gosling and John Dalton flew first class, while the rest of the cast and crew travelled in economy. 'If we were lucky, the lads sent back miniatures of drink for us or, occasionally, we were "allowed" into first class,' said Debi Doss. 'I remember climbing the spiral staircase up to Air India's bar area, but I don't remember climbing down! Dave hated flying and took pills to relax him on the flight, and drank. Often he would arrive at our destination the worse for wear. I also remember Dave going around on the baggage conveyor belt at one airport.'

By the time the plane touched down in New York on 22 November, the crew were in full party mode. 'I recall the drive from the airport to the hotel in the tour bus,' said Roden. 'It was like a big party, everyone drinking and laughing. Dave grabbed me and pulled me headfirst right over the back of his seat to sit next to him so he could talk to me. I couldn't believe I was being paid to party and have such fun – it all seemed so glamorous.' A Greyhound coach took the twenty-five-strong throng to the Warwick Hotel off Sixth Avenue on Fifty-Fourth Street. Built in 1926 by newspaper magnate William Randolph Hearst, and home to The Beatles during the Fab Four's first US visit in 1964, this was The Kinks' hotel of choice for many years.

The tour began on Saturday, 23 November in Hamilton, New York. With the horn section and singers, the band's numerous costume changes, the multi-media presentation of slides and films, and the lighting rigs, in all it took twelve hours to prepare the stage. At its worst, the tour resembled an overblown amateur dramatic production; at best, it would be described as a music hall version of Andy Warhol and The Velvet Underground's Exploding Plastic Inevitable 'happenings'. Regardless, this was the way it would be for the next few years and, slowly but surely, The Kinks began to win over bigger and bigger crowds, especially in North America. Their second coming was under way.

'I was so nervous that I'd had a couple of brandy and cokes before we went on stage,' said Debi Doss of her first performance with the band. 'I remember ever so slightly rocking back and forth with the house lights down, waiting to unfurl my canvas costume during the song "Daylight" when the spotlight hit and praying I'd reach the high starting note.'

At the time, New Yorkers had succumbed to a craze for writing messages for The Kinks on paper plates and sending them flying on to the stage. The effect was of a mass of oversized confetti cascading down as the band were cheered on. The first set of the night was made up of about a dozen songs from the back catalogue, with a good sprinkling of hits. Then, after an intermission, the *Preservation* part of the show kicked in: most of the two *Preservation Act* albums, played in order, straight through.

The theatricality of the shows was heightened by the appearance of The Kinks themselves who wore 'spivvy' pin-striped suits and took on character names: Dave Davies became Mr Twitch, Mick Avory was Big Ron, John Gosling was The Vicar, John Dalton was Mr Lugs and, of course, Ray was both Mr Flash and Mr Black.

Flash came from the working class and rose up to be a corrupt dictator. *Act 1* describes the country living under his rule, its village greens destroyed. Flash is planning further atrocities, but there are signs of a revolution. In *Act 2*, Mr Black leads the resistance against Flash and deposes the tyrant with an army. Once in power, however, he keeps a Big Brother-like watch on his people.

'The band was really tight,' said Ray Davies. 'I know The Kinks had a reputation of being unpredictable on stage, but oddly enough, on the shows that had themes to them the band was much tighter as they were playing to cues. There's less space for improvisation, so it's tight.'

'We had a lot of quick costume change things,' said Shirlie Roden. 'Add-ons and take-off bits, and I remember we girls started the show as villagers with other costumes over our floozy outfits. I drank far too much brandy before we went on that first night. I was swaying at the front of the stage as the curtain went up but quickly sobered up, especially when I got to my solo song, mainly because Dave Davies poured a pint of beer over my head while I was singing "Mirror Of Love". And for the next few nights, he tried a variety of tricks to throw me while I was singing, like lying on the floor playing guitar and looking up my skirt. I couldn't really understand what was going on. I was unaware at that time that they were feeling like some kind of backing band, because as far as I was concerned, I was just doing my job, what I was paid and asked to do. I wasn't trying to become a big star or something.'

Resentment, however, was slowly growing. Not only were The Kinks being outshone by the girls and the male singers, but Ray Davies was attracting ever more attention. Already firmly entrenched as singer, writer and producer, he now came into his own as the lead actor in the production. His on-stage performance was undeniably accomplished, and he played his two parts equally well, but he was succeeding at something that the other Kinks had never wanted. They would have been happier as a straightforward rock band, and were determined to behave like one off stage, where they still had their freedom.

While everyone else was partying, Ray rarely drank to excess or got involved in the revelries, partly because his new wife Yvonne was travelling with him, but also because he wanted to stay fresh for his difficult performance. He felt the weight of responsibility for the show and was shouldering the majority of the press work too. Despite the mediocre sales figures for the *Preservation* albums, the live show was well received by fans and critics alike. There wasn't really anyone else doing what The Kinks were doing and they made a refreshing change, as many reviewers agreed. 'One of the most enjoyable rock concerts I've ever seen,' wrote a reporter for the *Colgate News*.

'Ray was brilliant at connecting with the audience,' said Shirlie Roden. 'To front the band in those kind of big shows like he did, with a Kinks set first, he had to be on top form physically and mentally. He was the focal point, the lynchpin on which it all turned. When the band were really together, it was wonderful, the music, the atmosphere. I was a bit blown away by how much The Kinks were loved in America, absolutely revered. At that time in the mid-seventies, they were still remembered and known in England, but not in the same way as the US.'

For all its scale and the planning that had gone into making it happen, the full *Preservation* tour played just fourteen shows in the US that autumn, before returning home for a triumphant final outing at the Royalty Theatre, London. *Sounds* said this home-town gig had 'the best elements of a Christmas pantomime – extra evil villains and a degree of pathos, but no dull principal boy and girl – with a story which retains its interest'.

The experience of travelling as a large group would be invaluable for all concerned, as Ray was planning similar projects in future, though some problems persisted. Dave Davies continued to struggle with being on tour and confronted Ray about it during these dates. 'He was thoughtfully concerned,' said Dave. 'Especially when I told him that I wanted to leave before any further tours were planned, as it was mainly the touring that was getting me down, as well as the fact that I felt like a hired hand. We agreed to talk about it again when we got back to England.'

The women in the band were also unhappy with their treatment. 'Pam Travis had been working with the band as backing vocalist for some years and warned us in private of the attitude to women on the road and the continual rude comments,' said Shirlie Roden. 'But I was just exhilarated, especially when Ray gave me the song "Mirror of Love" to sing, I couldn't believe I was singing a solo in America with the Kinks.'

John Gosling was particularly unhappy about the large contingent on stage. 'My first impression of Baptist was of a dedicated musician, talented, serious about his work, really enjoying using his creativity,' said Roden. 'I think there were great depths to him that maybe were never drawn out of him in The Kinks because of all the aggro going on, which he really didn't enjoy or want to be part of.' Roden found Gosling's attitude during the tours especially surprising because she had met him previously on a recording project, where he had seemed very friendly and had treated her as a creative equal. But when she met him as part of the band, he went into what she calls 'playing the part', displaying a quite different attitude. 'The "part" being, women shouldn't be on the road and certainly shouldn't be fronting the band,' she said. 'He just joined in the general thing of ignoring the girls pretty much except to make rude comments when we came anywhere near socially.'

'Baptist would always go to throw a pint of beer over my head, but not waste the beer,' said Debi Doss. 'He would also stretch out both arms and mime strangling me. He once attacked me in a lift with a tequila sunrise and Shirlie had to pull him away. Even when we met up twenty-five years later he had to stop himself from tipping a beer over me, however, he finally apologised for his bad behaviour.'

Roden also remembers that when the girls were in costume (stockings and suspender belts, side-slit skirts and corset tops) the boys' reaction to them softened somewhat. On and off-stage introductions could still be cruel though: they were called The

Pointless Sisters, The Old Trouts, and The TWs (Titless Wonders). On one occasion, Ray Davies introduced Roden on stage to sing her solo with the memorable accolade: 'This is the orgasmic Shirlie. She farts a bit, but she's lovely.'

The taunting was not entirely nasty: there was a strong vein of boyish mischief in the band's behaviour. 'Mick Avory had an air of stability coming from him,' recalled Roden. 'In spite of the fact that he and Dave had had many rows. He wasn't interested in being a star or the centre of attention, no huge ego, just very down to earth. Also a great droll sense of humour and a talent for mimicking.' One night the girls followed him out of the hotel in New York, and he walked up to a silver limo parked outside. As the driver saw them coming he jumped out and opened the door. 'Thirty-fourth and fifth,' called Avory as they all piled in the back of the car. When they arrived at the restaurant he told the driver to take the rest of the night off. Once they were seated inside, Avory started laughing and explained that he had no idea to whom the car belonged.

In this period, The Kinks played so many shows in and around New York that the city became a second home for the band and its entourage. Ashley's nightclub was a regular haunt, where silly but mostly harmless hi-jinks were played out. Mick Avory would drag a potted plant onto the dance floor as his partner; Colin The Scrap would drop his trousers; and John Dalton would ride around on John Gosling's shoulders. Pam Travis's party trick was to eat the bar bill.

Of course the late nights and alcohol could be a problem when they had to get up early to travel the next day. 'Ken Jones would always have us up for ridiculously early flights,' said Debi Doss. 'We would all have to collect in the hotel reception and then sit for ages for various band members and, ultimately, the Great Raymondo!' Dave Davies hated flying so much that he would occasionally travel by train or car with one of the road crew. 'Occasionally, we got the best limo,' said Roden. 'In Los Angeles our security man, Tony Gibbing, ushered us girls into the first limo and, as it turns out, it was for Ray. It was white with a leopard skin interior, bar and sunroof. We travelled all the way to the Riot House with Pam sticking her head through the sunroof and hooting!'

With only one long-distance phone call per week allowed, relationships with partners and family back home could be strained. 'The atmosphere could become tense though because there were so many things that could go wrong,' said Roden. 'People sometimes called Ray a prima donna, but there were a lot of variables and a lot at stake too. If there's something wrong with the sound, reviewers don't blame the PA company but the performers.'

As with Ray, Shirlie Roden saw two very different sides to Dave Davies: on the one hand, a talented, creative guitarist, and very passionate; on the other, utterly insecure, moody and egocentric. 'My main and overriding impression of him was of a tortured soul,' said Roden. 'I think that's why I loved him so much, and I did grow to love him over the years, because I could see his pain and his goodness side by side, his anguish and his talent – and my heart went out to him. You can kind of hear that tortured soul in the sound of his singing voice. The other side of that was his wildness and his sexuality, which was a bit attractive too! Dave in his silver and black Mr Twitch jacket playing lead guitar solos on a good night was unbeatable.'

Debi Doss also got on well with Dave. 'He was quite easy to talk with and this was during his "spiritual awakening" time,' she said. 'He was always sending his "energy" across the stage. During one tour, he thought I was his "spiritual brother" and we nearly had a snog!'

Having worked with other sets of brothers in previous bands, Roden always expected the older sibling to dominate the creatively. 'Dave could be a pain in the arse with his behaviour and excesses,' but I don't know which came first,' she said. 'Because I observed Ray putting him down on stage too. One night he asked him to sing "Death of a Clown" and Dave forgot the words halfway through and gave up. Ray said, "Dave Davies, ladies and gentlemen. He doesn't perform solo very often and now you know why." At other times though, Ray would lovingly refer to him as Django and defend him to the death.'

In addition to his ongoing problems with Ray, the touring schedule, the voices in his head and the band's theatrical direction,

Dave once again started to fall out with Mick Avory around this time. His principal irritation with the drummer was that he tended to take Ray's side in discussions. 'Mick knew which side his bread was buttered,' said Dave, though he acknowledges that being between him and Ray couldn't have been easy for Avory.

The next US tour was still being advertised in some quarters as a continuation of the *Preservation Act* shows, but, with the *Soap Opera* album coming out in late April 1975, Ray Davies decided on a full stage production based around that record instead. After more rehearsals at Konk, and a delayed flight because of snow storms in the US, the band finally opened again in St Paul, Minnesota, on 13 April. The first half of the show now integrated some *Preservation* songs ('Here Comes Flash', 'Mirror of Love') alongside the greatest hits, while the second half was the *Soap Opera* set.

Despite the band playing larger venues and taking more money from ticket sales, costs were carefully managed. The best example of this came during the part of the show in which Ray was supposed to appear as if he was singing on a television show. In fact, a large model of a television, literally fashioned from a cardboard box, was placed on stage and Ray stood inside it. This was in stark contrast to the glam excesses of Elton John and David Bowie, and the overblown shows of Led Zeppelin and Pink Floyd which characterised the mid-1970s.

'Once those wretched shows took over I felt we lost our identity as one of the greatest bands in the world,' said John Gosling. 'The costumes were a bit of a giggle and it was fun when things went wrong because that was us, it was expected, but the very idea of being our own support band rushing through all those great songs at breakneck speed. How bizarre and downright depressing was that?'

One or two tours as a theatrical troupe might have been bearable, but, as they seemed to drag on, core members of The Kinks grew less tolerant. 'In later years I learned that Dave and Baptist began to feel they were being relegated to a backing band with the concept musicals and weren't very happy about it, feeling the band had lost direction,' said Shirlie Roden. 'They just wanted to be The Kinks doing rock music. It was a shame really as Ray was so phenomenally creative and I feel it was a very brave thing to do, take out such a huge entourage and perform those shows.'

'I've never really liked any blend of live music and drama,' said John Gosling. 'West End musicals, opera, any of it. So when The Kinks began to disappear into a sea of extra performers on stage, and our musical identity, which was unique, began to disintegrate, it became depressing. But it was Ray's dream and we went along with it.'

By the time the tour reached Florida in May, tempers were frayed and the friction sometimes got out of control. A silly fight by a swimming pool involving Dave Davies, John Gosling, Pam Travis and Shirlie Roden left the latter with a bloodied arm and Gosling injured, as wailing police cars arrived on the scene. Although no one appears to have been arrested or charged over the incident, it nonetheless demonstrates quite how brittle relationships between band members could become on tour. The tension was only exacerbated by wardrobe malfunctions, arguments over the show's sound, excessive alcohol, a seemingly endless succession of hotel rooms and general boredom.

Ray, however, sometimes appeared oblivious to such problems. 'Ray could be talkative, funny, hugely creative and talented, and attractive,' said Roden. 'He could also be shut off, totally insecure, moody, egocentric and manipulative.' Yvonne was with him, and the ex-cookery teacher seemed young and innocent, with Ray trying to shield her from some of the worst excesses of the rock and roll life. The couple's reticence to join in led to some jibes, with Colin The Scrap naming them The Glums, after characters from the long-running BBC Radio comedy *Take it From Here*.

Despite his outward demeanour, Ray was satisfied with the way these theatrical tours were going. 'I feel much better about myself,' he said. 'Now, after a show, I feel like I've done a good day's work, like I've actually achieved something at the end of the night. I'm not unhappy — it's just that I'm unhappy that people think that I'm unhappy. I felt that I was on top of the world the other night. When I was on stage I was the biggest star in the world. In the old days, we'd just go on stage and play the hits. We've done our loose shows, and I like that, but it doesn't really give me a buzz at the end of the evening. I don't think I could have ever toured again if I hadn't been able to do *Preservation* . . . do the concept shows.'

Shirlie Roden kept copious notes and diaries during her time on tour with The Kinks and she recorded the following dressing room exchange which gives a sense of the distance between Ray and the rest of the band at this time, as well as the pressure that he felt himself to be under:

Ken Jones (cagily): Some people are going to New York.

Ray Davies (pacing up and down): And why wasn't I told? Why wasn't I asked? Why is it I'm always the last person to know anything about what's going on? Why do I always find things out at the last minute? (Aggressively) Come on then, Ken. Tell me something I don't know.

Ken (shiftily): There's nothing you don't know.

Ray (getting angry): Come on, come on Ken. Just tell me something I don't know.

Ken: There's nothing to tell you.

(A short silence ensues, during which everybody stares intently at the floor and the walls.)

Ray: Tell me something I don't know, Ken, and then (threateningly) I'll be happy!

Ken: Alright then. The boys are going to New York tomorrow because their wives are flying in. They haven't seen New York before.

Ray (pacing up and down violently): Has my mother seen New York? Has my dad? Are you flying my dad in tomorrow as well? (Treads on an empty Coca-Cola tin and viciously crushes it) My God, you give some people an inch and they take a mile. He'll be running the whole band soon, taking it over, this man. (Walks over to his clothes bag and zips it venomously and turns to face the assembled and silent band) Well, I tell you what. Someone told me if I broke my neck to do *Soap Opera* instead of *Preservation* this tour, people would be behind me. I'll tell you something. I'll never break my neck for anyone to do anything again. (Exit stormily the great and temperamental Raymondo)

As you can imagine, a suitably depressing atmosphere settled in for the rest of the evening!

(The Kinks Present) A Soap Opera was released in the US in late April 1975, just as the tour was coming to an end, and then three weeks later in the UK, on 16 May, where it failed to chart. The dozen songs from the show were once again patchy and not really suited to a standalone album where, without the supporting stage act, they had to stand or fall on their own merits. Highlights were few and far between. The Bowie-glam promise of 'Everybody's A Star (Starmaker)' was swamped by brass-heavy production; 'Holiday Romance' was catchy but incredibly twee; and '(A) Face in the Crowd' leant towards being overly dramatic. The band played only ten UK shows to promote the album before taking a much-needed five-month break from the road.

During the summer pause, Dave Davies was visited by his father. Fred Davies had been ill but now seemed reasonably well. Dave, though, had an overwhelming foreboding about his father's health and found himself paralysed by fear. Fred and Annie were spending their summer weekends at Ray's house near Guildford, Surrey, and it was there, in July 1975, that Fred suddenly collapsed and died. 'Dad loved the garden in the big house,' recalled Ray Davies in *X-Ray*. 'He loved his life as a gardener.' Moments before Fred died, he had called Ray and asked him to put a bet on the Wimbledon Mens' Final for him. Ray had only just put the phone down when it rang again. Ray's mother, Annie broke the news and Ray was driven to meet them at the hospital by his sister, Gwen, and brother-in-law, Brian. Dave was full of regret that his fear had stopped him from spending more time with his father before it was too late. This was the first death in the immediate family since Rene's some eighteen years earlier.

Ray spent the rest of the summer writing new songs and, occasionally, the five Kinks would meet at his house to rehearse them. Greg Mitchell from *Crawdaddy!* caught up with Ray around this time, and reported on his average working day. It was a strict routine: work six days a week and some more on Sunday. Out at 8.30 a.m. for the day's paper, then breakfast and reading until 10 a.m., making a checklist of jobs for the day: 'Write verse for "School Days". Write verse for "First Time We Fall in Love". Write instrumental bridge for "No More Looking Back".' Then he would work at his piano with a notepad and guitar close to hand until 2 p.m., when he nipped to the local pub for a pint of Guinness and a cheese sandwich, before returning to work until 7 p.m. In this way, he completed around fifteen songs in a month.

The Kinks began recording at Konk in the latter part of August and continued through the early autumn. Ray's thoughts had turned back to childhood yet again and, this time, the result was an album's worth of material inspired by his and Dave's school days. He linked it back to the band's more recent past through a narrative outlining the origins of the Mr Flash character.

Roger Wake was appointed as the new engineer at Konk and his first task was to work on *Schoolboys in Disgrace*. Dave Davies was enjoying it more because, although they still had a brass section and singers, they were getting back to being a rock band again. Much of the narrative about getting expelled from school harked back to his own life story and, in particular, Sue's pregnancy. 'No More Looking Back' was the most obvious song to address his lost love: 'Yesterday's gone and that's a fact/ Now there's no more looking back/ Got to be hard/ Yeah, look straight ahead'.

'*Schoolboys in Disgrace* was a rebirth of the band,' said Dave Davies. 'As I was getting into my new internal, spiritual life, it wasn't as scary as I thought, it was empowering.'

Preparations for another ensemble tour began in late October and went on for a couple of weeks. Again, everyone had a character to play. 'Ray cast me as "Jack, the Idiot Dunce",' said Debi Doss. 'I had a solo dance to perform during the song, dressed in a schoolboy's uniform, clown mask and red curly wig. I remember the day that we went up to the high street in Wood Green and Ray directed me to dance down the street to a playback of the song so that it could be filmed for back projection. I was so glad that I was wearing a mask. I also had to do a photo shoot with Mick Avory in a shower cubicle at Konk. I was wearing stockings and suspenders, which seemed to be the ladies' "uniform" for nearly every tour, and holding a whip and Mick was kneeling in his boxers I recall!'

The tour began, as usual, with a cluster of dates up and down the east coast of the USA. The Kinks were based at the Warwick Hotel in New York. To the bemusement of the others, Ray and Yvonne brought along a camping stove so they could cook in their room. As New York could cater for any taste in food, it is likely that this was a money-saving measure.

The band were being supported by Steve Harley & Cockney Rebel, or 'The Rabble' as they were called by The Kinks' crew. As Dinky Dawson had observed in Chicago, Ray often delayed The Kinks' sound check, keeping the performers on stage for as long as he could, which left the support act scant time to set up. Sometimes they had as little as thirty minutes before the venue's doors opened. Either way, Cockney Rebel were unlikely to receive a warm reception. Sometimes they were greeted with apathy, which changed to jeering before the end of their set. 'You can't really be another English band,' said Shirlie Roden, 'when you're in front of a Kinks audience which is chanting "God Save the Kinks!" at full volume while you're playing.'

After a show, the various factions – The Juicers, the backing singers, Ray and Yvonne – would get picked up in limos and driven back to the hotel or on to a club. The journey time would be spent sifting through the piles of paper plates that had been collected from the stage and reading the messages scrawled on them by fans.

When The Kinks checked into hotels, they sometimes took over two whole floors and the party spread out into the corridors. 'I was rather taken aback at the American groupie scene,' said Shirlie Roden. 'We were often checked into hotels under pseudonyms so the groupies couldn't find the band, but they would follow us girls and sometimes sleep outside the doors in the hotel corridors hoping to find a band member. They were so persistent, wouldn't give up.' One night, 'Cynthia the Plaster Caster', who had been taking plaster cast moulds of rock stars' penises and breasts since the 1960s, turned up with a large leather bag, but it is not known whether she used her equipment on any of The Kinks. Certainly, none of them are listed on her official website.

A couple of weeks into the tour, tensions were once again running high. Ray had gained a reputation for impatience, and on occasion his behaviour would descend into shouting and bawling at bandmates. Shirlie Roden recalled one incident at a sound check in Boston. 'I had a big blow-up with Ray over the monitors,' recalled Roden. 'He yelled at me that there was, "a certain technique for singing rock with a rock and roll band, and you just haven't got it!" I threw my tambourine, which happened to be at hand, way up in the air, let it fall to the stage, and stalked off, just managing to hold back the tears while vague thoughts of being "a professional" skipped thorough my mind. As Scrap said to me afterwards, "You mustn't talk to God like that. You're not allowed to say things that are right, you know."' Roden described the next few days as a psychological stand-off. For her part, she simply tried to ignore Ray. After the next gig, he bought champagne for all the girls but Shirlie refused to drink any. Later, he tried to buy her another drink, but she walked out of the bar. 'Childish, isn't it?' she said. 'At least it gave everybody something to think about. Petty squabbling was in the air, anyway.'

During a show in New Jersey, someone stole one of Ray's jumpers from the dressing room while the band were on stage, and he exploded in anger on the coach back to the Warwick. 'It had been a particularly disorganised day anyway,' said Roden.

Ken [Jones] hadn't got an itinerary, and we were driving round for hours. We had to keep stopping the coach to ask if anyone knew where tonight's concert was! So after the gig on the way home, tired, weary, pissed, Ray comes storming down the coach from the back where he'd been sulking and swearing to himself, and launches into a verbal attack on poor, unsuspecting Ken, 'If the fucking support band can have a security man, why can't we? Do I ask very much of you, Ken? No, I don't. You're supposed to organise things. That's what you're paid for. I want someone in our dressing room while we're on stage. If they can have it, I want it too. I want a bodyguard. I want people around me that can break arms. I want to surround myself with people like that!'

By the time he'd finished, an aura of gloom and despondency had settled. Thereafter, trouble seemed to occur over the most insignificant incidents, as Roden recalled: 'Pandemonium broke loose one day when he got on the coach and spilled [his back-gammon set] all over the floor. "Stop the bus! The tour's off! I can't go on without my backgammon set. I got it in the Harrods sale!" he yelled.'

The tour headed off into the Midwest by a combination of plane and coach in mid-December. Tempers could be short with the long hours of travelling, which were not helped by heavy drinking. According to Roden, John Gosling threw a bottle at Pam Travis and caused a fracas. Listening to endless repeats of Peter Cook and Dudley Moore's foul-mouthed, drunken, stream-of-consciousness act 'Derek and Clive' only added to the tedium as the American winter took hold outside the sleet-splattered coach windows. The bus was like a powder keg: something was bound to spark a confrontation. It happened rather innocently when Pam Travis opened a can of coke, which exploded and splashed over John Dalton. The normally placid bassist retaliated by tipping Travis' glass of whisky over her and she replied by tipping more coke on him. He in turn splashed more drink on her. At first, it all seemed harmless and slapstick. Shirlie Roden had a good view of what happened next.

Pam sat there silently for a moment. Then, to the amazement of all, screaming, she jumped to her feet and kicks Nobby in the shin. He turned round and smacked Pam across the head and they both disappeared grappling viciously beneath the seat! Scrap and I jumped in to pull them apart and got involved in a sub-argument. ('Why don't I learn to keep my big mouth shut!', 'I've been hit around by people in this group too!') Pam was still screaming blue murder, refusing to sit down and ready to take anyone on. All the feelings of injustice and being insulted non-stop for two years had risen to the surface and she finally, and quite triumphantly, told the band that they were a 'load of sheep'.

No doubt fed up and emotionally exhausted, Travis would

complete the second leg of the *School Boys in Disgrace* tour and then leave the band.

Despite their discontents, The Kinks had arrived at the middle of the decade with a restored reputation in the US and a trio of theatrical productions behind them. Now *Schoolboys in Disgrace* had announced their trajectory for the second half of the 1970s: they were to get back to being a rock act, and would signal that shift by shedding more members, changing labels and turning their attention back to what had once been their natural territory: the singles charts.

CHAPTER 17: 1976 TO 1980

A Psychic Experiment

Never dedicated followers of fashion, The Kinks seemed ever more out of step with popular tastes when they released *Schoolboys in Disgrace* in 1976. The charts were dominated by disco and the perfectly crafted pop of Abba, while rock and roll was exhibiting the first spasms of what would later come to be seen as a transformative convulsion: punk. Nonetheless, *Schoolboys in Disgrace* received a general thumbs-up from the UK music press. *Melody Maker* called it 'a beautifully sustained concept', while *Sounds* weighed in with 'the most solid rock album The Kinks have made since the sixties'. Rosalind Russell, writing in the *Record Mirror*, called it a 'vast improvement on the style they adopted for the *Preservation* albums. There's more guts, more rock'n'roll and a little less pretension'.

The band returned to the USA for the *Schoolboys in Disgrace* tour between January and late February, before heading home for a handful of UK dates. Only four continental European shows, their first in eighteen months, were played to promote this album, as The Kinks were almost exclusively concentrating their efforts on America. In the US, disco was also the dominant force and punk had failed to make much of an impact on the rock scene, which remained resolutely traditional in both sound and appearance: The

Eagles, Fleetwood Mac, Boston, The Doobie Brothers and James Taylor were shifting millions of albums, and the average American record buyer remained more open to buying an album by The Kinks than the punters back in Blighty. This was highlighted by the album failing to chart in the UK but reaching number forty-five in the US.

The Kinks were, in fact, beginning to produce music in the new 'arena rock' style: big, metal-tinged guitar riffs, perfect for playing live in the 20,000-seat halls of North America. Thus began their commercial rebirth. And, though they turned their back on the burgeoning punk movement back home, Kinks albums from the late 1970s through to the mid-1980s would be carried along by punk's mainstream incarnation, 'new wave', and an ever-growing army of upcoming bands who would name-check them as an influence. To this day, The Kinks are perhaps better loved in America than any other British band, except The Beatles or the Stones. This represents a remarkable turnaround, given that most of their new American fans knew little of them before 'Lola', while in the UK the reverse was true.

The man behind the change in their fortunes was 44-year-old Clive Davis. He had already had an illustrious career. President of Columbia Records until 1973, he founded Arista in 1975, when he combined three smaller record labels – Bell, Colpix and Colgem. From the off, Arista was home to chart toppers like Barry Manilow and The Bay City Rollers. Davis was keen to sign The Kinks and determined to get them back into the US charts. The UK market, though influential, was tiny compared with North America and Ray only had eyes for the financial prize that the US could provide.

The Kinks said goodbye to RCA and signed with Arista in the summer of 1976, the hottest and driest British summer in living memory. A celebratory party was held at Konk and then the band set about recording an album for their new label. Davis's drive and energy was appreciated by both of the Davies brothers. 'Clive said, "You have a great touring base, I now want you to make hit albums in America,"' said Ray Davies. 'And we did. That was one of the happiest periods of my life. I moved to New York where I could walk over to Clive's office, play him some songs and then we'd go and record them with The Kinks.' Dave Davies concurred. 'Clive is a genius,' he said. 'He's got one of the best musical instincts of anyone I've ever met. He was really helpful to Ray as a writer and he helped galvanise the band.'

Recording their first album for Arista would be a long, slow process, with sessions taking place sporadically over the next seven months. Almost twenty new songs were worked on for what would become the *Sleepwalker* album, but, with no shows played during this hiatus, and no money coming in for the employee band members, relationships became strained. John Dalton decided that he'd had enough and resigned.

> My first child arrived while I was in The Kinks. It started off OK. I could take things home for them that we couldn't get in England. On one tour both Dave and I bought this toy American yellow bus which was electric and you could sit on it. No kids over here had seen anything like it. But as things got worse in the band, missing the kids got worse too. In the final days, personally I don't think I was getting enough money. We'd bought the studio and suddenly I wasn't so involved in it. I wasn't getting the money, there was aggravation in the band, I had three young kids and I was missing them growing up. I never played just for money but I could have been making something for my family. One time I couldn't even pay my gas bill, which was a bit silly for someone in The Kinks. There was nothing to look forward to.

In December 1976, auditions were held to find a replacement for John Dalton while Ray was commuting back and forth from New York. Andy Pyle was asked to join The Kinks as bass player. The 30-year-old was something of a rock veteran having played with Blodwyn Pig and Savoy Brown since the late 1960s, and as a session player on Rod Stewart's *Every Picture Tells a Story* in 1971. 'I don't know who else auditioned but I was brought in to help finish the *Sleepwalker* album,' he said. 'Everything else was an add on. Konk seemed like the perfect set up. It was never boring, they were The Kinks and I was the new boy, although Mick and John [Gosling] were always friendly and helpful.'

With Pyle on board, the sessions were wrapped up in January

1977, and right away the band set off to promote the record in America. But the entourage that flew off to New York had been trimmed down somewhat: just two horns and two backing singers meant a total of nine performers on stage – five fewer than the peak of the previous few years. The reduced numbers reflected the less theatrical turn in The Kinks' act.

The Kinks flew into one of the coldest winters Americans had experienced in years. By the time the tour reached Philadelphia, President Jimmy Carter had declared Pennsylvania a disaster area, with most of the shops and schools closed. A fuel shortage meant that around 70,000 people had to stay at home and the Delaware River was frozen solid. The Kinks found the Holiday Inn they were staying in had all heating turned off in communal areas, though surprisingly none of the shows were cancelled.

Andy Pyle had been warned by other members of the band that, before long, Ray would pick on him for something, and the time came in Chicago. When asked about the incident now he shrugs it off with, 'Everyone had their turn', but those who witnessed it knew how upsetting Ray's behaviour could be. 'We came off stage after a good gig,' recalled Shirlie Roden. 'Ray, who was feeling vindictive because his acoustic guitar didn't work, said that Andy was a turkey, all the bands he'd ever been in were turkeys, all the tuning problems in the band were Andy's fault and he wanted a new bass player before they got to Santa Monica for the next show.' Pyle just took it without making a big scene. There was a break of a few days to allow for travel before the Santa Monica show and, as usual, matters were left unresolved and simmering. In the meantime, Pyle was drinking heavily every night, and would tell anyone who would listen that Ray Davies was 'Shirley Temple' in view of his prima donna behaviour.

For others in the band, however, the situation was about to get even worse. Ray hadn't spoken to Pyle for five days. In Santa Monica, they were booked to play two shows in one night. Shirlie Roden's diary refers to Santa Monica as 'The Humiliation of Baptist and the Collapse of Dave'. 'I don't know where the band will go from now on,' she wrote. 'Even after all the arguments I've seen them undergo, I'll be surprised if they survive this one.' Her notes give an insight into what it was like to be on stage with The Kinks when one of the infamous battles broke out.

Although the band were putting in a sloppy performance, the crowd was enthusiastic and loving it, but, for some reason, The Kinks started bickering. Dave shouted at Mick, then Dave and John Gosling started trading insults. Much of this went unnoticed by the crowd, who couldn't hear the shouting over the noise of the songs. The insults got worse to the point where Dave and Gosling were almost fighting. At the end of the set, the combatants had to be held apart, and both refused to go back for an encore. Ray took his brother to one side and convinced him to go on, but Gosling refused. Ray tried to talk him round, but to no avail. Eventually, Ray resorted to threats: he'd hit him if he didn't. Gosling invited him to take a shot, which Ray did. Gosling sprawled backwards over the backing singers. Leaving Gosling backstage, the rest of the band went out for the encore.

Between the two shows, some of the band's wives and girlfriends arrived. Lisbet was asked to talk to Dave, but said there was nothing she could do. Much wrangling took place in the dressing room so that the second show of the night could go ahead. As the band returned to the stage later that evening, the tension was terrific. 'Baptist was sat at the piano like a stuffed dummy making feeble hand movements over the keyboards,' recalled Roden. 'Dave had a maniacal grin and looked ready to explode. Andy was clamped safely to his amplifier at the back of the stage and Ray, professional as usual, was selling heart and soul to the audience.' But even Ray Davies could crack on stage. After shouting back instructions to John Gosling, he eventually marched over and manhandled him off the keyboards so he could play them himself. Somehow the band staggered on to the end of the set before walking off stage. Roden took refuge behind the side-stage curtains and was surprised when Dave joined her. 'I went inside our "on-stage" changing room, built out of curtains into the wings, to avoid the violence,' she said. '[Dave] came in after me, threw his arms around me, hugged me to him, and said "I can't go on, I can't go on. All the meaning's gone from it, I can't go on." He was suddenly like a child. I tried to comfort him and say that he could, and he'd got the strength, and he believed in the right reasons for playing and he must go on. It was all very weird as Lisbet was sitting just the other side of the wings and I really don't know what was happening. Why couldn't he get any comfort from her, and why were they all destroying each other?'

When Dave had calmed down sufficiently, they returned to the stage, to perform – with some irony – 'Life on the Road'.

Although things had been getting worse for a while, the Santa Monica show was the breaking point for several members of the group. John Gosling had been feeling a little lost since John Dalton left, and Shirlie Roden was questioning her own participation: she only wanted to sing, but the atmosphere was becoming unbearable.

The final business of the trip was a slot on NBC's *Saturday Night Live* on 26 February. It was a major coup for The Kinks to secure nationwide coverage on such a hugely popular comedy show. Hosted that week by Steve Martin, a comedian at the height of his powers, The Kinks were the special musical guest stars. The band offered mainstream America a quick reminder of their past with a medley of 'You Really Got Me', 'All Day and All of the Night', 'A Well-Respected Man' and 'Lola', and ended with the brand new single, 'Sleepwalker'.

Barry Cain in *Record Mirror* was harsh on the new album. '"Stormy Sky" is OK, with its lazy guitar and pleasant vocals. The rest can go hang themselves. On this showing The Kinks might as well pack their bags and get outta town.' His was one of few dissenting voices though. Elsewhere, *Melody Maker* claimed the album 'emphatically testifies to the dramatic artistic revival of Raymond Douglas Davies'.

Released on 12 February 1977 in the UK, and exactly two weeks later in the US, the record was more accomplished than recent offerings, with the trimmed-down band getting back to the standards of the early seventies. The opening track, 'Life on the Road', was an autobiographical tale of Ray arriving in London. 'Sleepwalker', an upbeat rocker, edged into the *Billboard* top fifty in March, the first Kinks single to do so for seven years. The album itself was a number twenty-one semi-hit in the US, continuing the trend of its predecessors, which had seen higher chart peaks with every release since the low point of *Preservation Act 1* in 1973. *Act 1* reached 177 in the US, followed by 114 for *Preservation Act 2*, fifty-five for *Soap Opera*, and number forty-five for *Schoolboys in Disgrace*. In the UK, *Sleepwalker* failed to reach the charts just as all other Kinks albums had done during recent years.

Over the summer, two further legs of the *Sleepwalker* tour were dragged around America into the autumn. During these shows, Shirlie Roden and Dave Davies finally struck up a friendship after years of working together. They would chat about spiritual life, magic and philosophy. Davies wrote in *Kink*: 'After a few shows I decided to try a psychic experiment, with Shirlie's help.' He wanted to harness the energy from the audience into 'something else'. Without giving away his secret, he said that they performed the rite during a 'flat' show in Seattle, at which point the audience supposedly came alive. The sudden uplift in atmosphere was even mentioned in the following day's newspaper review, according to Dave. 'I would like to have discussed it with Ray,' he added. 'It is one of my greatest regrets that he has tended to be so unreceptive to my ideas. He has always been so unapproachable, so cautious. We've been close in some ways over the years and yet at the same time so far apart.'

The final US show was held in New Jersey on 14 December. Back in Britain, the year ended with a pair of performances at the Rainbow Theatre. These were recorded for the BBC and documented the end of an era. Shirlie Roden had already left and Debi Doss was about to join her. These would also be the last gigs to include John Gosling and Andy Pyle. During the Christmas Eve show, Ray donned a Santa Claus outfit for the encore, during which he planned to sing the new Christmas single, 'Father Christmas', but instead, Dave Davies started playing 'You Really Got Me', which Ray snarled his way through, throwing eye daggers at his brother before shouting him down backstage. In the season of goodwill, life continued as normal for the Davies brothers.

After a short break over the New Year period, the band went back to

Konk to wrap up the follow-up to *Sleepwalker*, but the break hadn't softened any feelings, or dispelled the lingering animosities.

Both John Gosling and Andy Pyle were ready to leave, but had not been able to make the final break. They had been playing in a side project together and had performed a couple of gigs. 'We rehearsed and held auditions at the Bridge House pub in Canning Town,' said John Gosling. 'It was exhilarating, like starting over. But Ray somehow found out and started giving me a hard time during my last overdub session for *Misfits*.' Things quickly got out of hand and Gosling simply walked out. He and Pyle formed United and were playing gigs around London by May 1978 with drummer Ron Berg, and both Dave Edwards and Dennis Stratton singing and playing guitars. 'It didn't happen quite the way I'd hoped,' said Gosling of leaving The Kinks.

> It was a very difficult decision, like leaving an extended family really, but we no longer seemed to be The Kinks I loved and was proud to be part of . . . I don't like to think about it, but it was very unpleasant . . . It was between Ray and me. Dave was there but didn't get involved. He knew how unhappy I was and had already tried to dissuade me from leaving. Negativity is infectious. Nobby was gone for good, and Mick was no longer active as a playing member and I missed them being there, I really did. The writing had been on the wall for quite some time. I had already been rehearsing hard with Andy Pyle. We'd written a lot of songs together and were anxious to get them aired in public as soon as possible. We landed both a record and a publishing deal within a year, and I went back to Morgan Studios and we did a great album for Phonogram right there, where I had auditioned for The Kinks.

Maybe it was just an excuse, feeling hurt at being rejected, but, as Gosling left, Dave Davies claimed that, as it happened, Gosling's keyboards has been limiting his guitar playing. 'I never wanted to cramp Dave's style – quite the opposite,' Gosling reflected years later. 'I know how frustrated he was because we were quite close for some time. We shared the same musical influences, and other interests as well – the paranormal, the occult, where to get a great curry. We had some great times though. Our hotel was always milling with transvestites, lunatics and every kind of misfit you could imagine. But then that's what we were, really.' After leaving, John Gosling kept in touch with Avory and Dalton, but not the Davies brothers. 'Dave and I haven't communicated since 1978, which is sad,' Gosling said. He later responded angrily to comments Ray made in an interview in *Record Collector*: 'He seemed to infer that on one occasion I couldn't finish a track because I was drunk, and that upset me. I'd also just read elsewhere that he was of the opinion that "the drinkers in the band" just wanted to get each new song over with so they could go down the pub! Not true, any of it. He had a loyal band of musicians working with him, but I don't think that at the time he realised it.'

Mick Avory, too, was also on the verge of walking away. He had been playing less of a role in the studio and left the last of the recordings to session drummer Nick Trevisick. Despite being a founder member, Avory had a closer bond with the 'hired hands', and saw going on tour with Dalton and Gosling almost as a lads' holiday with occasional gigs.

The mid-seventies Kinks, with their cliques and sub-groups, were now splintering apart. The brass section and backing singers had been discarded, and 'The Juicers' were no more. As each layer had been stripped back, the band's skeleton had looked more and more fragile. Yet again, The Kinks were faced with a massive personnel transition. The change of instrumentalists coincided with a change in management. With their aim still set on the US, they decided they wanted American management, and signed up Chicagoan Elliott Abbott, who had previously managed Ry Cooder and Randy Newman. With Ray already in New York, in a building next door to the Dakota, where John Lennon and Yoko Ono lived, and touring almost exclusively in the US, it was a natural progression.

Unlike other 1960s bands, who were seen as dinosaurs, The Kinks were never derided by the new, upstart generation of UK bands in the late seventies, perhaps because the youngsters recognised that

The Kinks had been 'punk' in their own way fifteen years before – aggressive, occasionally obnoxious and, musically, masters of the punchy, power-chord pop single. 'They knew they could never attack The Kinks because we could out-punk them,' said Ray Davies in 1988. 'If Sid Vicious ever came up to me, I would've killed him.'

Members of the punk movement and, soon after, the bands of the 'new wave' actually started gravitating towards The Kinks. 'Johnny Rotten came to Konk once,' said Ray Davies. '[He was] looking for somewhere to record the first Sex Pistols album. I wanted to sign them to my label, but as a comedy act.' When The Jam's Paul Weller visited Konk to talk to Dave Davies, he brought along a Kinks single for him to autograph. The Jam also recorded a typically energetic version of 'David Watts', sung by bassist Bruce Foxton rather than Weller, to release as a single in August 1978. It reached the top thirty. Their rough demo of a cover of 'Waterloo Sunset' only surfaced years later.

Meanwhile, The Kinks' 1978 album, *Misfits*, failed to chart at all in the UK, but made it to the top forty in the USA. The album showcased a collection of mainly three and four-minute songs which cemented the band's return to rock territory. In Andy Pyle's absence, a relatively unknown singer-songwriter from New Zealand, Zaine Griff, was employed on bass and the band tried to perk up the drums, with Mick Avory replaced by Nick Trevisick (a session man and friend of Dave Davies) on four songs, while the vastly experienced London session man Clem Cattini drummed on 'Live Life' and provided overdubs elsewhere.

For touring, The Kinks needed to replenish their line-up. Despite some reservations, Mick Avory agreed to tour again, while Gosling and Pyle were replaced by Gordon Edwards and Jim Rodford. The latter was hired after a chance meeting at Konk and had been known to the band since they'd shared bills with his various bands in the sixties. His enthusiastic style meshed well with Mick Avory to produce a formidable rhythm section; that he could sing was an added bonus. Rodford had started playing in skiffle and rock and roll bands back in the late 1950s, before moving to The Mike Cotton Sound in 1964, where he expanded his repertoire to jazz, soul and R&B. At the end of the sixties, he formed Argent with his cousin, Rod Argent, and they played together for the next six years. Gordon Edwards was a rock keyboard player, in contrast to the classically trained Gosling, and had played with The Pretty Things on their *Silk Torpedo* album in 1974. He, too, could sing, so they no longer needed backing singers. The five-piece incarnation of The Kinks was better suited to the harder 'arena rock' direction that the band would trace in the years to come.

The new line-up was tried out at the Roundhouse, London, on 19 May. They were so good that the crowd refused to go home, clapping after the house lights had gone up and the post-gig disco music began to pump through the speakers. Gone was the theatrical extravagance and, in its place, was a tight, hard-rocking style that breathed life into the *Misfits* songs which, on record, had failed to win over the critics. Even the *New Musical Express*, then cheerleading for punk, liked the show: 'A small triumph and, if I may say, I was too easily won, that's not to knock how good they were.'

The Kinks were back touring across America as soon as the album was in the shops on 19 May. The bands that supported The Kinks across the US in 1978 were a who's who of the emerging new wave: Blondie, Cheap Trick, Tom Petty and the Heartbreakers, and The Cars. And the fresh Kinks line-up was a success, with good reviews and packed concerts. 'The Kinks were at their most glorious,' said *The New York Times*. Perhaps surprisingly, given Ray Davies' competitive attitude toward past support acts, the new bands enjoyed playing with The Kinks, and the older band fed off the younger generation's energy and direction. 'Tom Petty always seemed so aloof and a bit wary of everyone,' said Dave Davies, 'but I liked his band's minimalist approach. Cheap Trick were funny and good company.'

The Kinks' first single of 1979 was heavily influenced by Blondie, as '(Wish I Could Fly Like) Superman' put Ray's vocals over a disco-rock fusion backing track. Clive Davis had been urging the band again and again to write songs that could be played on the radio because, otherwise, album sales would suffer. He was vindicated as 'Superman' opened the door for a new generation of fans, reaching forty-one in the *Billboard* chart, and pushing the album right up to number eleven in the US, a high-water mark for the band.

John Rollo worked on the single, having undergone a quick transition from teenage dreamer to studio engineer at Central Sound in London. 'It was incredible being at a major studio, and some of these bands didn't want to start until well into the afternoon and go through till six in the morning,' he said. 'My whole life was turned around. Back then sixteen-track had just started and that's where I learned to be an engineer.' Rollo was doing one session after another when he saw an advert for an engineer at Konk Studios. 'This was before they recorded *Misfits*,' he explained. 'I went up there and I didn't get the job, but a year later there was another advert so I tried again. I was told to go to Konk on a Sunday at a particular hour, and Ray walked in and asked me to edit on a quarter-inch tape and that seemed to be it. Suddenly I was hired, I was now working for The Kinks, at Konk.' No sooner had Rollo taken the job than The Kinks went away on tour for the best part of a year. 'They just said build it up as a studio, because it wasn't well known. So that's what I did, with the help of Sarah Murray, the studio manager at the time.'

Rollo worked around the clock to get the Konk name out and turn it into a commercial proposition, which it had never really been. One of Rollo's first jobs at Konk was with ex-Bay City Roller Les McKeown's solo album, sessions for which saw fans waiting outside the studio to catch a glimpse of their hero. 'I built it up to be busy but when the band came back from touring they wanted to use it whenever they liked. There was a little bit of tension with the clients because when Ray wanted it he'd just say, "Well, chuck em out."' Rollo was impressed that the band invested to keep Konk at the front of any new studio innovations: '[It had a] big Neve board, a twenty-four-track tape machine, we bought the first Necam automated board with moving faders, and Ray and Dave were really spending money to improve the studio and it was a great place.'

Rollo's first work with The Kinks, rather than outside clients, was on the tracks 'Superman' and 'Low Budget'. His approach was always that The Kinks were primarily a rock band and that they should be recorded as such, with everyone live, playing together in the studio. 'The album before was beautifully recorded, but not that rock and roll,' he said. 'I think the first two songs [I did] went extremely well and the band wanted to spend some time in New York, to get away from distractions and keep it as a raw band recording.'

Leaving Konk behind, everyone packed up and went to the Power Station in New York. Now known as Avatar Studios, the Power Station, on West Fifty-Third Street was relatively new when The Kinks worked there, having opened in 1977. Today, it is regarded as one of the world's great recording studios and has a client list second to none. Dave Davies, especially, got on well with John Rollo, and enjoyed working in New York. The respect was mutual. 'Dave had incredible natural instincts and knew what to play,' said Rollo. The band and their staff stayed at the Wellington Hotel on Seventh Avenue, a short walk from Central Park. New York was going through a period of high crime, dirty streets and a seedy culture, and the Wellington seemed to be a microcosm of the city.

Dave thought the hotel was dirty but he enjoyed New York, not least because a girlfriend he'd met on the west coast years before flew in to stay with him. 'Nancy [Evans] and I shared many unusual psychic experiences in the early years of our relationship and it was a time of great personal growth for both of us,' said Dave. 'It is strange how sometimes you are inexplicably drawn to certain people in your life by forces almost out of your control.' He was drinking much less, eating healthily and staying away from drugs. He enjoyed the sessions too.

The Kinks used the Power Station daily between 10 a.m. and 6 p.m. – a very different routine to the open-ended approach to recording they were used to at Konk. 'They were all very good about working to the schedule,' said Rollo. The New York sessions continued from May to mid-June, before the band headed back to London with most of the tracks laid down. The recordings were completed without Gordon Edwards, who failed to turn up for the final sessions and was kicked out of the band.

The resulting album was titled *Low Budget* and the US and UK release dates were again staggered, with the former being July 1979 and the latter September. In a further sign of the band's improving fortunes in the country from which they had once been banned,

Low Budget made it to number eleven in the US charts. Based on previous form, it almost goes without saying that it failed to chart at all in the UK, continuing the Kinks' dismal run in Britain, even though the *Melody Maker* enthused: '*Low Budget* is actually worth spending money on'.

'It was the most amazing time for me,' recalled Rollo. 'Ray is known as a great band leader and writer, but he's also a great producer. On "Superman" we must have mixed that song at Konk twenty times – and it was quite a long song – and to get it down for a 7-inch single version we had to do twenty edits. So every day we'd have to mix it and then do twenty edits. Then we were running out of days and [Ray] had to be out of the country. Clive Davis was always known as a totalitarian hands-on guy but Ray was having none of that, he was going to make the album he wanted.'

'*Low Budget* was overtly in the London vernacular,' said Ray Davies. 'It was a curious time because we were starting to make it in America, which was still Styx and big hair.' Looking back with more than thirty years of hindsight, the album seems lightweight compared with the band's best work, but it felt at home in the late 1970s. Ray Davies wrote the opening track, 'Attitude', as an address to a contemporary audience, explaining his need to constantly change and update. 'Take off your headphones/ Hear what's going on/ You can't live in a time zone/ You've got to move on,' he sang: 'The eighties are here, I know 'cos I'm staring right at them/ But you're still waiting for 1960s to happen'. The songs were recorded in the US again and intended to sell to an American audience, with titles like 'A Gallon of Gas'.

'Ray's writing was [previously] too subtle,' said Mick Avory. 'When we did the big arenas in the late seventies he was writing harder stuff that could come across. When we signed with Arista, Clive Davis would always talk about getting us into the bigger venues and the music changed so we could get them across in the large places. When we made *Low Budget*, that was a turning point really.'

With another US tour looming, a new keyboard player was needed. Auditions were held to replace Gordon Edwards and the down-to-earth, likeable Ian Gibbons was hired. Like Edwards, Gibbons could sing and had played in numerous bands. He had formed his first group at school, aged fourteen, and played with both Moonstone and Life, who released an album on Polydor. Before The Kinks' audition, he'd also played with The Nashville Teens and The Records.

Perhaps their Englishness exempted them from the rule, but The Kinks' rebirth in late 1970s America stands in defiance of F. Scott Fitzgerald's dictum that there are 'no second acts in American lives'. Reflecting on his band's salvation as stadium rockers, Ray Davies said, 'I think we appreciated it more when we made it back in America. We were kind of in shock when we first made it, and we'd been down when we came back to the States in 1969. It took a full decade to build up to what it became. I remember when we played the Spectrum in Philadelphia [in front of more than 16,000 fans], I said, "This is it guys, Just remember this night. All the hard work's finally paid off."'

'When you've got that many people in front of you, it does things to you,' said Dave Davies. 'It makes you feel huge. Makes you feel that's what you're born for.'

The band toured for the rest of the year and well into 1980. 'I went back to running the commercial studio and it was getting ridiculously busy,' said John Rollo. The band decided to record their concerts and send their tapes back to him. 'They used Showco, who did the sound for them on that tour, and they had a twenty-four-track system,' he recalled. 'They'd ship the tapes back to me weekly or monthly. It was a similar set but different performances and what I'd try to do was find the best performances of each song from about thirty or forty shows, so that when they came back they didn't have to go through that process.' The result was the double live album and videocassette release *One For The Road*. Twenty-one songs were spread over the four sides of vinyl, but only seven of them dated back to the 1960s, including an unfortunate reggae–tinged 'Till the End of the Day'. The theatrical period of the early seventies was skipped over, too, with the majority of the numbers being from *Misfits* and *Low Budget*. The bombastic performance of the songs was almost overpowering, with little finesse.

'At the end of the album I decided to leave,' said John Rollo. 'I wrote Ray a letter, and because I left he wouldn't put my name on the record, but with the re-releases my name has appeared so I must be forgiven.'

Before leaving, Rollo had also worked on Dave Davies' solo record, *AFL1-3603*, which was released in the US during July 1980. 'The first couple of songs were with a band but then he wanted to play everything himself, and so it was basically just me and him,' said Rollo. 'I think emotionally he need an outlet, because on most Kinks albums he only got one or two songs on. If he'd say "Can we get that better?" you'd want to try and he pushed you to your limit too.' Dave wrote of the experience in *Kink* that, 'It was an exhilarating, uplifting and freeing experience'. The songs were loud and carried more than a trace of heavy metal. Perhaps unsurprisingly, they also offered a not dissimilar experience to hearing The Kinks live at the end of the seventies.

After The Kinks' US dates had been completed, Dave's girlfriend, Nancy, had travelled back to London with him. She was pregnant. Naturally, Lisbet was upset. She had given birth to their fourth son, Russell, in May 1979. Dave's sisters descended and reminded him he had responsibilities to a wife and four children – advice to which he was less than receptive. When Nancy gave birth to a son, Daniel, in December 1980, Dave was still living with Lisbet. 'Inside I was so torn; my emotions were being pulled in different directions,' he said. 'I felt so bad about what was happening, yet I just couldn't help myself.' Dave had the idea that they could all live together under one roof, especially when Lisbet and Nancy agreed to meet each other. When Dave broached the idea to Lisbet, she was understandably upset. Man and wife continued to live together, but Dave would go off and visit Nancy whenever he could.

In the same month, Ray Davies was in Paris for an interview with an unusual format: he was to be played a record and then asked to respond to it. The interviewer played him John Lennon and Yoko Ono's 'Starting Over'. Ray said he thought it was good, but not as good as the music Lennon has made by himself. 'Don't you think it's as good?' asked the journalist. 'Not particularly,' Davies replied.

'Oh, that's interesting,' said the Frenchman, launching an ambush, 'because he got shot this morning. He's dead.'

'I felt really pissed off that he did it in that way,' said Ray. 'So I went with the people who I was with to Notre Dame and I lit a candle for him [Lennon]. It was the only thing I could do in the circumstances. It was a big sense of loss. You know sometimes the rivals are closer to you in life than the friends.'

Part 5

That was typical Ray, 'No you can't sue me for libel, it's a fictional character.'

Keith Altham discussing Ray Davies' autobiography, *X-Ray*

Cashing it In

The 1980s was a decade in which money was God. In the movie *Wall Street*, Michael Douglas's character, Gordon Gekko, famously declared that 'Greed, for lack of a better word, is good. Greed is right. Greed works. Greed clarifies.' In 1980, the US elected Ronald Reagan as its Republican president, espousing a 'voodoo economics' in which prosperity would 'trickle down' from the wealthy to the poor. The previous year, a British general election had seen the advent of Britain's first female prime minister, Margaret Thatcher – a Conservative who subscribed to an even more radical belief in the virtues of capitalism than her American ally. It was to be an era of yuppies and entrepreneurs, during which alternative comedian Harry Enfield would satirically taunt his audiences with the loutish catchphrase 'Loadsamoney!' Understandably, this state-sanctioned worship of cold hard cash stirred up much resentment amongst the 'have-nots' towards the 'haves'. The decade opened in recession, and with the difference between rich and poor widening. During the summer of 1981, as unemployment in the UK hovered around the three million mark, there were riots in Toxteth in Liverpool, the Handsworth area of Birmingham, and the south London district of Brixton. Three years later, Britain would be riven by the bitter miners' strike.

The Kinks avoided many of the troubles back home by doggedly touring the US, where they were now filling arenas across North America. They were a band with an influential past, a hip present and an exciting future. In 1978, the same year as The Jam's cover of 'David Watts', Van Halen put out 'You Really Got Me', a radio hit that propelled the American hard rockers to success, just as it had done for The Kinks fourteen years before. Dave Davies was not very impressed. 'Good art isn't always about having the comfiest technique,' he said. 'I shouldn't encourage him, but I'm sure Eddie Van Halen played better when he was drunk. But it must be a good record if people like it. Van Halen's version was very Middle America. It was like, "Hey man, look at me with my tight trousers!"' Ray Davies took a different view: he liked it because it made him laugh.

The Jam and Van Halen were joined by another young band singing The Kinks' praises when, in 1979, The Pretenders covered 'Stop Your Sobbing' and, two years later, another Ray Davies composition, 'I Go to Sleep'. The band was made up of Ohio-born Chrissie Hynde and a trio of Englishmen, and found great success riding the poppier end of the new wave. Hynde had briefly written for the *New Musical Express* and was a student of rock history, as well as a huge fan of The Kinks. She had tried to meet Ray Davies several times and had nothing but good things to say about him in the press. Ray had avoided any contact, later saying that he didn't want to ruin her illusion of him with the reality. Hynde was not easily deterred, however, and finally pinned him down in May 1980. Before too long, they were having an affair.

By the middle of 1981, both Davies brothers were seeing women other than their wives. Ray's wife, Yvonne, was still a secret outside his closest friends, but he was regularly seen out with Chrissie Hynde. Dave, meanwhile, had moved in with Nancy Evans. Initially, Dave failed to gel with Hynde, and wrote that he found her rude. He also resented those occasions when she joined the band on stage to sing. However, over time, as he got to know his brother's confident American girlfriend, he and Nancy began to spend more time with the other couple.

Though The Kinks were playing in arenas big enough for more than 15,000 people in the USA, the 1980 UK tour had ended in Nottingham, in the UK, on 19 December, at the newly opened Rock City, which had a capacity of less than 2,000. America was where the big money was and, almost two decades after they first tried to make it there, the band was finally getting some reward. It had taken a decade of hard touring but the results were worth it. With a new album to promote, *Give the People What They Want*, 1981 would once again be spent working back and forth across the United States.

The album, released on 26 August, comprised eleven tracks, most of them bombastic, unsubtle rockers – perfect for arena audiences in the US. The pop group of the 1960s and the music hall act of the seventies had been banished to rock and roll history. The cover showed Ray running past Konk Studios with the album's title – a blunt expression of the band's crowd-pleasing intent – painted on the wall behind him. The title track and 'Around The Dial' established the new Kinks as a power-chord propelled, semi-metal band; while 'Destroyer' represented a heavy take on their back catalogue, toying with the guitar riff of 'All Day and All of the Night', and name-checking 'Lola'. Only 'Yo Yo' and 'Art Lover' offered pause for breath and contemplation. The album closed with the optimistic anthem 'Better Things'.

US audiences lapped up the heavy Kinks and the record rocketed to number fifteen in the charts. *CREEM* magazine called it the best Kinks album since *Muswell Hillbillies*, while *Rolling Stone* enthused that they 'provide an exhilarating noise'. But while the big metal riffs The Kinks were using were popular in the US, the UK market was less interested. *Melody Maker* called it 'an unfortunate brand' and the British public, by and large, agreed.

With both The Kinks and The Pretenders often on tour in different parts of the world, Ray and Chrissie would sometimes fly to meet each other after their respective shows. Ray was juggling a wife, a girlfriend and a band, but also somehow found time to work on a musical, *Chorus Girls*, with Barrie Keefe. Keefe has had plays performed in more than twenty countries, but is perhaps best known for penning the script of British gangster movie *The*

Long Good Friday. He and Ray had been collaborating for two or three years, but only in 1981 did they get the opportunity to stage the show. Despite The Kinks' return to rock, Davies still harboured a yearning for the theatre, and this side project offered a perfect outlet for his feelings about England's worsening unemployment and deprivations. Ray attended many of the rehearsals during March before the show was opened in April at the Theatre Royal, Stratford, in east London. The story centred around Prince Charles being kidnapped to save a theatre from demolition. Marc Sinden (son of Sir Donald) was the star, supported by Michael Elphick (*Boon*) and Anita Dobson (*EastEnders*).

Dave Davies took the opportunity during the resulting downtime to work on some solo material, which would later be released as *Glamour* in the US on 1 July. Dave wrote in *Kink* that the album was a reaction to the Reagan/Thatcher era and that the songs addressed 'vanity, megalomania, illusion, control'. It got a good review in *Rolling Stone*, but other coverage was scarce and sales were low. The record was also found wanting in the UK where the *Melody Maker* slammed it as a 'truly depressing experience'.

At the end of August, The Kinks played the Reading Festival, and then Ray flew straight over to Los Angeles so he could join Chrissie Hynde on stage with The Pretenders. This was the first public sighting of them together. 'Obviously I'm besotted with him,' Hynde said. '[He's] a major part of my life.' The rest of The Kinks flew over shortly after Ray, and both bands had North American tours that ran at the same time that autumn.

On 25 September, The Kinks played in Toronto and were joined on stage for the encore by a special guest: Pete Quaife. He was living in Canada and this marked the first time in twelve years that the four original Kinks had shared a stage. They played 'Little Queenie', though Quaife remembered little about it. 'I was pissed drunk,' he said. 'It all happened by accident really. I was backstage and I was incredibly thirsty. I asked a roadie to get me a drink. He brought me what looked like a big glass of water with ice cubes. I took one gulp and the damn thing turned out to be vodka. I kept drinking it and by the time I joined them for an encore number I was out of it. Dave kept yelling at me, telling me I was playing in the wrong key.'

That autumn saw the Davies brothers fly their widowed mother to New York to see them play at Madison Square Garden, something Ray had promised himself he would do should The Kinks ever make it in the Big Apple.

After appearing again on NBC TV's *Saturday Night Live*, the band ended the year with the release of 'Better Things' as a single. Yet another US tour began on 8 January 1982 and, by February, the band were in Australia for the first time in eleven years. From there, they headed to Japan for a brief visit, before returning home later in the spring.

On the personal front, trouble was brewing. Ray and Chrissie were having frequent heated arguments, and things were going badly for Dave Davies too. He had moved to Exmoor with Nancy and son Daniel in November 1981, and was feeling depressed at the failure of *Glamour*. He had been dead set against the early 1982 shows and had to be cajoled into doing them. But it was during these January dates that he underwent an episode that changed his life – an event so profound that he spent more than fifteen pages of his autobiography discussing it.

'All I can expect of the reader,' he wrote, 'is to try and keep an open mind.' He explained that after arriving in Richmond, Virginia, on 13 January, he experienced visions, voices talking to him from unknown intelligences and a form of religious ecstasy. Captivated by the mystical and supernatural from an early age, Dave was perhaps more open to interpreting such an event as otherworldly. There were, he wrote, five 'intelligences' communicating with him, each of which had a distinct, pleasant aroma. They showed him the 'World of Ethers' and that humankind's next stage of development would come from the study and understanding of this world. 'Everything looked slightly different,' he said. 'As if there was a fine and delicate layer or web of matter over everything in the room.' The voices continued to communicate with Dave as he travelled to an afternoon sound check. During that night's show, they showed him how to project an invisible light from his forehead and chase away 'negative energies' from the audience. The events of that day continue to resonate with Dave and, no matter how others have regarded or interpreted it, the experience was undeniably 'real' for him.

Having been divorced in 1981 by Yvonne, who named Chrissie Hynde in her legal papers, Ray planned to marry the American, and they got as far as the Guildford registry office in on 21 April 1982. At that point, they were turned away, as they were arguing so furiously when they arrived. Neither party has ever spoken about what happened that day and why they didn't try again another time, despite plenty of interviewers having asked over the years. What is known is that Hynde was pregnant.

Ray went off on tour with The Kinks with tensions between him and Dave at a height. On 15 June in Louisville, Kentucky, the brothers exchanged several insults across the stage and, when Ray left at the end of the set, Dave started playing 'All Day and All of the Night', forcing Ray to return. It seemed that compelling Ray to perform in this way was one of the few methods Dave had of exercising power over his dominant older brother.

Chrissie Hynde was in London with The Pretenders – a band with its own problems. Bassist Pete Farndon was fired by Hynde because of his drug use, and then, on 16 June, guitarist James Honeyman-Scott died of a heart failure after taking cocaine. In the shadow of this tragedy, Hynde flew to join Ray, and was introduced on stage in Philadelphia, the last show of The Kinks tour. In the midst of his ongoing, festering dispute with Ray, Dave was far from pleased by her appearance, and wrote in *Kink* that he swung a punch at her. This represented a further escalation in hostilities between the brothers.

Later that year, Ray worked on a new song, 'Come Dancing', inspired by his memories of his older sisters going out on the town when he was a boy. Much of the lyrical imagery was autobiographical and nostalgic – mother and daughter arguing in the night, the Palais dance hall, and its demolition. The music, as befitted the theme, was eminently danceable. The song employed a brass section, which was briefly in vogue at the time, with Dexy's Midnight Runners having recently employed one to great acclaim, though Ray Davies twisted his closer to a big-band sound.

It was released in the UK that November but, initially, at least, failed to make any impression. It was only after the US release in April 1983 that it took off, where, helped by a charming, cinematic promotional video by Julien Temple, it was put into heavy rotation by the fledgling MTV channel. 'Julien was such a posey sod,' said Dave Davies. 'Walking around in a fur coat like he was Orson Welles, even though he was only doing a promo video.' In the film, The Kinks play the part of the dancehall band, while Ray is the boyfriend, with slicked-back hair, pencil-thin moustache and post-war pin-striped suit. After that, the song surged up the US charts to number six, the band's highest spot since the mid-sixties. Buoyed by this success, it was re-issued in the UK, and, this time, made it to number twelve.

By August 1983, The Kinks were back on *Top of the Pops*. Still the BBC television's flagship music programme, the show looked rather different to when the band had last appeared in 1971. Now it was all neon shapes, dancing girls in ra-ra skirts and men in sleeveless T-shirts. Ray sported a mullet and pin-striped suit, while the rest of the band wore white tuxedos. Ian Gibbons had his hair slicked back, and Jim Rodford's bass seemed to be almost as big as him as he beamed from behind it, apparently very pleased to be there. The brass section spent their time reading newspapers until they were needed for the song's finale, at which point Ray took a girl from the crowd and danced with her centre stage – mirroring the closing scenes of Temple's video.

On January 22 1983, Chrissie Hynde gave birth to Ray's daughter, Natalie Rae Hynde. Ray, while working on songs for a new album, kept the first part of the year relatively free.

Though not as heavy as its predecessor, The Kinks' 1983 album, *State of Confusion*, was still a radio and arena-friendly collection. Crunching guitars and gang vocals appear here and there throughout the album, and several of The Kinks' best songs from the eighties are featured. The aforementioned, keyboard-led 'Come Dancing' sits a little uneasily among the pounding beats evident on other tracks. Title track 'State of Confusion' dashes along with the best pop-rockers of the era, such as 'Footloose', while 'Heart Of Gold' is more restrained, with jangly rather than overpowering guitars. It is all the better for it, in fact, and sounds not unlike a

Pretenders' song from the same period. Ray said it was inspired by the birth of Natalie.

Once the album had been completed, Dave Davies, feeling hard done by on previous records, was determined to make sure he was properly credited for the work he had put in on the arrangements. He went through the liner notes and cleared them with Arista but, when the album came out on 24 May, he was staggered to discover that his name didn't appear. He immediately called the record company offices demanding an explanation. In *Kink* he claims that Ray, had called Arista the night before the album sleeve was due to be printed and made a final set of changes, in the process discrediting his brother. Whether the change was deliberate or not, Dave was furious. To him it appearred that Ray had twisted public perception to his own advantage. In light of what felt to Dave like a betrayal, he backed away from his brother's next project, *Return to Waterloo*.

It was during the summer of 1983, that Dave Davies started talking openly about metaphysics and his beliefs about extra-terrestrials, while promoting another solo album, *Chosen People*, which had been inspired by a book by a Native American called Black Elk. Perhaps unsurprisingly, the shutters started going up with interviewers; he even heard people laughing at him – the experience proved profoundly disenchanting. 'When old Kinks start droning on about the inner self shining through,' wrote the *New Musical Express*, 'it's time to get worried.' Dave promptly cancelled the upcoming Kinks tour of the US. This time, there was no touching brotherly reconciliation. The occasional spats were becoming longer and more serious.

In Dave's absence, Ray was left to work on *Return to Waterloo*, a film commissioned for Channel 4, as a genuine solo project. Meanwhile, his private life was falling apart. By 1984, the often tempestuous relationship between Ray and Chrissie Hynde finally came to an end. 'She was someone who was on a journey that she found difficult to cope with,' said Ray. 'She thought that I could help her. Then she realised I was more difficult than the journey she was on.' Though she had left him, and taken Natalie with her, Ray was stunned when, on 5 May, she married Simple Minds lead singer Jim Kerr. In one last shot, she dedicated 'Stop Your Sobbing' to Ray during the final Pretenders show before her wedding.

Dave wrote in *Kink* that it was a 'relationship doomed for disaster from the outset', and that Hynde and Ray had awful fights in which furniture would be smashed up. After the break-up, Ray was distraught, and tried everything to get her back, though late-night calls to The Pretenders on tour eventually came to a stop when she refused to talk to him. Ray sank to such a dire state that he had to have a psychiatric nurse stay with him twenty-four hours a day. When Dave went to visit, he bore the brunt of his brother's anger, and found himself being blamed for the break-up during one of Ray's aggressive rambles.

When Ray's thoughts eventually turned back to the band, he made a surprising decision: he called Larry Page and asked him to come back as manager, almost two decades after their acrimonious bust-up. This time there were no contracts, however, and everything was agreed with a handshake. Keith Altham's connections with The Kinks were also rekindled in 1984. The former journalist was now running his own PR company. 'I didn't sign them up to anything,' he said.

> They rang me up and said would I do their PR? I think it was Larry who got in touch with me. It was while they were shooting *Return to Waterloo*. I'd always had a good working relationship with Larry, with The Troggs or whoever he was working with, and when he got them back on board he rang me up . . . I came from the backwoods of PR before it developed into the racket that it has in certain areas now, where people just do deals all the time. Now a PR is a protector, a defence against the journalists, almost the role of a minder.

Altham was 'poacher turned gamekeeper', and understood the problems that could arise between bands and the press. 'I tried to get as sympathetic a response as I could from journalists that I knew were empathetic with the artist,' he said. 'When the bridge became a wall I opted out because people write on walls, they forget that. You put a wall up between you and the media, and you watch what they write on your wall!' Altham's reunion with the band only lasted for about a year before it petered out. 'My relationship with Ray was always at a distance,' said Altham. 'I think it's better that way, he's quite a private individual and if he gets into a personal relationship it usually gets very intense. I think he gets confused when people want to be his friend and then all kinds of problems occur as the edges get blurred.'

It wasn't just the management of The Kinks that had changed. After twenty years in the band, and plenty of agonising over the years, Mick Avory finally 'retired' from the group in 1984. His departure came in the wake of new trouble between him and Dave – yet another fist fight between the two. They'd been fighting and arguing on and off since they'd shared a flat in the mid-sixties, but this was the final straw.

'The situation between Dave and Mick had got so bad that I couldn't bear to be in the same dressing room with both of them,' said Ray. Ray took Mick out for a drink and a heart-to-heart. 'I said to Mick "You're gonna have to do a lot of touring if we make another album,"' he recalled. 'Mick said, "I just can't face arguing anymore."'

'I had about six years of arenas and then I'd had enough,' Avory said. 'We couldn't play a concert without aggravation . . . I felt we'd already done everything so what was the point in carrying on.' Dave, for his part, had long held the view that Avory took Ray's side in disputes just to keep himself in a job, and now he felt the drummer was being arrogant as well. Dave wrote in *Kink* that, 'I was starting to tire of his attitude. He was always acting like a buffoon.' Avory's last show was in Leicester in April 1984. Despite moving away from recording and touring, he did stay close to the group, taking up a job at Konk. 'I was part of the company so it was a natural thing to fall into," he said. 'I did a bit of administration but I'm not a businessman and it wasn't a proper job.'

Avory's departure from the band and the company led to the formation of a new entity, Kinks 85 Ltd, owned by Dave and Ray, a replacement for Kinks Productions Ltd. His place in the line-up was filled by Bob Henrit, who made his Kinks debut in New Orleans at the end of November at the start of a tour promoting a new album,

Word of Mouth. It was Dave, who had felt Avory's playing was getting sloppy anyway, who suggested to Ray that they recruit Henrit, a crack session drummer who had worked on some of Dave's solo recordings.

The new album, *Word of Mouth,* was released on 19 November 1984, with an almost stereotypical mid-eighties design – bright pink with lipstick smudges on the front, like a David Bowie or Duran Duran sleeve from the same period. The music, however, is less obviously of its time. 'Do It Again' provides an excellent opener, agilely fusing Bob Henrit's big drum sound and Dave's soaring guitars with a great melody. Indeed, the best song on the album came from Dave. He wrote 'Living on a Thin Line' for Ray to sing but, when his brother showed little interest, Dave performed it himself. If it had been released as a single, it might have produced another hit, but despite lots of radio play, it was confined to the album. While making no impression in the UK, *Word of Mouth* reached number fifty-seven in the US charts. In *Billboard*, the album was described as being 'full of the quirks, turns and sleight-of-hand that have endeared them to diehard fans', but the reviewers lamented that it was 'devoid of a single to rival "Come Dancing" or "Superman"'.

Adding to the ever-ratcheting tension between the brothers, Dave probed why 'Living on a Thin Line' wasn't being released as a single, and found out that Ray had struck a deal which ensured the first three singles from any album would be his compositions. One consequence of this was that Dave's songwriting – for The Kinks at least – stood less chance of getting major airplay.

In November 1984, *Return to Waterloo* was screened on Channel 4 in the UK. Written and directed by Ray Davies, the film simply follows a commuter on a train journey from the Surrey town of Guildford north into London. Ken Colley played 'the Traveller', who the viewer is invited to suspect is a secret rapist. Ray also makes a brief cameo appearance. Rather than dialogue, the story is told through music. Tim Roth ('Boy Punk'), Claire Parker ('Walkman Girl') and Sallie Anne Field ('Girl Punk') all have parts, while BBC weatherman Michael Fish and agony aunt Claire Rayner appear as themselves.

The film was well received, and *The Listener*'s critic was impressed:

'It could have been a load of pretentious rubbish, instead it was like a long and very good poem.' Dave Davies also liked the finished cut but revealed in *Kink* that, 'Ray and Chrissie were going through some "domestic strife" to put it mildly.' He added, 'I always thought that if he'd been less emotionally distracted, the film would have turned out even better.'

The *Return to Waterloo* soundtrack album was released in the US only on 1 July 1985, during an otherwise quiet year for The Kinks. There were just a handful of shows, across the south and west of the US, and then again during September, followed by three months of silence to end the year, as record label negotiations took place. It became clear that the band would be leaving Arista for MCA.

If 1985 was quiet, 1986 was even more subdued. It later surfaced that Ray had married Pat Crosbie, a dancer, on 25 January 1986. She was the daughter of the owner of the *Cork Examiner*, an Irish newspaper, and Ray took to living in Ireland for six months of the year. During the wedding reception at Ray's house, there was a performance from a band that included his daughter Victoria and Dave's son Simon.

The Kinks' first album for MCA, *Think Visual*, was released in November. Ray Davies wanted to make it a concept piece based around his character from the *Come Dancing* film, now older and running a video rental shop, making illegal copies in the back room. MCA, however, wanted the band to concentrate on touring and promoting the album. The compromise is possibly The Kinks' weakest ever collection. 'How Are You' and 'Lost And Found' struggle to rise above mediocrity and, while the rest of the album isn't awful, it pales in comparison with The Kinks at their best. By the summer of 1987, *Think Visual* had crept up to number eighty-one on the *Billboard* chart.

That autumn came the news that the brothers' mother, Annie, was seriously ill. Following an operation for cancer, she was told she had only weeks to live. Dave and other family members, including his ex-wife Lisbet, were at her hospital bedside every day, but there was one notable absence. Ray was working in New York and didn't fly in to see his mother but, instead, phoned and wrote letters. He only returned after she had died. 'I could have killed him for not coming home to see her before she went,' wrote Dave in *Kink*. Although Ray gave a moving speech at the funeral, Dave only felt further resentment as his brother took centre stage. 'How typical of Ray,' Dave added. 'All the hard work had already been done and then he waltzes in for the spoils.'

Soon afterwards, Ray suffered health problems of his own and, in January 1988, was admitted for what he expected to be a heart bypass operation. The problem was found to be a blood clot which doctors dispersed. It was only reported two years later in the *Sun*, under the typically subtle headline MY TERROR ON THE NIGHT I CHEATED DEATH. 'The doctor said there was something wrong with my heart and to assume the worst,' Ray was quoted as saying. 'I feared I would lose everything that I had worked for all my life. The doctor told me that I had nearly died and was lucky to be alive.'

In light of this event, it is unsurprising that The Kinks were quiet for the first three months of 1988. Thereafter, there were a handful of North American shows in late spring, before a short UK tour to promote a live album, *The Road*, which had been recorded in the US the previous year. For the second half of 1988, The Kinks fell silent again, while Ray, in California, worked on a musical based on Jules Verne's *Around the World in 80 Days*.

The hiatus continued into 1989. The band were older, had suffered health scares and financially were in a position where they didn't have to do anything unless they really wanted to. And what more was there to achieve?

In August 1989, after more than a year without any outward signs of life in The Kinks' camp, it became apparent that much had been going on behind the scenes. Personnel changes had taken place and a new album had been recorded.

UK Jive saw the return of another of the band's oldest collaborators, engineer Alan 'Irish' O'Duffy. 'By the late 1980s I had my own studio,' says O'Duffy. 'After finishing with The Kinks at Pye I was offered a job working with Andrew Oldham at the beginning of his Immediate Records label, and then I got call from Keith Grant who ran Olympic Studios and he asked me if I wanted to work as a tape operator. I wanted to be a recording engineer and Pye had this idea that you couldn't be one until you were 21 and I was 19 at the time.'

By the time Ray Davies asked O'Duffy to come back and work with The Kinks on the new album at Konk, more than twenty years had passed, during which time O'Duffy had made three American number one albums and put nine others in the US top thirty. He had also undertaken sound recording work for television.

'There was a fantastic fellow named Joe Gibb,' said O'Duffy. 'He was the studio engineer and knew more about the studio than I did, and it was a kind of a co-engineering thing but it was fantastically annoying. Ray didn't believe in eating and you could be there from ten in the morning until five in the afternoon, and you'd think "Well I would quite like a sandwich" and you'd end up starving. He'd become a more difficult chap to work with, except when you gave him a microphone and then he'd be fantastic.'

As The Kinks had their own studio, it was a big change in working environment for O'Duffy. 'They could take as long as they'd want,' he says. 'There were the most extraordinary and tough production concepts. Like recording the drums on an analogue machine and then transferring the whole lot to digital, so we had an analogue drum compression on a tape machine and then copied to digital to make it sound like analogue, and Joe Gibb was brilliant at that sort of stuff.'

After recording *UK Jive*, Ian Gibbons had walked out, to be replaced by Mark Haley, then Larry Page left too, because of a disagreement over his commission. Finally, after so many years of tension, the inevitable happened: Dave Davies quit, too. The trigger for this event was Ray's unilateral decision to cut two of Dave's songs from the album's running order. The younger Davies simply couldn't take any more. He was sick, as he saw it, of being undermined all the time. 'We had already had a minor fist fight on the roof of the studio,' said Dave. 'I had been away for a few days while Ray was mixing. I said, "How the fuck could you do this to me, did you think I'd never find out?"'

This falling out, serious as it was, was short lived. By the time of the tour to promote the album in September, Dave was back with the band, although the wounds continued to fester. Ray claimed he had cut the tracks for the good of the album, while Dave believed his brother had been motivated by rivalry – by a desire to prevent his younger sibling from having too much input into the band's sound. Dave later wrote in *Kink* that Ray had told him, 'Dave, I'm a perfectionist, I'm a genius.' To which Dave replied, 'You're not, you're an arsehole.'

In the decades that followed, the Davies brothers were to enter a new, more poisonous phase in their relationship. Where, once, there had been collaboration punctuated with occasional disputes, from here on, it would be outright warfare with periodic truces.

CHAPTER 19: 1990 TO 2004

The Kinks are Dead! Long Live The Kinks!

In the 8 February 1990 edition of *Rolling Stone* magazine, Joan Jett was asked about The Kinks. She called them 'perhaps the greatest and most underrated rock and roll band of all time'. She joined a growing call for the critical rehabilitation of the band, the need for which had rather crept up on them in the preceding decade.

During the second half of the 1980s, The Kinks' stock had fallen, both in terms of their artistic reputation and at the cash register. In 1990, however, yet another turnaround began with their induction into the Rock and Roll Hall of Fame, in Cleveland, Ohio. The Hall had opened its doors to its first inductees, who included Elvis Presley, Little Richard and Fats Domino, in 1986, and, by the start of the new decade, many of the big names from the 1960s had been celebrated: The Beatles, The Rolling Stones, The Beach Boys, Bob Dylan, The Supremes and Roy Orbison, among others.

'I didn't like it at first,' said Dave Davies of the invitation, 'but then I thought, everyone else is in there so why not us?' The Kinks joined the 'Performers' Class of 1990 alongside The Who, Hank Ballard, Bobby Darin, The Four Seasons, The Four Tops, The Platters and

Simon and Garfunkel. The induction ceremony took place at the Waldorf Astoria hotel in New York on 17 January 1990, but, as the event was due to begin Ray, as Dave had done, felt uneasy. 'I got to the Hall of Fame dinner and saw what a big schmoozing event it was, and went back to my room,' he said. 'I ordered sandwiches in my room. A guy who was with me, Kenny Laguna, came up and talked me into going back down. It all kind of resolved itself. Mick [Avory] dragged me up on stage. He had a terrible suit on, this terrible tuxedo.'

Eventually all went well. Pete Quaife was invited as a founder member, and joined Mick Avory and the Davies brothers in tuxedos to collect their awards. After an introduction from Graham Nash, The Kinks took to the stage to say a few words. 'They called us up and everyone did their respective numbers,' recalled Avory. 'The Who were there. Keith Moon's daughter took the award for him and said, "Sorry Keith couldn't be here tonight but he's banned from this hotel." It was a big deal, radio and TV networks all over the place. We all had to go up and each say something, luckily Pete was on before me so I said, "That was Pete Quaife, ladies and gentlemen, you may not have recognised him because they always used to stick the price label over his face," and that got a little laugh.' Quaife had actually castigated the selection panel from the stage, asking what had taken them so long to induct The Kinks.

Ray then passed Dave a note to read, muttering 'Don't fuck up' as he did so. Dave ad-libbed for a few moments, leaving with, 'Thank you very much for the award, we really do deserve it!' Not surprisingly, Ray had the most to say. He opened his speech by saying, 'I'm Ray Davies, I'm the Beatle of the group.' He produced a sheet of paper and explained it was an intra-departmental memo from their record label. He started to read from it: 'We all know that The Kinks are a unique band, but difficult to promote. I recommend, and this is to the A&R, promotion and business affairs, that if this new Kinks record is not a success, that we drop The Kinks from our label and not renew our option.' Then came the punch line: 'Now, this letter was sent twenty-five years ago!' It was a moment of triumph – of complete acceptance into the rock music establishment – and Ray, typically, couldn't help harking back to a decades-old insult.

During the early nineties, The Kinks toured little and recorded less. Ray worked on a documentary about jazz legend Charles Mingus, while the sessions for a new Kinks album ran on interminably at Konk. Nigel Thomas, who had previously managed the likes of Joe Cocker and Alexis Korner, signed up as the band's new manager in the spring of 1991. He became a stabilising influence on the Ray-Dave relationship, which sorely needed it. That summer, MCA issued a US-only compilation of material The Kinks had released on their label, after the band agreed to release their next new album through Columbia Records, a deal which Thomas and the Davies brothers had worked hard to seal. The band played fewer than ten shows during 1992 and still their next album remained stubbornly unforthcoming. That record, when it finally emerged, was to be *Phobia*, The Kinks' last genuine studio album.

At the same time, the guitar was making a comeback: in the US, grunge would revolutionise and revitalise rock while, in the UK, Britpop was gathering momentum. And though there were undoubtedly connections between The Kinks and grunge, via punk, it was in the latter that the line of descent was most clearly evident. Blur, in particular, emerged with their debt to The Kinks writ large. Lead singer Damon Albarn wrote songs very much after Ray Davies' manner, most noticeably in the lyrics to tracks such as 'Stereotypes' ('The suburbs they are dreaming/ They're a twinkle in her eye/ She's been feeling frisky since her husband said goodbye'); 'Charmless Man' ('Educated the expensive way/ He knows his Claret from his Beaujolais/ I think he'd like to have been Ronnie Kray'), and 'Tracy Jacks' ('Tracy Jacks works in civil service/ It's steady employment'), all of which feature English suburban characters. 'Country House', from 1995's *The Great Escape*, bears striking similarities with 'House in the Country' from The Kinks' 1966 album *Face to Face*, and when on an early tour of the US, Albarn would endlessly play 'Waterloo Sunset' to remind him of home. He and Davies would cement the mentor-pupil relationship in 1995 by singing that song together on *The White Room* television programme.

Blur's big mid-nineties rivals, Oasis, also took a lead from The Kinks. Their debut album title, *Definitely Maybe,* was a corruption of the title to The Kinks' 1983 track 'Definite Maybe', and their 2004 single 'The Importance of Being Idle' was promoted with a video that looks like an homage to The Kinks' film for 'Dead End Street'. Keen students of sixties pop, perhaps Noel and Liam Gallagher also appreciated their own re-enactment of British rock and roll's first great sibling rivalry? But as Liam and Noel were just beginning to play out their brotherly drama in the public eye, the dispute between Dave and Ray was reaching a crescendo.

At the outset, the Davies brothers collaborated happily together on *Phobia*. 'The first song we worked on was "Close to the Wire",' recalled Dave.

> It worked really well. I thought, 'this is fun', we're really doing something together. I suppose I'd got into the habit before, of Ray coming in with loads of songs, and me thinking, 'Well, let's do an album', without much enthusiasm or effort. But I soon became frustrated that it was taking so long – it was like, we had this song finished three months ago and we're still doing it. Ray would say, there's something wrong with it, and I'd say that what's wrong is that we've been doing it for three months! There was a point where I thought the album would never come out.

Recording was beset by bad luck, poor decision making and over-thinking. First, the sessions went on for too long; then the label asked for different song sequences; and, finally, just before the record was released, the band's manager, Nigel Thomas, died. 'I have considered the possibility that Nigel died rather than taking another call from me,' said Ray Davies. 'I hope he's actually somewhere in the Bahamas laughing at me.' Rather than wait to appoint a new manager, Ray kept the project on its agreed schedule and took over some management duties himself.

Phobia was released, eventually, as a long, seventeen-track collection designed to fill a CD. It featured just four principal players – Ray, Dave, Jim Rodford on bass and Bob Henrit on drums. It was probably the band's best album for a decade and, though the title track may have regressed to the worst metal excesses of the 1980s, overall, the songwriting and production represented a return to form. It was a concept album in all but name. The cover showed burning cities and animals hanging from trees, and the songs had an edge to them that had been missing from the band's more recent offerings.

On 'All Of Fire' and 'Drift Away', Ray sang of social meltdown and natural catastrophes. 'Don't' is a melodic walk through New York while someone stands on the ledge of a skyscraper. 'The Informer' is a warm, mid-paced track that ends with a vicious lyrical kick. One of the most talked about songs on the album was 'Hatred (A Duet)', which many people saw as being a comment on the brothers' relationship. 'Hatred, hatred,' sang Ray, 'Is the only thing that keeps us together.' When asked about it he said, 'I would not like to see Dave come to any actual harm. Dave pisses me off, awfully. I mean, Dave's a complete jerk. But I did write him a birthday card today that asked, "Why do I love you?"'

At the end of the *Phobia* sessions, John Rollo was again called in to help finish off the project. 'I did a lot of overdubs and mixed the whole thing,' he said. 'Then they brought in Bob Clearmountain and he mixed four songs. They'd changed drummers, which in my opinion was a big step backwards. I thought Mick was the perfect drummer for The Kinks, nothing against Bob Henrit.'

Phobia, The Kinks' twenty-fourth studio album, was issued on Columbia in both the UK and the US in March 1993. Ray greeted its release in a strikingly optimistic frame of mind, whilst also looking back on the previous few years with apparent regret: 'That was the most evil and insidious time in my life. I lost all confidence that I even knew how to make a record. Now with Columbia I'm encouraged again. I believe I've made a hit record. If the public tells me that *Phobia* sucks, I'll still believe I've done good work. What bothers me is that . . . it's been too many years since we've even been given a shot at reaching our audience. We know they are out there. There's a song on the record called "Still Searching" and we are still searching.'

The album stumbled to only number 166 in the US and did not chart at all in the UK, although it did garner some positive reviews, in the specialist rock press, at least. With hindsight, Ray's own view changed somewhat. 'I thought our last album . . . was good,' he later said of *Phobia*. 'But it was misconceived by the record company. The Kinks are a rock band and it's very hard to put the songs in that context. They wanted songs in it that were more my sort of songs. I think they wanted a solo record, quite frankly. But you can't compromise a rock band. You've got to go in there and make a rock record.' Tensions between Ray and Dave were never as bad as in the aftermath of failed projects, and so it proved with *Phobia*.

Things came to head when Ray and then Dave published autobiographies within eighteen months of each other. Perhaps reflecting how far apart the two brothers had drifted since their shared childhood in north London, the books couldn't have been more different in their approach.

Ray got in first with his 'unauthorised autobiography', *X-Ray*, published in the UK in September 1994. It was a project that had been bubbling under for six years. The publisher, Viking, had first made an approach in 1988, and Ray started writing it in Ireland in the late eighties. Characteristically, he was determined to tell his story in an unconventional manner. 'I came up with the idea of me as a young person meeting me as an old person, which allowed me to step back and look at myself objectively, and the band, as well, more objectively,' explained Davies. 'I found that in the interviews that I'd done before I always phoned up the next day and asked the press person to cut bits out. So I adopted a journalistic style in pulling bits I might cut out.' Tracing his story up to 1973, the book jumps back and forth between the young version of Ray, working for 'the corporation', visiting Konk, where the older version provides reminiscences about his life. 'People think *X-Ray* is fiction,' said Davies, 'but the bits that appear to be fiction are actually the most truthful parts of the book.'

He ran it past some friends and family. Of all his sisters, he was closest to Gwen and her views were particularly important to him. 'The big thrill for me is that she read the book,' said Ray. 'She was one of the first people to buy it. She phoned me up and told me she liked it.' Ray had insisted that Mick Avory also read the book, or at least the parts about him, and, apart from requesting some minor changes, Avory was happy with it. Dave, however, didn't get to read it before it was published. In fact, it took him completely by surprise.

There had been talk of Ray writing an official history of The Kinks, but, as far as Dave knew, the idea had petered out. Dave himself had shown little interest in writing a book about the band. Instead, he wanted to pen a tale that married science fact and science fiction, but was persuaded that to build up to such a book he should write an autobiography. 'The only real writing I'd done up until then had been screenplay writing, which is totally different,' he said. 'I'd never been a great reader, never a very attentive novel reader. During this time, Ray was very quiet about his book and I thought I'd just get on with mine.'

Dave had been living in Los Angeles with Nancy, but he came back to England in late 1994 to sell the book to a UK publisher. On arrival in London, he got a shock. 'I set up all these meetings with publishers, and all of a sudden there were ads everywhere for Ray's book,' he said. 'I didn't know anything about it! And a lot of publishers backed off immediately. When I read Ray's book, and I really enjoyed it, it was so totally different from mine, that I was very relieved.'

Simply titled *Kink*, Dave's book was published in the UK in February 1996, and was equally characteristic of its author. Unlike Ray, Dave held nothing back and made no attempt to shroud the story in mystery. Indeed, *Kink* is an unvarnished and largely straightforward rock and roll memoir, but one which closely addresses his sexual encounters, openly discusses his bisexuality and psychic experiences and, of course, talks about his relationship with Ray. *Kink* was called 'a work of considerable cultural significance' by the *Mail on Sunday*, while *Billboard* said it was a 'shockingly candid and poignant book'.

X-Ray's unorthodox approach was also lauded in parts of the press. 'The process allows the author to declare himself both a nincompoop and a genius, and to write a novel and a true story, all at the same time. Pretentious? Perhaps. But clever with it,' said the *Mail on Sunday*. Elsewhere the literary approach was too elusive for some. The *Sunday Times* said 'the book would be more interesting if we heard less of the laddish capers and more about how the music was made'.

When Dave was asked whether he thought Ray had been truthful in *X-Ray*, he answered that 'when he got into difficult areas, he was a bit more evasive. That probably says a lot about our different personalities. I tried to keep it fairly factual. It helped having a diary.' Neither did Dave shy away from questioning on the book's revelations about his own psychic episodes. 'The whole process of writing is schizophrenic,' he explained. 'Look at Ray and the imaginary characters in his book. If something productive comes out of it, what's wrong with that? We're so afraid of the mind. Schizophrenia is quite normal, I think – I'm sure people will blast me for saying that, but I feel that it's a necessary part of the mind. The voices were just like you and me talking.'

When Ray was asked if he had read Dave's book he said 'no' and also made the evidently counterfactual claim that his brother had 'refused to read' *X-Ray*. Whether Ray had read *Kink* or not, he was certainly unhappy about its contents. 'I probably shouldn't tell you this,' confided Dave in an interview published in April 1996, 'Ray phoned up someone at our office and said, "Have you seen Dave's book?" They said they'd seen bits and pieces. He said, "You know, I think this is going to be the end of The Kinks."'

The band had toured hard to promote *Phobia* throughout 1994 and 1995 but, after Dave's book hit the shelves in early 1996, The Kinks were all but defunct. Ray had started playing shows under the title '20th Century Man: An Evening with Ray Davies', in which he read from *X-Ray* and performed songs from across The Kinks' discography, accompanied only by guitarist Pete Mathison.

The Kinks played an outdoor show in Sweden at the start of June – a festival promising 'twelve hours of seventies music' – but bad weather meant that, by the time the band took to the stage for an uninspired performance, there was almost no one left in the stadium to hear them. Two weeks later, on 15 June, in Norway, they played another festival, this time putting in a good performance in front of 5,000 fans. Local paper *Dagbladet*, reported that 'The Kinks appeared as very old men. Say what you like about Ray Davies, but elegant he is not. Nevertheless it was a lot of fun.' The final song that night was 'You Really Got Me' and the crowd sang along. No one, the band included, knew that they had just witnessed The Kinks' last show. It was a fitting song to conclude their career as a live band.

Ray continued his solo shows and Dave returned to Los Angeles to start work on his own material. Rodford and Henrit waited for the call that never came: there was not to be another tour.

In the autumn of 1996, the final Kinks collaboration was released, *To The Bone*. It came as both a single and double CD set, and contained live songs recorded at gigs during 1993 and 1994, along with a smattering of 'new' songs from the archive. It didn't chart anywhere, despite offering a decent record of the band's later live performances.

As time passed, people wondered if The Kinks were finished or not. There was never an official announcement either way, just an ever-lengthening silence. In November 1996, Ray was asked about Dave and replied, 'We're trying to make it so that we don't have any business dealings together any more, which will hopefully make it easier for us to work as musicians.' Reading between the lines, this was an ominous statement – were they in legal dispute? – but the band still technically had one album left to deliver on their contract with Guardian Records, who had issued *To The Bone*.

In the immediate aftermath of The Kinks unceremonious disintegration, the UK was caught up in a massive wave of optimism, as 1997 saw Tony Blair lead the Labour party to its first general election victory since 1974. A new generation of exciting young bands had already broken through under the umbrella of Britpop, all honorary standard-bearers, willing or otherwise, of a media construct dubbed 'Cool Britannia'. Pop stars were invited to receptions at Downing Street; the new prime minister played the electric guitar in his spare time; and the Union Flag adorned everything from clothes to magazine covers. The feeling was that the nation was living through the second coming of the swinging sixties. Helped by knowing tips of the hat from Britpop's leading lights, The Kinks were undeniably cool and influential, but weren't around to enjoy the accolades.

If they had any mind to capitalise on the potential for a post-Britpop Kinks comeback tour, their efforts were half-hearted. In 1997, Pete Quaife was approached by Ray with a view to working on a final Kinks album, but nothing came of it. Dave was virtually in exile and spent the year promoting his book and playing sporadic solo shows in the US. During the same year, Ray and Pat Crosbie had a daughter, Eva, but shortly afterwards, the couple separated and eventually divorced.

On 21 April 1998, Ray Davies released *Storyteller*, a live solo recording of his shows. The thirty-track CD, which included dialogue segments between the songs, was book-ended by two new studio takes. The album opened with 'Storyteller', a rolling rocker which offered a glimpse into Ray's future solo recordings; and closed with 'London Song', a love letter to his home town with almost spoken-word vocals, in which Ray picks out random people (Sherlock Holmes, Henry Cooper, William Blake, Thomas Moore and the Kray twins), places (Newham, Streatham and East Ham) and landmarks (Crystal Palace, Clapham Common, Chiswick Bridge). Mick Avory played drums on four of the songs and Jim Rodford gets a 'special thanks' in the credits, but that's as far as The Kinks' involvement went.

'It is what it is and I think the audiences have enjoyed it,' said Davies of his solo show. 'It's always been important to have a special bond between the band and the audience. I've got to be able to trust the audience, and also the audience has to be able to trust me because I'm going on stage reading from a book and explaining a lot about yourself.'

As the century neared its end, The Kinks had become yet another sixties act destined for a future of nothing but 'best of' and 'greatest hits' compilations.

*

'Not many people know this, but I was living alone in 2000/2001,' said Ray Davies. 'I was living in an isolated place and drinking heavily. I watched the same film over and over again for three weeks. It comforted me, because I knew every line. I'm not going to tell you what it is. It's a foreign movie . . . But alcohol did get the better of me. I was having sleep problems. But drink doesn't cure sleep.'

Having separated from Pat Crosbie, Ray eventually broke out of his malaise by deciding he needed to challenge himself and seek out new territory. He headed for post-9/11 America, the land where the blues and R&B music he loved had originated. He journeyed to the south, the homeland of the songs that had first made him want to pick up a guitar. Travelling across several states and down the Mississippi river, he ended up in the Big Easy, New Orleans, where he stayed and lived with a girlfriend for three years. His next-door neighbour was Alex Chilton, formerly of the Box Tops and Big Star. They bonded over their enjoyment of cycling around historic areas of the city. Both singers were seen as somewhat grumpy old men – rock and roll recluses who wanted to be left alone.

On the evening of 4 January 2004, Ray Davies was walking with his girlfriend along Burgundy Street in the French Quarter shortly before 8.30 p.m. The streets were quiet because a big American football game was taking place. Davies and his partner were looking for a restaurant when they were approached by two men. One drew a gun and fired a shot into the ground before demanding all of their money. Ray refused, at which point one of the men grabbed the woman and pointed the gun at her. Davies immediately handed over his money and the pair ran off with the woman's handbag. Without thinking of the possible consequences, Ray set off in pursuit. The muggers turned and one of them fired a shot that went straight through Ray's right thigh. His girlfriend managed to get the number plate of the escape car and called 911. Four hours later, an arrest was made. The suspect was named as Jerome Barra, 25, who had been stopped while driving a car with the reported number plate. He was charged with armed robbery and aggravated battery. A police spokesman said the second suspect was still being sought.

Davies was taken to Charity Hospital on Tulane Avenue, a public establishment administered by the Louisiana State University. He likened the experience to 'being shot in a Johannesburg shanty town' and healthcare in New Orleans left him indignant: 'It's almost Third World conditions – and that was before [Hurricane] Katrina.' He was also anxious. He had heard stories of shooters going back to finish off witnesses and was fearful during his stay: 'I told the hospital to say it was a flesh wound and that I'd gone back to England, and they did, and everyone believed it. I actually stayed incognito with some friends.' In fact, Davies was in and out of hospital for months. He had an infection in his leg and, when he was awarded a CBE, he collected it at Buckingham Palace, on 17 March, with the aid of a walking stick. A month later he was back in hospital.

The case went to trial twice. On each occasion it was dismissed and the charges against Barra were eventually dropped. An assailant has to be able to face his accuser under US law, but Ray repeatedly failed to appear: 'The day I had to go to court, I was here mixing a track,' said Davies. 'I didn't discover until later that you have to be there in person.'

Less than six months after Ray Davies was shot in New Orleans, Dave Davies suffered a stroke, at the age of 57. Dave was living in Los Angeles with his partner, Kate, but was back in London to promote his new solo album, *Bug*, during June 2004. On the 30 June, he spent the morning at the BBC's Broadcasting House in central London with his publicist and his son, Christian. He was in a lift leaving the building when he suddenly lost the ability to speak and the right side of his body seized up, but he managed to remain conscious. Christian called for an ambulance and Dave was immediately taken to hospital.

The stroke had not come entirely without warning. One morning, just days earlier, Dave woke up and struggled to move his right hand, and also had trouble speaking. A few hours later, this happened again, but after a visit to a doctor, who hadn't seemed too concerned, he went home and carried on as normal. 'It was a wake-up call,' said Dave, speaking of those first 'mini-strokes'. 'I was touring, flying, I thought I was still 20. It was like a stroke that goes away, I was totally disabled for several hours. So that gave me an introduction to it.'

Dave was initially taken to the University College Hospital in Euston and, after examination, he was transferred to the National Neurological Hospital in Queen's Square. Kate, who was now also Dave's manager, had been in California arranging tour dates to promote *Bug*. She flew to London and spent every day of the next two months at the hospital until Dave was discharged. He couldn't move his right hand, so his family left it resting on a guitar while he slept in the hope that his unconscious mind would reconnect the fingers with the strings. He was in very poor shape and no one could predict if and when he would fully recover.

'The doctors told me I had high blood pressure and that this was what had caused the stroke,' Dave explained. 'They thought I'd probably had high blood pressure for at least ten years. I remember thinking this was strange as I'd eaten healthily for nearly forty years.' Years of drink and drugs, and a stressful regime of touring and recording, had worn his body down over time. He has since said that he believes his use of amphetamines as a young man may have had long-term effects.

After a few days, he was able to eat some soft foods with a spoon, and a week later he was allowed outside in a wheelchair. Though he knew he might never be able to play the guitar again, he found ideas for songs striking him even as he lay in his hospital bed. By the time he was let out of hospital, he had some movement back in his right hand. He needed voice training and, as a result, now says he has more of a 'posh' accent than before. He also underwent an intensive regime of physical therapy. 'Nearly eighteen months after my stroke,' he said, 'I was about 85 per cent back to normal with my guitar playing. I believe my stroke was meant to happen to slow me down. I'd like to write and make films, and start a foundation where I can help people be more spiritual.'

During his convalescence, Dave spent time at his sister Dolly's, but also, tellingly, with Ray. The older Davies brother was quoted as saying that he had helped coach Dave back to fitness, but while Dave confirms that he stayed with Ray and that his brother was a quite good cook, he rejects Ray's 'coaching' claim outright: 'What a load of bollocks,' said Dave. 'That is so Ray. He likes to think he's the good guy. I had not seen him for about ten months then. He was very sympathetic when I became ill, of course, but I've had great therapists. Ray's not been part of that.'

In the aftermath of the shooting and the stroke, any chances of The Kinks reuniting seemed gone forever. Physically it would be extremely difficult and emotionally the Davies brothers were as far apart as ever, despite their concern for each other's health. Communication was now done by fax and email, and only when a business issue needed resolving. Dave would have to complete his rehabilitation before recording again. The chances of Ray Davies continuing with new material seemed slim, but he was about to surprise everyone.

After the Fall

I t may have come surprisingly late in their career, but Ray Davies and The Kinks finally seem to have secured their legacy as great songwriters, innovators and performers. This was made evident during the glorious Olympic Games in London in 2012 – a time it would be right to compare with the great sporting summer of 1966, when The Kinks were at their peak and England won the football World Cup. Ray Davies took a central role in the Olympic closing ceremony, something that would have seemed impossible seven years earlier, in the aftermath of his shooting. The road from hospital bed to centre stage in the biggest show on Earth was a long one.

In 2005, Ray was recovering from the injuries he'd sustained in New Orleans and, in February, had a metal rod removed from his leg. Though he continued to feel unwell, mentally he felt stronger than he had in a long time. He hadn't released an album of new material in over a decade, but the trauma of the incident, that confrontation with death, seemed to have freed him musically. In fact, it sparked a period of creativity that he hadn't experienced since The Kinks stopped working. 'Having lost three years recovering from the shooting, I'm more determined to see all of my ideas through. I also want the lifespan of The Kinks' material to be enduring,' he said.

Davies spent much of 2005 recording a solo album that had been anticipated since The Kinks' final show nine years earlier. By late summer, it was ready to be mastered, although the much-rumoured release date slipped from September into early 2006. When *Other People's Lives* finally arrived in February 2006, on V2 Records, it was a pleasant surprise. Twelve of the thirteen songs had been written before the shooting, and they were undeniably good – certainly an improvement on the final Kinks albums. They sounded modern while retaining that special Davies charm.

The scene-setting 'Things Are Gonna Change (The Morning After)' is backed up by 'After The Fall', one of the record's highlights. From the title, many casual listeners might have believed the song referred to the shooting but, as it pre-dated the attack, it's more likely about the break-up of Ray's third marriage. If the slightly hypnotic vibes of 'The Tourist' took Davies away from his usual territory, it was to good effect. The character studies for which he had become so renowned in the sixties and seventies were present in the form of 'Next Door Neighbour' ('Mr Smith, another story/ I wonder what became of him?/ They say he threw the telly through the window/ He went berserk and jacked the whole world in'); and 'Creatures of Little Faith' ('I didn't mean to follow you/ But I suspected you were meeting somebody/ I was playing detective').

Other People's Lives, however, has been sadly overlooked, and was harshly treated by the critics. 'Davies has produced an album that delights as much as it disappoints,' said the *Guardian*. 'Leaving the listener not celebrating the rebirth of one of England's greatest songwriters, but slightly confused.' The BBC's Chris Long was less impressed and positively brutal in his comments: 'There's little that stands out from a disturbingly average collection which can only be compared to a mid-Atlantic version of Del Amitri. For a songwriter of Davies' calibre, *Other People's Lives* is nothing short of a failure.' It edged briefly into the top forty but seems to have been largely forgotten since.

Because of his long career and 'national treasure' status, rather than his recent recordings, Ray Davies was asked to headline a concert as part of the BBC's October music festival, the Electric Proms — a short-lived rock and roll extension of the corporation's more famous classical music season. It was a big event and Ray pulled out all the stops to make it a memorable night. In the run up, there was even excited talk of Dave joining him on stage after the brothers had met in the West Country, but nothing came of it. Instead, Ray was accompanied by the sixty-piece Crouch End Festival Chorus on several songs.

That same month, having waited a decade for the first solo Ray Davies album, fans were treated to the second in one year, *Working Man's Café*, recorded in Nashville. He had written almost three-dozen new songs, paring the final track-listing down to ten, adding a couple of bonus tracks on some versions. Unfortunately for Ray, V2 Records, experiencing financial problems, hatched a deal with the *Sunday Times*: *Working Man's Café* was given away free with the newspaper a day before it was due to hit the shops. It may have eased the label's problems in the short term, but it was commercial suicide for the album, which sank without a trace.

It is sad that it failed to garner more attention, because it's a great record. The rocky 'Vietnam Cowboys' could be his best opening song since '20th Century Man' on *Muswell Hillbillies*. 'You're Asking Me' is the updated harder-hitting cousin of a song like 'Picture Book' and could easily have sat alongside many of the tracks from the *The Kinks are the Village Green Preservation Society*. The title track was poignant both lyrically and musically — even more so to those who know that the bridge comes from a telephone conversation Ray had with Dave while trying to find a parking space on the way to one of their last meetings, and that, by this time, the two brothers were barely speaking. 'It's lonely,' Ray admitted of his solo career. 'You need to upset people, have a bit of conflict. Great music, drama and literature have conflict. I miss being in a band, I'm at my best when I cast songs for the people around me. I like to take people on a journey, trust me and I'll get you there in the end.'

Ray's belief that the next song is going to be his best yet drives him forward on a never-ending journey, and the remaining tracks on *Working Man's Café* demonstrate that he is right to believe in his own ability. 'Morphine Song' is a truly majestic piano-driven effort with an infectious chorus, while 'Imaginary Man' is possibly his best composition in a generation. It has the kind of play-it-at-my-funeral poignancy which can't help but make the listener think back on all that Ray Davies and The Kinks have achieved: 'Is this really it?/ Is this the final station?/ It's really been quite a trip'. While this might sound like a sad goodbye, retrospection has been one of the recurring themes of Ray's work in recent years, not just on his second solo album, but in other musical projects.

In 2008, his most recent theatrical endeavour, the *Come Dancing* musical, enjoyed a run at London's Theatre Royal. Written in 1997, the show took over a decade to get to opening night. This wasn't a run-through of the band's greatest hits, like the Queen-inspired *We Will Rock You*, but featured new music written by Ray specifically for the show. Set in the Ilford Palais, the kind of Saturday-night venue Ray's sisters used to visit, the new songs were woven into a story of 1950s dance halls and the transition from ballroom dancing to the rock and roll era. The press were understandably upbeat about its prospects and it received several warm reviews, including one from the *Telegraph*, which called it 'a winning show that deserves a bright future'. *The Times*, however, dismissed it as 'a ragged and sentimental montage of scenes sorely in need of narrative'. The show's run was extended into 2009 but then plans for a West End version in 2010 were shelved.

Ray's thoughts turned next to revisiting The Kinks' past. First, he called again upon the Crouch End Festival Chorus, this time to record a whole album of material, and spent the late spring of 2009 at London's AIR Studios fleshing out versions of more than a dozen Kinks classics. Ten made it onto the album, *The Kinks Choral Collection*, which was never likely to become a favourite amongst rock purists, but did contain some highlights. 'Days' was reworked fairly successfully, but the new version of 'Waterloo Sunset' proved that, sometimes, an original recording is just perfect and shouldn't be tinkered with. The out-and-out rockers like 'You Really Got Me' and 'All Day and All of the Night' did not really fit at all, but 'See My Friends' floats angelically and 'Shangri-La' could have been written for this kind of arrangement. 'When you break things down and build them up in a different way,' explained Ray Davies, 'you discover nuances to the harmonics that you hadn't realised were there.' It did not, in conclusion, do The Kinks' reputation any favours and prompted questions: why was Ray doing this? Had he, finally, run out of new ideas?

Apart from a brief burst of internet activity at the turn of the century, exciting Kinks fans by posting on message boards and taking part in 'question and answer' sessions, Pete Quaife had dropped out of sight. It came as something of a surprise, then, when news began to circulate that he, too, had written a book. It was to be called – perhaps ominously for those who had found Dave Davies *Kink* rather too frank – *Veritas*, Latin for 'the truth'.

Quaife spoke openly about what he had written. 'My hope is that, when the reader is finished he or she will have an educated idea of what it was like in those days,' he said. 'I have based everything on truth – so everything you read actually happened! I have left no stone unturned – life on the road, the tedium of one-night stands, groupies, drugs, other groups and musicians. All of these characters are based on real-life friends of mine – they all existed and lived exactly as described in the book. Many people will believe that this is a faintly veiled story of The Kinks. I have never alluded, in the book, to The Kinks in any way, shape or form.'

That last disclaimer rang hollow. By the summer of 2010, Quaife still hadn't secured a publishing deal for the book. Then, on 23 June, in the midst of preparations for his marriage to Elisabeth Bilbo, very suddenly, he died. The cause was renal failure; he was just 66 years old.

News of his death was covered in many major publications, but few people had any idea where he had been, or what he had been doing for the past thirty years. *The Times* gave half a page to its tribute, saying that he had 'provided the throb and muscle to some of the greatest pop songs of the 1960s'. *Rolling Stone* magazine ran a piece in its 5 August issue which quoted Dave Davies' reaction: 'He was part of the essential DNA of the band . . . In addition to the bass, he gave a lot of input into the arrangement, and blending and backing vocals and riffs and other ideas. We were never the same after he left.' Of a solo show at which Quaife made a guest appearance, Davies said: 'After the show my bassist said to me, "It's so strange, I played virtually the same thing as Pete and that song sounds so much better the way he does it."' Ray, however, seemed bemused. 'It made me realise how little I knew him,' he said. 'I had to look him up on Wikipedia to find out about him. *The Kinks are the Village Green Preservation Society* was his favourite album. I didn't know that. He never told me.'

'Pete was extremely good at hiding,' said his brother David Quaife. 'Be it for two or three months or two or three years. Things would just get too much for him and he'd shut off completely, and that happened after the breakdown, he'd go into exile.' So where *had* he been since walking out for the second time in 1969? 'Pete and I kept in touch but we went off on different career paths,' explained long-time friend Jeff Bailey. 'We met up occasionally but kind of lost track of each other. Through mutual friends we knew each other's circumstances. However, I tracked him down in Denmark in late 2009. He rang me and I last wrote to him at the beginning of April 2010.'

Quaife spent the 1970s living in Denmark, working, where he could, as a graphic artist. He did work for Lego, Saab and Sadolin, among others, and produced sleeve designs for obscure albums by bands such as Flair, Olsen, and Kjeld and the Donkeys. He also worked for local newspapers producing cartoons; as an 'employee', he was not allowed to sign the pieces, but always tried to hide the letter Q in them somewhere.

Pete's second wife, Hanne, though of Danish descent, also had Canadian citizenship and, in 1980, the couple decided to emigrate there. They married on 1 May and made preparations. '[Pete] knocked on my door and said, "I'm going to live in Canada,"' recalled David Quaife. 'He'd had a couple of jobs that he could never hold down because he wasn't allowed to express his own ideas.' Pete and Hanne arrived in Canada in September 1980 and lived there for the next fifteen years, settling in Belleville, Ontario. He continued to work in graphic arts and enjoyed drawing as a hobby, combining his skills as a draughtsman with a love of astronomy to produce some wonderful star charts. He also began writing what would become *Veritas*.

'He did fairly well in Canada,' said David Quaife. 'When my son was 15 I sent him over to stay for three months, and he had a jolly old time but when he came home he said, "Pete's still upset about what happened in The Kinks." I said, "You're joking, that was years ago." When he'd had a few too many he could get quite bitter about it.'

After The Kinks stopped working in the mid-nineties, there were rumours of the original line-up getting back together for a show, or to record a new album. The usual problems soon surfaced. 'Ray doesn't want to do it without me, and Dave doesn't want to do it with me,' said Mick Avory. 'And I don't particularly want to do it with him [Dave]. So where do you go from there?' Any lingering hopes for a reunion seemed to come to an end in 1998 when Pete Quaife first suffered kidney failure and had to begin dialysis. He also required heart surgery as a result of a blood clot.

During the many hours spent in clinics and hospitals undergoing dialysis, Quaife started drawing cartoons about the subject. These led to the book *The Lighter Side of Dialysis Volume 1*, published in Canada in 2005. By now, Quaife and Hanne had divorced, and Quaife headed back to Denmark, where he moved in with girlfriend Elisabeth Bilbo.

'He'd called up Elisabeth and she was so pleased that he was OK,' said David Quaife. 'She met us at the airport and we drove to the farm, but he looked terrible. He was emotionally dead, he looked a million years older. At four in the morning I was rushing around trying to set up his dialysis and do you know how difficult it is? You have to get the cash up front and God knows what before they'll do it. Elisabeth said, "He can come and live with me and I'll look after him." They were the genuine sweethearts and so he ended his days there, but the last two years were so difficult. He couldn't even go to the toilet by himself, which was hard for someone as proud as Pete.'

Four days after Quaife's passing, Ray Davies appeared in the afternoon slot at Glastonbury Festival. He took to the stage at the same time that England were playing Germany in the football World Cup. Ray said a few words and dedicated his appearance to

Pete. 'I wanted to acknowledge what had happened, obviously,' he explained. 'Then suddenly it occurred to me that it was live on TV, there were 120,000 people there, and I had a song to sing next. It nearly got to me for a moment.'

The year ended with Ray as the subject of a film by Julien Temple for the BBC's *Imagine* series. The resulting documentary, *Imaginary Man*, follows Ray around north London as he muses on his past and sings snippets of The Kinks' back catalogue. An entirely separate companion piece featuring Dave was also produced, the brothers being no more able to share a screen than a stage.

Ray also picked up a *GQ* magazine Outstanding Achievement award, following in the footsteps of recent recipients such as Elvis Costello, Led Zeppelin and The Clash. But why did he get the award and not the whole band? He was the most visible surviving member, had written most of the songs and was undoubtedly the key creative force – but he hadn't done it alone and The Kinks were not merely his backing band.

He was also given the honour of curating the 2011 *Meltdown Festival* on London's South Bank, while the fiftieth anniversary of the Festival of Britain was celebrated around him. He arranged a series of shows which saw him recreate an episode of *Ready, Steady, Go!* from the early days of The Kinks, and showcased gigs by Madness, one of the many bands he'd directly inspired, along with Wire and Nick Lowe.

Concert duties over, Ray went back to The Kinks catalogue: it was as though he couldn't leave it alone. This time, he invited a series of guest performers to re-record the old songs with yet more choral backing and other embellishments. Under the title *See My Friends*, Davies presented fourteen songs performed by artists such as Bruce Springsteen, Jon Bon Jovi, Alex Chilton, Amy MacDonald, Paloma Faith and Jackson Browne. Most reviewers asked the same question: why? In *The Times*, the record was reviewed alongside projects by Neil Diamond and Rod Stewart, with the leader 'Should have died before they got old'. *Mojo* gave it just one star and called the version of 'You Really Got Me' with Metallica a 'travesty'. Of 'Lola', performed as a duet with singer Paloma Faith, *Q*'s critic was almost cruel, suggesting it 'might be the worst thing to happen to Davies since he was shot in the leg'. In fact, while that particular track didn't measure up to the original, it did have some novelty value. Elsewhere in the collection, the Springsteen version of 'Better Days' outshines The Kinks version, and the collaboration with Mumford & Sons on 'Days/This Time Tomorrow' offers an interesting interpretation of the originals. Despite the critical slamming, the album sold well, and reached twelve in the UK charts, Ray's highest album placing in more than thirty years.

In May 2012, Ray appeared at the Barbican as a collection of diverse musicians and singers gathered together to recreate Big Star's *Third/Sister Lovers* album. Davies sang his own song, 'Till The End of the Day', which the Americans had covered on the 1975 album, and a version of 'The Letter', which had been a worldwide hit for Alex Chilton's pre-Big Star band, The Box Tops.

Many groups of the 1960s have tribute bands. The Kast Off Kinks, however, is a tribute with a twist: it's made up largely of ex-members of the original, including drummer Mick Avory. Could you imagine a Beatles tribute act with Ringo Starr on drums? The Kast Off Kinks have had almost every ex-Kink play with them at one time or another. Even Ray has joined them on occasion, as has Rasa, but Dave is firmly set against the project, which plays twenty to thirty shows a year. 'We were going to play in America but Dave was over there and he got the promoter to put a block on it like he owned the territory,' said Mick Avory. 'He hates it because he thinks it's downgrading the hallowed name.' The band has now been around for so long that there are ex-members of the Kast Off Kinks who joke that they will form the Kast Off, Kast Off Kinks. The current line-up comprises Mick Avory, Jim Rodford, and Ian Gibbons, with Dave Clarke on vocals. John Dalton and John Gosling have previously played with the band.

Ray Davies is almost 70 years old now and still packs out the Royal Albert Hall on a semi-regular basis. He has such a vast repertoire that he can pull out neglected gems from the 1970s seemingly at will. But rock music, almost by definition, is made by young people for young people, and was never meant to get old. Davies is part of the first British rock and roll generation to reach pensionable age. Along with Jagger, Richards and Bowie, he ignores the march of time, refusing to get old, or to dress and act as those in their seventies would have done when he was a child in post-war Britain.

Now he's the elder statesman and bands two generations younger are paying homage. Brighton rockers The Kooks went to record at Konk and named an album after the studio; while Razorlight's Johnny Borrell said of his visit, 'I was surrounded by Ray's stuff from the past thirty years and it was weird standing there and knowing I was in the midst of reels to reels of all these great songs.' In a September 2009 issue of the *NME*, Gary Jarman of The Cribs cited 'Waterloo Sunset' as the song he most wished he'd written: 'It's my favourite song. It seems sad in some ways, but without being in any way soporific. It's a perfect pop song.' Craig Finn from The Hold Steady picked *The Kinks are the Village Green Preservation Society* as one of the ten greatest albums from his life in music.

Kinks material continues to be mined from the archives, with even rejects from their heyday sounding exciting to true devotees. Re-releases of their decades-old albums with additional tracks and alternative recordings are welcomed by music critics with much excitement. A massive 131-track collection of The Kinks' many BBC recordings was issued in Autumn 2012, spreading over six discs. Elsewhere, the gradual drip of 'best of' and 'greatest hit' CDs continues.

Proof, if it were needed, that The Kinks' best music still resonates today can also be found in the use of their songs in commercials and the revenue that generates. A 2006 study named the band as the highest-earning UK act in US adverts, gathering a massive £6 million over the previous twelve months, with Led Zeppelin in second place at £4 million. The most popular song used by advertisers was 'All Day and All of the Night', employed by SAAB, Kohl's department stores, General Motors and Tide washing powder. Other companies promoted their products to the strains of songs such as 'Ev'rybody's Gonna Be Happy' (Abbott Laboratories), 'I'm Not Like Everybody Else' (IBM), 'Picture Book' (Hewlett Packard), 'Gotta Be Free' (Toyota), 'Everybody's a Star' (Converse) and 'Days' (Volkswagen). All this from a collection of songs which were mostly released three decades previously, and recorded by rock's ultimate dysfunctional family.

That dysfunction has been there for all to see from the start. Personalities that were virtual opposites helped trigger the energy of the early recordings, but in later life, having been through so much together, the tension ceased to prompt creativity and, instead, saw the band shatter into pieces. Today, Ray and Dave communicate rarely, and even then it is usually by that most casual, impersonal of methods, email.

National newspapers, such as the *Observer*, now call Ray Davies a 'national treasure' and he still meets interviewers in and around Highgate, within miles of where he grew up. He spends his time observing people, looking for inspiration for his next song. Dave Davies wanders the moors of south-west England each morning, looking for a place to sit and contemplate life, farther than ever from his brother, both geographically and emotionally. 'There is more good than bad in the relationship,' Ray Davies said recently. 'It's the damage it does the immediate family. My older sisters get upset when they hear about the squabbling. And Dave's boys, sometimes it poisons the offspring. They might have heard a bad rap about me and it kind of instils it into them as they're growing up.'

It's usually the bad that gets reported and quoted. 'I don't see anything wrong with doing some Kinks shows, but I don't know if I'd feel too happy about going back into the studio with Ray, because he's off his head, man,' said Dave in 2008. 'He's, like, spoiled. He doesn't even know what an asshole he is. He's the first person on the planet who would own up to thinking he's a genius. But real geniuses don't realise they are.' More recently Ray countered with, 'You know Dave did invent the wheel don't you? I think that feeling's grown, depending which woman he's been with.'

And so it goes on. But who should get the final word? Dave has slipped away from his past in The Kinks but says 'I've always loved the idea about The Kinks being misfits . . . being an outcast and not fitting in, but celebrating the fact. "Fuck it. I'll be who I want to be. And that's who I am, take it or leave it."' For Ray's part, he seems to have accepted his past and now, in 2013, is the most settled he has ever been. He describes himself as 'abstract and motivated. Discovering the value of all the stuff I've put out so far and the body of work that defines me.'

It is Dave, however, who offers the best summary of their relationship: 'How could I not love my own brother?' he asks. 'I just can't stand to be with him.'

And so Ray Davies left the dressing room, took a long walk down to the black cab and climbed inside. Almost a billion people would be watching him sing in a few moments' time and he wasn't even sure if his microphone and earpiece were working properly. Outside, a multitude of costumed dancers were backed by a pre-recorded Beatles soundtrack. The middle of the stadium had been transformed into a Gulliver's London, with iconic landmarks such as Big Ben, Battersea Power Station, the Gherkin, and the centrepiece of the London Eye. As the music faded down, a lone black cab drove up a ramp to the front of the Eye. Guitarist Bill Shanley stood by as the taxi door opened and a grinning Ray stepped out to sing 'Waterloo Sunset'. While he was obviously concerned about the earpiece, and despite the pressure of the occasion, he gave a great vocal performance and even managed to lead the crowd in singing the 'sha-la-las'.

He had found fame as a member of The Kinks, but he stood there alone, an elder statesman surveying his estate. Finally content that his legacy was sealed, Ray sang his most famous song to the world. With Union Flags waving in the background around the mini-London skyline, Ray was briefly something only the greatest figures in rock and roll have ever been: the centre of the world's attention.

Author's Note, Thanks and Acknowledgements

You could say that this book was easily conceived, but had a difficult birth. I've been researching and writing it on and off for around five years and during that time a lot happened in both the world of The Kinks and my own life. Ray Davies has undergone something of a re-birth as an eccentric national treasure, Pete Quaife unfortunately passed away and any chances of an original Kinks reunion died with him. During the same period I've been lucky enough to have two amazing children, the oldest of which now asks for Kinks songs to be played in the car (alongside The Beatles and Johnny Cash) so I must be doing something right as a father.

For a book that took so long to write and covered so much ground it's not surprising that I needed much help along the way. I could have written a book about The Kinks without tracking down new interviewees and stories, but the resulting work wouldn't have offered much different to what has gone before. I was lucky enough to interview nearly two-dozen band members, producers, engineers and friends of The Kinks. Many of those listed below have never been interviewed about the band before and each provided fresh and illuminating insights, I am seriously indebted to them all. To secure these interviews I also had help from many people along the way who freely gave their time and energy to aid my cause. My sincere thanks goes out to them too.

My interviewees were: journalist, press agent and long-time Kinks observer, Keith Altham. Original Kinks drummer Mick Avory. Friend of the band since the 1960s, Jeff Bailey. Singer and friend of Ray Davies, Dave Berry. Kinks bassist, John Dalton. Backing singer and photographer, Debi Doss. Early Kinks promo photographer, Bruce Fleming. Kinks keyboard player, John Gosling. Konk artist and backing singer, Claire Hammill. Singer and prolific songwriter, Tony Hiller. Sound engineer on and off for the Kinks over three decades, Alan O'Duffy. Backing singer, Maryann Price. Kinks bassist, Andy Pyle. Pete Quaife's brother, David Quaife. Touring companion in the 1960s, from Goldie & The Gingerbreads, Genya Ravan. Backing singer, Shirlie Roden (her original 1970s notes were extremely useful). Studio engineer, John Rollo. Choreographer, Dougie Squires. Hit producer, Shel Talmy. Photographer, Barrie Wentzell. Band assistant, Brian Wilcock.

Others provided time and effort to help secure the interviews above while yet more people gave advice, help and encouragement. They include: Dave Clarke, Dave Emlen, Joe Gibb, Patrick Harrington Q.C., Doug Hinman, Alan Holmes, Geoff Lewis, Larry Page, Graham Palmer, Steve Phillips, Ed Pyle, Jim Rodford, Rachel Ruderman, Olga Ruocco, Marianne Spellman, Nick Trevisick, and Mark Volman.

I would also like to thank Tim Bates and all at Pollinger and Sam Harrison, Ray Newman, Melissa Smith, Lucy Warburton, Anabel Briggs, Maxine Baker, Emily Kearns and all at Aurum for the encouragement and patience in getting this book to print. With so many helpers in so many different ways over the years it is quite likely that I have missed someone out, so apologies to you. All mistakes, of course, are mine.

Source Notes

Chapter 1

p12: 'Ray never drinks', Marion Rainford to the *New Musical Express*, 13 October 1973

p12: 'The doctor had given me pills', Ray Davies to *Mojo*, March 2006

p12: 'He was very subdued backstage', Mick Avory to *Mojo*, July 2000

p13: 'There wasn't even a stunned silence', Roy Carr to *Mojo*, July 2000

p13: 'We didn't know what to expect', Dave Davies to *Mojo*, July 2000

p13: 'I should have died', Ray Davies to *Mojo*, July 2000

p14: 'I finished it then for a good reason', Ray Davies to *Goldmine*, 1 March 1996

p14: 'When I got there he looked lost', Dave Davies to *Mojo*, July 2000

p15: 'The only thing to do', Dave Davies to *Mojo*, July 2000

Chapter 2

p19: 'Ray's probably resented me', Dave Davies to *Magnet* magazine, summer 2008

p20: 'From an early age', Ray Davies to *Mojo* magazine, March 2006

p20: 'I remember the fifties', Ray Davies to the *Observer*, 1 May 2011

p21: 'When we were children', Dave Davies to *Rave* magazine, 11 November 1965

p23: 'During the time when Ray', Dave Davies to *Rave* magazine, 11 November 1965

p24: 'Boyfriends always came to the house', Ray Davies to the *Observer*, 1 May 2011

p25: 'I called Rosie "Mum"', Ray Davies to *Goldmine* magazine, 1 March 1996

p25: 'The only time there was any', Dave Davies to *Rave* magazine, 11 November 1965

Chapter 3

p28: 'I think that says a lot', Dave Davies to *Mojo*, September 2000

p29: 'I came from quite a happy', Ray Davies to *Mojo*, March 2006 p30: 'I remember drinking beer', Ray Davies to the *Telegraph Magazine*, date unknown

p30: 'I started to improve', Dave Davies to *Rave* magazine, 11 November 1965

p31: 'I said, "Yeah, I play guitar".' Pete Quaife to *Q* magazine, September 1989

p32: 'I knew Pete from', Jeff Bailey interview with the author, 2010

p32: 'We found an old oxygen cylinder', Pete Quaife to the *New Musical Express*, 2 April 1965

p32: 'As a teenager I was', Pete Quaife to the *New Musical Express*, 2 April 1965

p33: 'They were a Jewish family', David Quaife interview with the author, 2011

p34: 'It makes me giggle', David Quaife interview with the author, 2011

p37: 'You carry that around', Dave Davies in the film *Mystical Journey*, 2010

p37: 'They said I was a Ted', Pete Quaife to the *New Musical Express*, 28 August 1964

p37: 'Pete and I', Jeff Bailey interview with the author, 2010

Chapter 4

p42: 'It was not often that a bunch of scruffy', Pete Quaife to Jean-Pierre Morisset, *Jukebox* magazine, May 2006

p43: 'When we first started out', Ray Davies to the *Telegraph Magazine*, date unknown

p43: 'Superficially they were upper-class twits', Dave Davies to *Q* magazine, September 1989

p44: 'I was doing my four numbers', Robert Wace to Johnny Rogan, *The Kinks*, page 10

p45: 'We were still so young', Ray Davies to *Q* magazine, 1989

p45: 'It's one of those skeletons in the cupboard', David Quaife interview with the author, 2011

p46: 'I told Ray and Dave', Mickey Willett to *Mojo*, September 2000

p46: 'He seemed to get on', John Turney to Johnny Rogan, *The Kinks*, page 7

p47: 'I was General Professional Manager', Tony Hiller interview with the author, 2010

p48: 'They were dandies', Larry Page to *Mojo*, September 2000

p48: 'I started by going for the biggest', Larry Page to *Mojo*, September 2000

p49: 'I worked for the *Melody Maker*', Bruce Fleming interview with the author, 2011

p49: 'They'd got some new clothes', Bruce Fleming interview with the author, 2011 p50: 'I was having a chat with Larry', Bruce Fleming interview with the author, 2011

p50: 'The image we settled on', Larry Page to *Q* magazine, 1989

Chapter 5

p54: 'That was a life-changing experience for me', Shel Talmy interview with the author, 2011

p54: 'I was 12', Shel Talmy interview with the author, 2011

p54: 'Three days later', Shel Talmy interview with the author, 2011

p55: 'The first person I saw', Shel Talmy interview with the author, 2011

p55: 'It was unbelievable', Shel Talmy interview with the author, 2011

p55: 'They were public school stereotypes', Shel Talmy interview with the author, 2011

p55: 'I was at Mills Music', Shel Talmy interview with the author, 2011

p56: 'I chose all the songs to be recorded', Shel Talmy interview with the author, 2011

p56: 'Ray was certainly', Shel Talmy interview with the author, 2011

p56: 'I was charged for the studio time', Shel Talmy interview with the author, 2011

p57: 'I remember sitting', David Quaife interview with the author, 2011

p57: 'I was present at the Camden Head', Jeff Bailey interview with the author, 2010

p57: 'So when I went down to the pub', Dave Davies to *Rave* magazine, 11 November 1965

p58: 'I went for some piano lessons', Mick Avory interview with the author, 2011

p58: 'I discovered Elvis Presley', Mick Avory interview with the author, 2011

p58: 'The guy who'd played with a stick', Mick Avory interview with the author, 2011

p59: 'The worst problem', Mick Avory to the *New Musical Express*, 28 August 1964

p59: 'He wasn't actually a drummer', Mick Avory interview with the author, 2011

p59: 'I went to see what it was all about', Mick Avory interview with the author, 2011

p60: 'I practised with them', Mick Avory interview with the author, 2011

p60: 'I didn't really have any direction', Mick Avory interview with the author, 2011

p61: 'I wanted to pursue it', Mick

Avory interview with the
author, 2011

p62: 'Our manager said', Ray
Davies, unknown source

p65: 'It was quite a small, pokey,
Victorian terrace', Allan
Ballard to *Mojo Collections*, 2002

p65: 'When I first heard it', Shel
Talmy to *Musician* magazine,
July 1997

p66: 'It was a slower and much
bluesier version', Shel Talmy
to *Musician* magazine, July 1997

p67: 'I was floundering', Ray
Davies, unknown source

Chapter 6

p69: 'I Like them both for different
reasons', Ray Davies to *Circus*
magazine, 1974

p69: 'There was a six-month
period', Ray Davies to *Circus*
magazine, 1974

p72: 'I heard that song for the first
time', Tom Petty to *Rolling
Stone*, 9 December 2010

p72: 'We just knew we were
going to make a great
record', Ray Davies to *Uncut*,
September 2004

p73: 'Once "You Really Got
Me" was a hit', Shel Talmy
interview with the author,
2011

p74: 'I did some of my own
engineering', Shel Talmy
interview with the author, 2011

p74: 'Pete Quaife was my favourite',

Shel Talmy interview with the
author, 2011

p74: 'Mick was our drummer', Pete
Quaife to *Jukebox* magazine,
May 2006

p74: 'Ray I think it's fair to say
probably', Shel Talmy
interview with the author,
2011

p75: 'They found the band', Shel
Talmy interview with the
author, 2011

p75: 'We were in a 707', Ray Davies
to the *Telegraph Magazine*, date
unknown

p75: 'Ray used to come in', Shel
Talmy interview with the
author, 2011

p76: 'A few months ago', Ray
Davies to *Rave* magazine,
December 1964

p77: 'The whole EP was pretty
dreadful', Ray Davies to *Ugly
Things*, summer 2010

p77: 'I'd gone from £9 a week',
Mick Avory interview with the
author, 2011

p77: 'I really enjoyed that tour',
Mick Avory interview with the
author, 2011

Chapter 7

p80: 'At the end of the show', Dave
Davies to *Rave* magazine,
11 November 1965

p81: 'One night in a Brisbane
hotel', Dave Davies writing in
Kink

p82: '[Pete] liked meeting people', Dave Davies on the *Mojo* blog, 2010

p82: 'Everyone would be there', David Quaife interview with the author, 2011

p85: 'We were innocent bystanders really', Ray Davies to *Uncut*, September 2004

p86: 'I'd had all the praise', Ray Davies to *Q* magazine, September 1989

p87: 'We were a good band', Genya Ravan interview with the author, 2010

p87: 'It was very draining', Genya Ravan interview with the author, 2010

p87: 'I know that the drummers', Genya Ravan interview with the author, 2010

p88: 'We got on well', Keith Altham interview with the author, 2011

p89: 'We were all the same age', Keith Altham interview with the author, 2011

p89: 'On the night of the incident', Keith Altham interview with the author, 2011

p89: 'Though everyone says', Keith Altham interview with the author, 2011

p89: 'The Kinks were', Genya Ravan interview with the author, 2010

p89: 'The incident with Dave and Mick', Ray Davies to the *Independent*, 1994

p89: 'I'm not sure if there was a warrant', Keith Altham interview with the author, 2011

p90: 'Everything was a bit upside down', Pete Quaife to *Jukebox* magazine, May 2006

Chapter 8

p91: 'It was the first time', Ray Davies to Sky Arts TV, 2010

p92: 'Larry [Page] fell out with them', Keith Altham interview with the author, 2011

p94: 'I was surprised how old-fashioned', Dave Davies to *Vanity Fair*, November 2002

p94: 'Once The Beatles had opened', Keith Altham interview with the author, 2011

p94: 'It certainly wasn't the American tour', Pete Quaife to *Mojo*, September 2000

p95: 'It was like landing on another planet', Mick Avory interview with the author, 2011

p96: 'When I turned 21', Ray Davies to *Q* magazine, 'Cash for Questions', February 2005

p96: 'There was some concert', Keith Altham interview with the author, 2011

p97: 'Larry Page went with us', Mick Avory interview with the author, 2011 p98: 'When we asked where Larry had gone', Ray Davies in *X-Ray*

p99: 'Our biggest problem, it seemed', Dave Davies in *Kink*

p99: 'All this turned me into a less innocent person', Ray Davies in *X-Ray*

p99: 'Visiting America and LA was great', Mick Avory interview with the author, 2011

p100: 'I said they sounded like a proper band', Dave Berry interview with the author, 2010

p100: 'I'd be at the Sunderland Empire', Dave Berry interview with the author, 2010

p101: 'At that time', Dave Berry interview with the author, 2010

p101: 'It was massive', Dave Berry interview with the author, 2010

p101: 'I was staying in a hotel', Ray Davies to *Record Mirror*, 8 January 1966

p102: '"See My Friends" I really liked', Shel Talmy interview with the author, 2011

p102: 'I got that idea from being in India', Ray Davies to *Rolling Stone*, November 1969

p104: 'He was an Irish Tenor', Alan O'Duffy interview with the author, 2011

p104: 'When I was about 12', Alan O'Duffy interview with the author, 2011

p104: 'The first band', Alan O'Duffy interview with the author, 2011

p104: 'I remember that the playback', Alan O'Duffy interview with the author, 2011

p105: 'I was the new boy', Alan O'Duffy interview with the author, 2011

p105: 'Shel Talmy was the first man', Alan O'Duffy interview with the author, 2011

p105: 'We didn't do many takes', Alan O'Duffy interview with the author, 2011

p106: 'Nicky Hopkins looked so thin', Ray Davies to *The New York Times*, 1 January 1995

p106: 'We all, with the exception of Mick', Pete Quaife to *Jukebox*, May 2006

p106: 'Rasa is a very sore point with me', Pete Quaife to *Jukebox*, May 2006

p106: 'She used to fancy herself', said Dave Davies to *Record Collector*, November 2012

p107: 'This mad, druggy New Yorker', Ray Davies to *Magnet*, summer 2008

p107: 'At this time', Pete Quaife to *Jukebox*, May 2006

p108: 'Everyone had roots in England', Mick Avory interview with the author, 2011

Chapter 9

p110: 'I got pissed off with him', Ray Davies to *Ugly Things*, summer 2010

p110: 'A terrible brawl, I kicked him', Ray Davies to *Ugly Things*, summer 2010

p110: 'That guitar clanging at the beginning', Pete Quaife to *Mojo '60s, Issue 2*

p111: 'It was a fairly straight-forward recording', Alan O'Duffy interview with the author, 2011

p111: 'There's a lot of venom in that song', Ray Davies to *Magnet* magazine, summer 2008

p111: '[I would dress up] with these girls', Mick Avory to *Record Collector*, November 2012

p111: 'I came up with a line, a riff or two', Dave Davies writing in *Kink*

p113: 'If I'd made contact', Ray Davies to *Ugly Things*, summer 2010

p113: 'Ray was on the razor edge', Allan McDougall in *Kinks Kronikles*, 1985

p113: 'Stuck in England I just wanted to write for us', Ray Davies to Sky Arts TV, 2010

p114: 'At the time I wrote "Sunny Afternoon"', Ray Davies to *Rolling Stone,* November 1969

p114: 'I didn't exclude adults from my audience', Ray Davies to *Music Connection,* 1996

p114: 'Nothing was really planned', David Quaife interview with the author, 2011

p115: 'I always wanted to be a mod', David Quaife interview with the author, 2011

p116: 'I had some pads made up my', Mick Avory interview with the author, 2011

p116: 'I started to play and sing', Dave Davies writing in *Kink*

p116: '"Sunny Afternoon" was made very quickly', Ray Davies to *Rolling Stone*, November 1969

p117: 'A lot of the time Shel wasn't too fussy', Mick Avory interview with the author, 2011

p117: 'The accident was the crescendo', David Quaife interview with the author, 2011

p118 'I went to the same school as Cliff Richard', John Dalton interview with the author, 2011

p119: 'I remember a film coming out', John Dalton interview with the author, 2011

p119: 'I was at a party', John Dalton interview with the author, 2011

p119: 'We had a road manager', John Dalton interview with the author, 2011

p119: 'I said I can't play with a band like that', John Dalton interview with the author, 2011 p120: 'I just went to the audition and it was awful', John Dalton interview with the author, 2011

p120: 'Wace and Collins were very very funny', John Dalton interview with the author, 2011

p120: 'I think it was the get-out', John Dalton interview with the author, 2011

p122: 'He didn't like it, having time off', David Quaife interview with the author, 2011

p122: 'Pete was a bit of a strange character', Mick Avory to *Record Collector*, November 2012

p123: 'Making good music', Shel Talmy interview with the author, 2011

p123: '[It was] inspired partly by', Ray Davies to *The New York Times*, January 1 1995

p123: 'I liked *Face to Face*', Mick Avory to *Record Collector*, November 2012

p124: 'We allowed ourselves to experiment', Ray Davies to *Record Collector*, October 2012

p124: 'I didn't like that sleeve', Ray Davies in *The Kinks: The Official Biography*, 1984

p125: 'I'd got on very well with the band', John Dalton interview with the author, 2011

p125: 'That accident had smashed me up quite badly', Pete Quaife to *Jukebox*, May 2006

p125: 'I've been away all this time',

Pete Quaife to the *New Musical Express*, 3 December 1966

p125: 'I don't like it when', Ray Davies to *Record Mirror*, 28 October 1967

p126: 'I wasn't overly impressed with him', Ray Davies to *Record Collector*, October 2012

p126: 'I liked Shel and I remember', Dave Davies to *Record Collector*, November 2012

p127: 'I'm very proud', Shel Talmy to *Sound on Sound*, September 2009

Chapter 10

p132: '*Kelvin Hall* was done three-track', Alan O'Duffy interview with the author, 2011

p133: 'I got so upset about not going', Ray Davies to *Ugly Things*, summer 2010

p134: 'One of my memories is the Wimpy bar', Alan O'Duffy interview with the author, 2011

p134: 'I was only 17 or something', Alan O'Duffy interview with the author, 2011

p135: 'It painted a picture', Mick Avory to *Uncut*, January 2009

p136: 'They had a tack piano', Alan O'Duffy interview with the author, 2011

p137: 'There was a boy called Denton', Ray Davies to *Ugly Things*, summer 2010

p137: 'I suppose I tend to be rather

cruel to my friends', Ray
Davies to *New Musical Express*, 4
November 1967

p138: '[You] have to arrive at 9 a.m.',
Pete Quaife to *Record Mirror*,
1965

p139: 'I like autumn things',
Ray Davies to *Rolling Stone*,
November 1969

p139: 'It's a miniature movie',
Andy Partridge to *Musician*
magazine, May, 1997

p140: 'Pete was outgoing like me',
Dave Davies to the *Mojo* blog,
2010

Chapter 11

p142: 'I played football with him
a few times', Keith Altham
interview with the author,
2011

p143: '"Wonderboy" was horrible',
Pete Quaife in Andy Miller's
book, *The Kinks Are the Village
Green Preservation Society*, 2003

p143: 'In that song is all the
layers', Ray Davies to *Mojo*,
September 2012

p144: 'I said, "Don't be an
arsehole"', Ray Davies to *Ugly
Things*, summer 2010

p146: 'I wrote it to be a flop', Ray
Davies to Sky Arts TV, 2010

p146: 'I wanted it to be *Under Milk
Wood*', Ray Davies to *Rolling
Stone*,
10 November 1969

p146: 'Making that album was the

high point of my career', Pete
Quaife to *Jukebox*, May 2006

p146: 'It was more collaborative',
Mick Avory in 2004 CD liner
notes

p146: 'I was freelance', Barrie
Wentzell interview with the
author, 2011

p147: 'I didn't know at the time',
Barrie Wentzell interview
with the author, 2011

p147: 'There was no wall or
distance', Barrie Wentzell
interview with the author,
2011

p150: 'I wrote for the way
something should sound',
Ray Davies to *Magnet*,
summer 2008

p150: 'I had the whole idea of the
record in my head', Ray
Davies in 2004 CD liner notes

p150: 'I stood around the piano',
Ray Davies to *Record Collector*,
October 2012

p150: 'On "Wicked Annabella"',
Mick Avory to *Record Collector*,
November 2012

p151: 'I was upset', Ray Davies
interview from an unknown
source

p151: 'It was so Ray', Keith Altham
interview with the author,
2011

p151: 'For me, *Village Green
Preservation Society*', Pete
Townshend in 2004 CD liner
notes

Chapter 12

p154: 'Ray always had that', Keith Altham interview with the author, 2011

p154: 'Pete and I never sat down', Dave Davies to *Mojo* blog, July 2010

p154: 'I know from our discussions', Jeff Bailey interview with the author, 2010

p155: 'Pete did enjoy the band', Jeff Bailey interview with the author, 2010

p155: 'Peter liked his Scotch', Stan Endersby to the *Toronto Globe and Mail*, 1 July 2010

p156: 'I used to drive a little bit for them', David Quaife interview with the author, 2011

p156: 'As *Village Green Preservation Society*', Pete Quaife to *Jukebox*, May 2006

p156: 'Beden's family was paying for everything', David Quaife interview with the author, 2011

p156: 'I stayed in his bedsit', David Quaife interview with the author, 2011

p157: 'Ray asked me if I could get John Dalton', Mick Avory interview with the author, 2011

p157: 'I never had a contract', John Dalton interview with the author, 2011

p158: 'I decided to make it about

one person', Ray Davies to *Rolling Stone*, 10 November 1969

p158: 'That gave us the opportunity', Ray Davies in 2011 CD liner notes

p159: 'I liked the idea of brass', Ray Davies to *Record Collector*, October 2012

p160: 'I played "Shangri-La"', Ray Davies to *Rolling Stone*, 10 November 1969

p161: 'I was disappointed, but not devastated', Ray Davies in 2011 CD liner notes

p163: 'We're presently planning', Dave Davies to *Rolling Stone*, 27 December 1969

p163: 'I've been overwhelmed with the response', said Ray Davies to *New Musical Express* 29 November 1969

p164: 'I was bringing up a family', John Dalton to *Record Collector*, November 2012

Chapter 13

p166: 'He was great to me', Keith Altham interview with the author, 2011

p167: '"Plastic Man" was my death knell', Ray Davies to *Record Collector*, October 2012

p168: 'We used the piano so much on the records', Mick Avory interview with the author, 2011

p168: 'We found a keyboard player

in a church', John Dalton interview with the author, 2011

p168: 'I was taught by a vicious old crone', John Gosling interview with the author, 2011

p168: 'We were inspired to do that', John Gosling interview with the author, 2011

p169: 'I also played a few well-known Tube stations', John Gosling interview with the author, 2011

p169: 'Grenville Collins and Robert Wace were like', John Gosling interview with the author, 2011

p169: 'Ray was friendly but guarded', John Gosling interview with the author, 2011

p169: 'We put down several', John Gosling to the Kast Off Kinks website

p169: 'It was certainly an education', John Gosling to the Kast Off Kinks website

p170: 'I wore the whole [gorilla] suit', John Gosling interview with the author, 2011

p170: 'I've always been a great believer', John Gosling to the Kast Off Kinks website

p170: 'John [Dalton] is a great bass player', John Gosling interview with the author, 2011

p170: 'We'd always used keyboards',

John Gosling interview with the author, 2011

p171: 'Grenville said, "This has got to stop"', Mick Avory in, *You Really Got Me*, 2011

p173: 'Ken was king of the roadies', John Gosling interview with the author, 2011

p173: 'In the studio', John Dalton interview with the author, 2011

p173: 'Somebody came up to us', Ray Davies to *New Musical Express*, unconfirmed date, 1973

p175: 'I didn't see the funny side of that at all', Robert Wace to Johnny Rogan, June 1982

Chapter 14

p177: 'I felt stranded', Dave Davies in *You Really Got Me*, 2011

p177: 'I'd always been into The Kinks', Brian Wilcock interview with the author, 2010

p178: 'That was one of the most chaotic gigs', John Gosling interview with the author, 2011

p178: 'The following night in Providence', John Gosling interview with the author, 2011

p178: 'Internally and spiritually', Dave Davies in *You Really Got Me*, 2011

p179: 'The Scrap came on the road', John Gosling interview with the author, 2011 p179: 'What a great bunch of blokes', John Gosling interview with the author, 2011

p179: 'At the end of our Australian tour', John Gosling interview with the author, 2011

p180: 'We just signed a deal with RCA', Ray Davies to *RockBill*, May 1988.

p180: 'Recording sessions in the early', John Gosling to the Kast Off Kinks website

p181: 'I would come up with the odd intro', John Gosling to the Kast Off Kinks website

p182: 'It is as difficult as it looks', John Gosling to the Kast Off Kinks website

p184: 'I wake up reasonably early', Ray Davies to *Record Mirror*, 8 January 1972

p185: 'The three-man brass line-up', Mick Avory to *New Musical Express*, 2 September 1972

p185: 'We all went to see Elvis', John Gosling to the Kast Off Kinks website

p188: 'That was a big, big turning point', Dave Davies in *You Really Got Me*, 2011

p188: 'Ken Jones, an old friend', Dinky Dawson to *Crawdaddy!*, 20 May 2009

p188: 'Ken and I went at it for a few minutes', Dinky Dawson to *Crawdaddy!*, 20 May 2009

p189: 'Just before the sound check',

Dinky Dawson to *Crawdaddy!*, 20 May 2009

p190: 'I'd always been the one', Dave Davies to *Record Collector*, November 2012

p190: 'It used to be a tobacco warehouse', Mick Avory to *Record Collector*, November 2012

p191: 'Once Konk was operational', John Gosling to the Kast Off Kinks website

p191: 'Inevitably things took more time', Mick Avory to *Record Collector*, November 2012

p191: 'We spent a lot of time in there', John Dalton to *Record Collector*, November 2012

p191: 'I didn't think it was necessary', Mick Avory interview with the author, 2011

p192: 'It was an exciting idea', John Gosling interview with the author, 2011

Chapter 15

p193: 'I was there with Roy Hollingsworth', Barrie Wentzell interview with the author, 2011

p194: 'I came to London in 1972', Debi Doss interview with the author, 2011

p194: 'It was a bad time, of course', Ray Davies to *Record Review* magazine, April 1996

p195: 'I really felt I was getting',

Rasa Davies in *The Kinks: The Official Biography*, 1984

p196: 'We all had to pretend', John Gosling in *Well Respected Men*, 2002

p196: 'That's when it almost became', Mick Avory to *Mojo*, March 2006

p196: 'On *Preservation*, Mr Black overthrows', Ray Davies to *Mojo*, March 2006

p196: 'I miss the Cold War', Ray Davies to *Mojo*, March 2006

p197: 'I loved The Kinks', Maryann Price interview with the author, 2011

p197: 'I saw a little bit of the show', Maryann Price interview with the author, 2011

p198: 'He addressed it to Maryann Price', Maryann Price interview with the author, 2011

p198: 'I called the number', Maryann Price interview with the author, 2011

p198: 'I was on stage as window dressing', Maryann Price interview with the author, 2011

p199: 'I was an old hand', Maryann Price interview with the author, 2011

p199: 'Pam was easy as pie', Maryann Price interview with the author, 2011

p199: 'They communicated in the studio', Maryann Price interview with the author, 2011

p200: 'John Gosling was a loveable drunk', Maryann Price interview with the author, 2011

p200: 'My husband was in California', Maryann Price interview with the author, 2011

p201: '*Preservation* is about what a mass of people will do', Ray Davies to *Circus* magazine, 1974

p201: 'We'd have a load of strangers on stage', John Gosling interview with the author, 2011

p201: 'Tony brought Ray', Claire Hammill interview with the author, 2010

p202: 'I had no intention of moving', Claire Hammill interview with the author, 2010

p202: 'Ray sang backing vocals', Claire Hammill interview with the author, 2010

p203: 'Like the whole of my generation', Dougie Squires interview with the author, 2011

p203: 'I was given the tape', Dougie Squires interview with the author, 2011

p203: 'June Ritchie was a joy', Dougie Squires interview with the author, 2011

p203: 'I hated the whole experience', John Gosling to the Kast Off Kinks website

p204: 'I hung around with some

guys', Brian Wilcock interview with the author, 2010

p204: 'Tony was keen', Brian Wilcock interview with the author, 2010

p205: 'I was just there', Brian Wilcock interview with the author, 2010

p205: 'In those days', Brian Wilcock interview with the author, 2010

p206: 'I answered ads in *Melody Maker*', Shirlie Roden interview with the author, 2010

Chapter 16

p207: 'John Gosling and Dave Davies were', Shirlie Roden interview with the author, 2010

p207: 'I was nervous', Shirlie Roden interview with the author, 2010

p207: 'Konk Studios seemed very dark', Debi Doss interview with the author, 2010

p208: 'There was no written music', Shirlie Roden interview with the author, 2010

p208: 'It was great fun', Shirlie Roden interview with the author, 2010

p210: 'The band was really tight', Ray Davies to *Mojo*, September 2012

p208: 'It was terribly exciting',

Debi Doss interview with the author, 2011

p208: 'If we were lucky', Debi Doss interview with the author, 2011

p209: 'I recall the drive from the airport', Shirlie Roden interview with the author, 2010

p209: 'I was so nervous', Debi Doss interview with the author, 2011

p210: 'We had a lot of quick costume change things', Shirlie Roden interview with the author, 2010

p211: 'Ray was brilliant at connecting', Shirlie Roden interview with the author, 2010

p211: 'He was thoughtfully concerned', Dave Davies in *Kink*, 1996

p212: 'My first impression of Baptist', Shirlie Roden interview with the author, 2010

p212: 'Baptist would always go to throw', Debi Doss interview with the author, 2011

p213: 'Mick Avory had an air of stability', Shirlie Roden interview with the author, 2010

p213: 'Ken Jones would always have us up', Debi Doss interview with the author, 2011

p213: 'Occasionally, we got the best limo', Shirlie Roden

interview with the author, 2010

p214: 'The atmosphere could become tense', Shirlie Roden interview with the author, 2010

p214: 'My main and overriding impression', Shirlie Roden interview with the author, 2010

p214: 'Dave could be a pain in the ass', Shirlie Roden interview with the author, 2010

p215: 'Mick knew which side', Dave Davies in *Kink*, 1996

p215: 'Once those wretched shows took', John Gosling to the Kast Off Kinks website

p215: 'In later years I learned', Shirlie Roden interview with the author, 2010

p216: 'I've never really liked any blend', John Gosling interview with the author, 2011

p216: 'Ray could be talkative', Shirlie Roden interview with the author, 2010

p216: "I feel much better about myself", Ray Davies to *Crawdaddy!*, 1975

p219: 'Ray cast me as "Jack, the Idiot Dunce"', Debi Doss interview with the author, 2011

p220: 'You can't really be another English band', Shirlie Roden interview with the author, 2010

p221: 'I had a big blow-up with Ray', Shirlie Roden interview with the author, 2010

p221: 'Childish, isn't it?' Shirlie Roden interview with the author, 2010

p221: 'It had been a particularly disorganised day', Shirlie Roden interview with the author, 2010

p222: 'Pam sat there silently for a moment', Shirlie Roden interview with the author, 2010

Chapter 17

p225: 'Clive said, "You have a great"', Ray Davies to *Mojo*, March 2006

p225: 'Clive is a genius', Dave Davies to *Mojo*, March 2006

p226: 'My first child arrived', John Dalton interview with the author, 2011

p226: 'I don't know who else', Andy Pyle interview with the author, 2011

p227: 'Everyone had their turn', Andy Pyle interview with the author, 2011

p227: 'We came off stage after a good gig', Shirlie Roden interview with the author, 2010

p228: 'Baptist was sat at the piano', Shirlie Roden interview with the author, 2010

p228: 'I went inside our "on stage"', Shirlie Roden interview with the author, 2010 p231: 'We rehearsed and held auditions', John Gosling to the Kast Off Kinks website

p231: 'It didn't happen quite the way I'd hoped', John Gosling interview with the author, 2011

p231: 'It was a very difficult', John Gosling interview with the author, 2011

p231: 'I never wanted to cramp Dave's style', John Gosling to the Kast Off Kinks website

p232: 'Dave and I haven't communicated', John Gosling to the Kast Off Kinks website

p233: 'They knew they could never attack', Ray Davies to *RockBill*, May 1988

p233: 'Johnny Rotten came to Konk once', Ray Davies to *Vox*, January 1993

p234: 'Tom Petty always seemed so aloof', Dave Davies in *Kink*, 1996

p235: 'My whole life was turned around', John Rollo interview with the author, 2010

p235: 'This was before they recorded *Misfits*', John Rollo interview with the author, 2010

p235: 'They just said build it up as a studio', John Rollo interview with the author, 2010

p235: '[It had a] big Neve board', John Rollo interview with the author, 2010

p235: 'The album before was

beautifully recorded', John Rollo interview with the author, 2010

p236: 'Dave had incredible natural instincts', John Rollo interview with the author, 2010

p236: 'Nancy and I shared many unusual', Dave Davies in *Kink*, 1996

p236: 'They were all very good', John Rollo interview with the author, 2010

p237: 'It was the most amazing time for me', John Rollo interview with the author, 2010

p237: '*Low Budget* was overtly in the London vernacular', Ray Davies to *Mojo*, September 2012

p237: 'Ray's writing was too subtle', Mick Avory interview with the author, 2011

p238: 'I think we appreciated it more', Ray Davies to *Record Collector*, January 2008

p238: 'When you've got', Dave Davies in *Kink*, 1996

p238: 'I went back to running', John Rollo interview with the author, 2010

p238: 'They used Showco, who did the sound', John Rollo interview with the author, 2010

p239: 'At the end of the album', John Rollo interview with the author, 2010

p239: 'The first couple of songs', John Rollo interview with the author, 2010

p240: 'I felt really pissed off', Ray Davies to *Goldmine* magazine, 1 March 1996

Chapter 18

p244: 'Good art isn't always', Dave Davies to *Classic Rock*, August 2010

p250: 'She was someone who was on a journey', Ray Davies to *Uncut*, September 2004

p251: 'I didn't sign them up to anything', Keith Altham interview with the author, 2011

p251: 'They rang me up', Keith Altham interview with the author, 2011

p251: 'I tried to get as sympathetic a response', Keith Altham interview with the author, 2011

p252: 'My relationship with Ray', Keith Altham interview with the author, 2011

p252: 'The situation between Dave and Mick', Ray Davies to *Record Collector*, January 2008

p252: 'I said to Mick', Ray Davies to *Record Collector*, January 2008

p252: 'I had about six years of arenas', Mick Avory interview with the author, 2011

p252: 'I was part of the company', Mick Avory interview with the author, 2011

p255: 'The doctor said', Ray Davies

quoted in the *Sun*, 20 April 1990

p255: 'By the late 1980s I had my own studio', Alan O'Duffy interview with the author, 2011

p266: 'There was a fantastic fellow', Alan O'Duffy interview with the author, 2011

p256: 'They could take as long as they'd want', Alan O'Duffy interview with the author, 2011

Chapter 19

p258: 'I didn't like it at first', Dave Davies on the Bio Channel

p259: 'I got to the Hall of Fame dinner', Ray Davies to *Goldmine* magazine, 1 March 1996

p259: 'They called us up', Mick Avory interview with the author, 2011

p261: 'The first song we worked on', Dave Davies to *Record Review* magazine, April 1996

p262: 'I did a lot of overdubs', John Rollo interview with the author, 2010

p262: 'That was the most', Ray Davies to *Rolling Stone*, 13 May 1994

p263: 'I thought our last album we did', Ray Davies to *Goldmine* magazine, 1 March 1996

p263: 'I came up with the idea of me', Ray Davies to *Goldmine* magazine, 1 March 1996

p263: 'People think X-*Ray* is
fiction', Ray Davies to *Mojo*,
September 2012

p264: 'The big thrill for me is
that', Ray Davies to *Goldmine*
magazine, 1 March 1996

p264: 'The only real writing I'd
done', Dave Davies to *Record
Review*, April 1996

p264: 'I set up all these meetings',
Dave Davies to *Record Review*,
April 1996

p265: 'When he got into difficult
areas', Dave Davies to *Record
Review*, April 1996

p265: 'The whole process of
writing', Dave Davies to
Record Review, April 1996

p265: 'I probably shouldn't tell you
this', Dave Davies to *Record
Review*, April 1996

p266: 'We're trying to make it', Ray
Davies to the *New York Post*,
November 1997

p267: 'It is what it is', Ray Davies to
Island Ear, 5 February 1996

p268: 'Not many people know this',
Ray Davies to *Mojo* magazine,
September 2012

p269: 'Being shot in a Johannesburg
shanty town', Ray Davies to
Uncut, May 2006

p269: 'The day I had to go to
court', Ray Davies to *Uncut*,
December 2010

p269: 'It was a wake-up call', Dave
Davies to *Uncut*, December
2010

p270: 'The doctors told me', Dave

Davies to the *Daily Mail*, 10
October 2006

p270: 'Nearly 18 months after my
stroke', Dave Davies to the
Daily Mail, 10 October 2006

p270: 'What a load of bollocks',
Dave Davies to the *Sunday
Express*, 4 December 2005

Chapter 20

p273: 'Having lost three years
recovering', Ray Davies to
the *Independent*, 19 June 2009

p274: 'It's lonely', Ray Davies on
Songbook, Sky Arts TV, 2009

p275: 'When you break things
down', Ray Davies to *Record
Collector*, July 2009

p276: 'My hope is that', Pete Quaife
to *Rejected Quarterly*, Issue 8

p277: 'It made me realise how little
I knew him', Ray Davies to
Uncut, December 2010

p277: 'Pete was extremely good
at hiding', David Quaife
interview with the author,
2011

p277: 'Pete and I kept in touch',
Jeff Bailey interview with the
author, 2010

p277: '[Pete] knocked on my door',
David Quaife interview with
the author, 2011

p278: 'He did fairly well in Canada',
David Quaife interview with
the author, 2011

p278: 'Ray doesn't want to do it
without me', Mick Avory in
Uncut, September 2004

p278: 'He'd called up Elisabeth', David Quaife interview with the author, 2011

p279: 'I wanted to acknowledge', Ray Davies to *Uncut*, December 2010

p280: 'We were going to play in America', Mick Avory interview with the author, 2011

p281: 'I was surrounded by Ray's stuff', Johnny Borrell to the *New Musical Express*, 21 August 2004

p282: 'There is more good than bad', Ray Davies to the *Big Issue*, 13 June 2011

p282: 'I don't see anything wrong', Dave Davies to *Magnet*, Summer 2008

p282: 'You know Dave did', Ray Davies to *Uncut*, February 2013

p282: 'I've always loved the idea', Dave Davies to *Record Collector*, November 2012

p283: 'abstract and motivated', Ray Davies to *Uncut*, February 2013

p283: 'How could I not love my own brother?', Dave Davies to the *Daily Telegraph*, 12 October 2011

Bibliography

Listed below are the editions of the books that I referred to during the preparation of this biography. Some were more useful than others, but all were worthwhile in their different ways:

Ackroyd, Peter. *London: The Biography*. Vintage, London, 2001

Crampton, Luke and Rees, Dafydd. *Rock & Pop, Year by Year*. Dorling Kindersley, London, 2003

Davies, Dave. *Kink*. Boxtree, London, 1996

Davies, Ray. *Waterloo Sunset*. Viking, London, 1997

Davies, Ray. *X-Ray*. The Overlook Press, New York, 2007

Erlewine, Michael, et al. Eds. *All Music Guide*. Miller Freeman Books, San Francisco, 1997

Gay, Ken. *Muswell Hill*. Tempus, Stroud, 2002
——*Muswell Hill Revisited*. The History Press, Stroud, 2009

Hasted, Nick. *You Really Got Me*. Omnibus Press, London, 2011

Heylin, Clinton. *All The Madmen*. Constable, London, 2012

Hinman, Doug. *All Day And All Of The Night: Day-by-day concerts, recordings and broadcasts,1961-1996*. Backbeat, San Francisco, 2004

Kilgarriff, Michael. *Grace, Beauty & Banjos*. Oberon Books, London, 1999

Kitts, Thomas M.. *Ray Davies: Not Like Everybody Else*. Routledge, New York, 2008

Marten, Neville and Hudson, Jeff. *The Kinks: Well Respected Men*. Sanctuary, London, 2001

Mendelssohn, John. *The Kinks Kronikles*. Quill, New York, 1985

Miller, Andy. *The Kinks Are The Village Green Preservation Society*. Continuum, London, 2003

Quaife, Peter. *Veritas Volume 1*. Hiren, Herts, 2011

Rogan, Johnny. *The Kinks: A Mental Institution*. Proteus, London, 1984
    —*The Complete Guide to the Music of The Kinks*. Omnibus Press, London, 1998

Romanowski, Patricia and George-Warren, Holly, Eds. *The New Rolling Stone Encyclopedia of Rock & Roll*. Fireside, New York, 1995

Savage, Jon. *The Kinks: The Official Biography*. Faber and Faber, London, 1984

Schwitzer, Joan and Gay, Ken. *Highgate and Muswell Hill*. Tempus, Stroud, 2006

Shearman, Colin (Intro.). *The Kinks: Virgin Modern Icon Series*. Virgin, London, 1997

Discography

For a band like The Kinks, whose career spanned almost half a century, a worldwide discography could easily fill a book by itself. Below you will find details of their studio and live albums and a selection of significant compilations, accompanied by the original and most-recent track listings for each.

Kinks Studio Albums

Kinks
Original 1964 track list:
Beautiful Delilah / So Mystifying / Just Can't Go to Sleep / Long Tall Shorty / I Took My Baby Home / I'm a Lover Not a Fighter / Cadillac / Bald Headed Woman / Revenge / Too Much Monkey Business / I've Been Driving On Bald Mountain / Stop Your Sobbing / Got Love If You Want It

Two-disc 2011 re-issue:
Disc 1: Beautiful Delilah / So Mystifying / Just Can't Go to Sleep / Long Tall Shorty / I Took My Baby Home / I'm a Lover Not a Fighter / You Really Got Me (alt. Mix) / Cadillac / Bald Headed Woman / Revenge / Too Much Monkey Business / I've Been Driving On Bald Mountain / Stop Your Sobbing / Got Love If You Want It / I Believed You / I'm a

Hog for You Baby / I Don't Need You Anymore / Everybody's Gonna Be Happy / Long Tall Sally / You Still Want Me / You Do Something to Me / It's Alright / All Day and All of the Night / I Gotta Move / Louie, Louie / I've Got That Feeling / I Gotta Go Now / Things Are Getting Better

Disc 2: (first 14 tracks in mono) Beautiful Delilah / So Mystifying / Just Can't Go to Sleep / Long Tall Shorty / I Took My Baby Home / I'm a Lover Not a Fighter / Cadillac / Bald Headed Woman / Revenge / Too Much Monkey Business / I've Been Driving On Bald Mountain / Stop Your Sobbing / Got Love If You Want It / Don't Ever Let Me Go / I Don't Need You Anymore / Bald Headed Woman (mono) / Too Much Monkey Business (Alt.) / Got Love If You Want It (Alt.) / "Meet the Kinks" (BBC intro) / Cadillac (live at BBC) / "Ray Talks About 'You Really Got Me'" (live at BBC) / You Really Got Me (live at BBC) / Little Queenie (live at BBC) / I'm a Lover Not a Fighter (live at BBC) / All Day and All of the Night (live at BBC) / "Ray Talks About the USA" (BBC Interview) / I've Got That Feeling (live at BBC)

Kinda Kinks
Original 1965 track list:

Look for Me Baby / Got My Feet on the Ground / Nothin' in the World Can Stop Me Worryin' 'Bout That Girl / Naggin' Woman / Wonder Where My Baby Is Tonight / Tired of Waiting for You / Dancing in the Street / Don't Ever Change / Come On Now / So Long / You Shouldn't Be Sad / Something Better Beginning

Two-disc 2011 re-issue:

Disc 1: (all mono) Look for Me Baby / Got My Feet on the Ground / Nothin' in the World Can Stop Me Worryin' 'Bout That Girl / Naggin' Woman / Wonder Where My Baby Is Tonight / Tired of Waiting for You / Dancing in the Street / Don't Ever Change / Come On Now / So Long / You Shouldn't Be Sad / Something Better Beginning

Disc 2: (first ten tracks in mono) Ev'rybody's Gonna Be Happy / Who'll Be the Next in Line / Set Me Free / I Need You / See My Friends / Never Met a Girl Like You Before / A Well Respected Man / Such a Shame / Wait Till the Summer Comes Along / Don't You Fret / I Go to Sleep (Demo) / When I See That Girl of Mine (Demo) / Tell Me Now So I'll

Know (Demo) / A Little Bit of Sunlight (Demo) / There's a New World Just Opening for Me (Demo) / This I Know (Demo) / See My Friends (Alt.) / Come On Now (Alt.) / You Shouldn't Be Sad (live at BBC) / Tired of Waiting for You (live at BBC) / Ev'rybody's Gonna Be Happy (live at BBC) / This Strange Effect (live at BBC) / Hide and Seek (live at BBC)

The Kink Kontroversy

Original 1965 track list:

Milk Cow Blues / Ring the Bells / Gotta Get the First Plane Home / When I See That Girl of Mine / I Am Free / Till the End of the Day / The World Keeps Going Round / I'm on an Island / Where Have All the Good Times Gone / It's Too Late / What's in Store for Me / You Can't Win

Two-disc 2011 re-issue:

Disc 1: (all mono) Milk Cow Blues / Ring the Bells / Gotta Get the First Plane Home / When I See That Girl of Mine / I Am Free / Till the End of the Day / The World Keeps Going Round / I'm on an Island / Where Have All the Good Times Gone / It's Too Late / What's in Store for Me / You Can't Win

Disc 2: Dedicated Follower of Fashion (mono) / Sittin' on My Sofa (mono) / I'm Not Like Everybody Else (mono) / Mr. Reporter (outtake) / Dedicated Follower of Fashion (alt.) / Time Will Tell (outtake) / And I Will Love You / I'm Not Like Everybody Else (alt.) / All Night Stand (demo) / Milk Cow Blues (live at BBC) / "Ray Talks About Song writing" / Never Met A Girl Like You Before (live at BBC) / Wonder Where My Baby is Tonight (live at BBC) / "Pete Talks About Records" / Till The End of The Day (live at BBC) / A Well Respected Man (live at BBC) / Where Have All The Good Times Gone (live at BBC)

Face To Face

Original 1966 track list:

Party Line / Rosie Won't You Please Come Home / Dandy / Too Much on My Mind / Session Man / Rainy Day in June / A House in the Country / Holiday in Waikiki / Most Exclusive Residence for Sale / Fancy / Little Miss Queen of Darkness / You're Lookin' Fine / Sunny Afternoon / I'll Remember

Two-disc 2011 re-issue:

Disc 1: (tracks 1 – 18 in mono) Party Line / Rosie Won't You Please Come Home / Dandy / Too Much on My Mind / Session Man / Rainy Day in June / A House in the Country / Holiday in Waikiki / Most Exclusive Residence for Sale / Fancy / Little Miss Queen of Darkness / You're Lookin' Fine / Sunny Afternoon / I'll Remember / Dead End Street / Big Black Smoke / This Where I Belong / She's Got Everything / Little Miss Queen of Darkness (alt.) / Dead End Street (alt.)

Disc 2: Party Line / Rosie Won't You Please Come Home / Dandy / Too Much on My Mind / Session Man / Rainy Day in June / A House in the Country / Holiday in Waikiki / Most Exclusive Residence for Sale / Fancy / Little Miss Queen of Darkness / You're Lookin' Fine / Sunny Afternoon / I'll Remember / This Where I Belong / Big Black Smoke / She's Got Everything / You're Looking Fine (alt.) / Sunny Afternoon (alt.) / Fancy (alt.) / Little Miss Queen of Darkness (alt.) / Dandy (alt.)

Something Else
Original 1967 track list:
David Watts / Death of a Clown / Two Sisters / No Return / Harry Rag / Tin Soldier Man / Situation Vacant / Love Me Till the Sun Shines / Lazy Old Sun / Afternoon Tea / Funny Face / End of the Season / Waterloo Sunset

Two-disc 2011 re-issue:

Disc 1: (original mono album) David Watts / Death of a Clown / Two Sisters / No Return / Harry Rag / Tin Soldier Man / Situation Vacant / Love Me Till the Sun Shines / Lazy Old Sun / Afternoon Tea / Funny Face / End of the Season / Waterloo Sunset / Act Nice and Gentle / Mr. Pleasant / Susannah's Still Alive / Harry Rag (Alt.) / David Watts (Alt.) / Afternoon Tea (Alt. Mono) / Sunny Afternoon (live on BBC) / Autumn Almanac (live at BBC) / Mr. Pleasant (live at BBC) / Susannah's Still Alive (live at BBC) / David Watts (live at BBC) / Love Me Till the Sun Shines (live at BBC) / Death of a Clown (live at BBC) / Good Luck Charm (live at BBC) / Harry Rag (live at BBC) / Little Women

Disc 2: David Watts / Death of a Clown / Two Sisters / No Return / Harry Rag / Tin Soldier Man / Situation Vacant / Love Me Till the Sun Shines / Lazy Old Sun / Afternoon Tea / Funny Face / End of the Season

/ Waterloo Sunset / Susannah's Still Alive / Autumn Almanac / Sand on My Shoes / Afternoon Tea (Alt.) / Mr. Pleasant (Alt.) / Lazy Old Sun (Alt.) / Funny Face (Alt.) / Afternoon Tea (Alt.) / Tin Soldier Man (Alt.)

The Kinks Are The Village Green Preservation Society
Original 1967 track list:

. The Village Green Preservation Society / Do You Remember Walter? / Picture Book / Johnny Thunder / Last of the Steam-powered Trains / Big Sky / Sitting by the Riverside / Animal Farm / Village Green / Starstruck / Phenomenal Cat / All of My Friends Were There / Wicked Annabella / Monica / People Take Pictures of Each Other

Three-disc 2004 re-issue:

Disc one: The Village Green Preservation Society / Do You Remember Walter? / Picture Book / Johnny Thunder / Last of the Steam-powered Trains / Big Sky / Sitting by the Riverside / Animal Farm / Village Green / Starstruck / Phenomenal Cat / All of My Friends Were There / Wicked Annabella / Monica / People Take Pictures of Each Other / Mr. Songbird / Days / Do You Remember Walter? / People Take Pictures of Each Other

Disc two: (mono) The Village Green Preservation Society / Do You Remember Walter? / Picture Book / Johnny Thunder / Last of the Steam-powered Trains / Big Sky / Sitting by the Riverside / Animal Farm / Village Green / Starstruck / Phenomenal Cat / All of My Friends Were There / Wicked Annabella / Monica / People Take Pictures of Each Other / Mr. Songbird / Days / Do You Remember Walter? / People Take Pictures of Each Other / Days / Mr. Songbird / Polly / Wonderboy / Berkeley Mews / Village Green (without strings)

Disc three: Village Green (with orchestral overdub) / Misty Water / Berkeley Mews / Easy Come, There You Went / Polly / Animal Farm (Alt.) / Phenomenal Cat (mono instrumental) / Johnny Thunder (remix) / Did You See His Name (mono) / Mick Avory's Underpants / Lavender Hill / Rosemary Rose / Wonderboy / Spotty Grotty Anna / Where Did My Spring Go / Groovie Movies / Creeping Jean / King Kong / Misty Water (mono) / Do You Remember Walter (BBC remix) / Animal Farm (BBC remix) / Days (BBC remix)

Arthur (Or The Decline and Fall of The British Empire)
Original 1969 track list:
   Victoria / Yes Sir, No Sir / Some Mother's Son / Drivin' / Brainwashed
   / Australia / Shangri-La / Mr. Churchill Says / She's Bought a Hat Like
   Princess Marina / Young and Innocent Days / Nothing to Say / Arthur

Two-disc 2011 re-issue:
   Disc 1: (tracks 1 – 18 in mono) Victoria / Yes Sir, No Sir / Some Mother's
   Son / Drivin' / Brainwashed / Australia / Shangri-La / Mr. Churchill Says
   / She's Bought a Hat Like Princess Marina / Young and Innocent Days /
   Nothing to Say / Arthur / Plastic Man / This Man He Weeps Tonight /
   Mindless Child of Motherhood / Creeping Jean / Lincoln County / Hold
   My Hand / Victoria (live at BBC) / Mr. Churchill Says (live at BBC) /
   Arthur (live at BBC)

   Disc 2: Victoria / Yes Sir, No Sir / Some Mother's Son / Drivin' /
   Brainwashed / Australia / Shangri-La / Mr. Churchill Says / She's Bought
   a Hat Like Princess Marina / Young and Innocent Days / Nothing to Say
   / Arthur / Plastic Man / This Man He Weeps Tonight // Plastic Man / This
   Man He Weeps Tonight / Drivin' (alt.) / Mindless Child of Motherhood
   / Hold My Hand (alt.) / Lincoln County / Mr. Shoemaker's Daughter /
   Mr. Reporter / Shangri La (backing track)

Lola vs. Powerman and the Moneygoround, Part One
Original 1970 track list:
   The Contenders / Strangers / Denmark Street / Get Back in Line / Lola
   / Top of the Pops / The Moneygoround / This Time Tomorrow / A Long
   Way From Home / Rats / Apeman / Powerman / Got to Be Free

2004 re-issue:
   The Contenders / Strangers / Denmark Street / Get Back in Line / Lola
   / Top of the Pops / The Moneygoround / This Time Tomorrow / A Long
   Way From Home / Rats / Apeman / Powerman / Got to Be Free / Lola /
   Apeman (demo) / Powerman (demo)

Percy
Original 1971 track list:
   God's Children / Lola (instrumental) / The Way Love Used to Be /
   Completely (instrumental) / Running Round Town (instrumental) /

Moments / Animals In The Zoo / Just Friends / Whip Lady (instrumental) / Dreams / Helga (instrumental) / Willesden Green / God's Children – End (instrumental)

2004 re-issue:

God's Children / Lola (instrumental) / The Way Love Used to Be / Completely (instrumental) / Running Round Town (instrumental) / Moments / Animals In The Zoo / Just Friends / Whip Lady (instrumental) / Dreams / Helga (instrumental) / Willesden Green / God's Children – End (instrumental) / Bonus mono mixes from the film: Dreams / Moments / The Way Love Used To Be / The Way Love Used To Be / The Way Love Used To Be

Muswell Hillbillies

Original 1971 track list:

20th Century Man / Acute Schizophrenia Paranoia Blues / Holiday / Skin and Bone / Alcohol / Complicated Life / Here Come the People in Grey / Have a Cuppa Tea / Holloway Jail / Oklahoma U.S.A./ Uncle Son / Muswell Hillbilly

2004 re-issue:

20th Century Man / Acute Schizophrenia Paranoia Blues / Holiday / Skin and Bone / Alcohol / Complicated Life / Here Come the People in Grey / Have a Cuppa Tea / Holloway Jail / Oklahoma U.S.A. / Uncle Son / Muswell Hillbilly / Mountain Woman / Kentucky Moon

Everybody's in Show-Biz

Original 1972 track list:

Here Comes Yet Another Day / Maximum Consumption / Unreal Reality / Hot Potatoes / Sitting in My Hotel / Motorway / You Don't Know My Name / Supersonic Rocket Ship / Look a Little on the Sunny Side / Celluloid Heroes / [the remaining tracks were recorded live at Carnegie Hall, New York on 2nd and 3rd March 1972] Top of the Pops / Brainwashed / Mr. Wonderful / Acute Schizophrenia Paranoia Blues / Holiday / Muswell Hillbilly / Alcohol / Banana Boat Song / Skin and Bone / Baby Face / Lola

2004 re-issue:

Here Comes Yet Another Day / Maximum Consumption / Unreal

Reality / Hot Potatoes / Sitting in My Hotel / Motorway / You Don't Know My Name / Supersonic Rocket Ship / Look a Little on the Sunny Side / Celluloid Heroes / [the remaining tracks were recorded live at Carnegie Hall, New York on 2nd and 3rd March 1972] Top of the Pops / Brainwashed / Mr. Wonderful / Acute Schizophrenia Paranoia Blues / Holiday / Muswell Hillbilly / Alcohol / Banana Boat Song / Skin and Bone / Baby Face / Lola / Till The End of The Day / She's Bought A Hat Like Princess Marina

Preservation Act I
Original 1973 track list:

Morning Song / Daylight / Sweet Lady Genevieve / There's a Change in the Weather / Where Are They Now? / One of the Survivors / Cricket / Money and Corruption / I Am Your Man / Here Comes Flash / Sitting in the Midday Sun / Demolition

2002 re-issue:

Preservation / Morning Song / Daylight / Sweet Lady Genevieve / There's a Change in the Weather / Where Are They Now? / One of the Survivors / Cricket / Money and Corruption / I Am Your Man / Here Comes Flash / Sitting in the Midday Sun / Demolition / One of the Survivors

Preservation Act II
Original 1974 track list:

Announcement / Introduction to Solution / When a Solution Comes / Money Talks / Announcement / Shepherds of the Nation / Scum of the Earth / Second-Hand Car Spiv / He's Evil / Mirror of Love / Announcement / Nobody Gives / Oh Where Oh Where Is Love? / Flash's Dream (The Final Elbow) / Flash's Confession / Nothing Lasts Forever / Announcement / Artificial Man / Scrapheap City / Announcement / Salvation Road

2004 re-issue:

Announcement / Introduction to Solution / When a Solution Comes / Money Talks / Announcement / Shepherds of the Nation / Scum of the Earth / Second-Hand Car Spiv / He's Evil / Mirror of Love / Announcement / Nobody Gives / Oh Where Oh Where Is Love? / Flash's Dream (The Final Elbow) / Flash's Confession / Nothing Lasts Forever / Announcement / Artificial Man / Scrapheap City / Announcement /

Salvation Road / Mirror of Love / Slum Kids (Take 1)

A Soap Opera
Original 1975 track list:

Everybody's a Star (Starmaker) / Ordinary People / Rush Hour Blues / Nine to Five / When Work Is Over / Have Another Drink / Underneath the Neon Sign / Holiday Romance / You Make It All Worthwhile / Ducks on the Wall / (A) Face in the Crowd / You Can't Stop the Music

2004 re-issue:

Everybody's a Star (Starmaker) / Ordinary People / Rush Hour Blues / Nine to Five / When Work Is Over / Have Another Drink / Underneath the Neon Sign / Holiday Romance / You Make It All Worthwhile / Ducks on the Wall / (A) Face in the Crowd / You Can't Stop the Music / Everybody's A Star (Starmaker) (mono) / Ordinary People (live) / You Make It All Worthwhile (live) / Underneath The Neon Sign (live)

Schoolboys in Disgrace
Original 1976 track list:

Schooldays / Jack the Idiot Dunce / Education / The First Time We Fall in Love / I'm in Disgrace / Headmaster / The Hard Way / The Last Assembly / No More Looking Back / Finale

[The 2004 CD re-issue had the same track list as the 1976 version of the album.]

Sleepwalker
Original 1977 track list:

Life on the Road / Mr. Big Man / Sleepwalker / Brother / Juke Box Music / Sleepless Night / Stormy Sky / Full Moon / Life Goes On

2004 re-issue:

Life on the Road / Mr. Big Man / Sleepwalker / Brother / Juke Box Music / Sleepless Night / Stormy Sky / Full Moon / Life Goes On / Artificial Light / Prince of the Punks / The Poseur / On the Outside (1977 mix) / On The Outside (1994 mix)

Misfits
Original 1978 track list:

Misfits / Hay Fever / Live Life / A Rock & Roll Fantasy / In a Foreign Land

/ Permanent Waves / Black Messiah / Out of the Wardrobe / Trust Your Heart / Get Up

2004 re-issue:

Misfits / Hay Fever / Live Life / A Rock & Roll Fantasy / In a Foreign Land / Permanent Waves / Black Messiah / Out of the Wardrobe / Trust Your Heart / Get Up / Black Messiah / Father Christmas / A Rock 'N' Roll Fantasy / Live Life

Low Budget
Original 1979 track list:

Attitude / Catch Me Now I'm Falling / Pressure / National Health / (Wish I Could Fly Like) Superman / Low Budget / In a Space / Little Bit of Emotion / A Gallon of Gas / Misery / Moving Pictures

2004 re-issue:

Attitude / Catch Me Now I'm Falling / Pressure / National Health / (Wish I Could Fly Like) Superman / Low Budget / In a Space / Little Bit of Emotion / A Gallon of Gas / Misery / Moving Pictures / A Gallon of Gas / Catch Me Now I'm Falling / (Wish I Could Fly Like) Superman

Give The People What They Want
Original 1981 track list:

Around the Dial / Give the People What They Want / Killer's Eyes / Predictable / Add It Up / Destroyer / Yo-Yo / Back to Front / Art Lover / A Little Bit of Abuse / Better Things

[The 2004 CD re-issue had the same track list as the 1981 version of the album.]

State Of Confusion
Original 1983 track list:

State of Confusion / Definite Maybe / Labour of Love / Come Dancing / Property / Don't Forget to Dance / Young Conservatives / Heart of Gold / Clichés of the World (B Movie) / Bernadette / Long Distance [on cassette copies]

2004 re-issue:

State of Confusion / Definite Maybe / Labour of Love / Come Dancing /

Property / Don't Forget to Dance / Young Conservatives / Heart of Gold / Clichés of the World (B Movie) / Bernadette / Don't Forget To Dance / Once A Thief / Long Distance / Noise

Word Of Mouth
Original 1984 track list:

Do It Again / Word of Mouth / Good Day / Living on a Thin Line / Sold Me Out / Massive Reductions / Guilty / Too Hot / Missing Persons / Summer's Gone / Going Solo

2004 re-issue:

Do It Again / Word of Mouth / Good Day / Living on a Thin Line / Sold Me Out / Massive Reductions / Guilty / Too Hot / Missing Persons / Summer's Gone / Going Solo / Good Day / Summer's Gone

Think Visual
Original 1986 track list:

Working at the Factory / Lost and Found / Repetition / Welcome to Sleazy Town / The Video Shop / Rock 'n' Roll Cities / How Are You? / Think Visual / Natural Gift / Killing Time / When You Were a Child

UK Jive
Original 1989 track list:

Aggravation / How Do I Get Close? / UK Jive / Now and Then / What Are We Doing? / Entertainment / War Is Over / Down All the Days (Till 1992) / Loony Balloon / Dear Margaret / Bright Lights / Perfect Strangers

Phobia
Original 1993 track list:

Opening / Wall of Fire / Drift Away / Still Searching / Phobia / Only a Dream / Don't / Babies / Over the Edge / Surviving / It's Alright (Don't Think About It) / Informer / Hatred (A Duet) / Somebody Stole My Car / Close to the Wire / Scattered / Did Ya

Kinks Live Albums

Live at Kelvin Hall
Original 1967 track list:

Till the End of the Day / A Well Respected Man / You're Lookin' Fine

/ Sunny Afternoon / Dandy / I'm On An Island / Come On Now / You Really Got Me / Medley: Milk Cow Blues-Batman Theme-Tired of Waiting for You

2004 re-issue:

(Tracks 1-9 in mono) Till the End of the Day / A Well Respected Man / You're Lookin' Fine / Sunny Afternoon / Dandy / I'm On An Island / Come On Now / You Really Got Me / Medley: Milk Cow Blues-Batman Theme-Tired of Waiting for You / (tracks 10-18 in stereo) Till the End of the Day / A Well Respected Man / You're Lookin' Fine / Sunny Afternoon / Dandy / I'm On An Island / Come On Now / You Really Got Me / Medley: Milk Cow Blues-Batman Theme-Tired of Waiting for You

One For The Road

Opening / Hard Way / Catch Me Now I'm Falling / Where Have All the Good Times Gone / Intro: Lola / Lola / Pressure / All Day and All of the Night / 20th Century Man / Misfits / Prince of the Punks / Stop Your Sobbing / Low Budget / Attitude / Superman / National Health / Till the End of the Day / Celluloid Heroes / You Really Got Me / Victoria / David Watts

Live: The Road

The Road / Destroyer / Apeman / Come Dancing / Art Lover / Clichés Of The World (B Movie) / Think Visual / Living On A Thin Line / Lost And Found / It (I Want It) / Around The Dial / Give The People What They Want

To the Bone

Two-disc 1996 issue:

Disc 1: All Day and All of the Night / Apeman / Tired of Waiting for You / See My Friends / Death of a Clown / Muswell Hillbilly / Better Things / Don't Forget to Dance / Sunny Afternoon / Dedicated Follower of Fashion / Do It Again (Acoustic) / Do It Again

Disc 2: Celluloid Heroes / Picture Book / Village Green Preservation Society / Do You Remember Walter / Set Me Free / Lola / Come Dancing / I'm Not Like Everybody Else / Till the End of the Day / Give the People What They Want / State of Confusion / Dead End Street / A Gallon of Gas / Days / You Really Got Me / Animal / To the Bone

Selected Kinks Compilations

The Kink Kronikles [US only release]

Victoria / The Village Green Preservation Society / Berkeley Mews / Holiday In Waikiki / Willesden Green / This Is Where I Belong / Waterloo Sunset / David Watts / Dead End Street / Shangri-La / Autumn Almanac / Sunny Afternoon / Get Back In Line / Did You See His Name? / Fancy / Wonderboy / Apeman / King Kong / Mr. Pleasant / God's Children / Death of a Clown / Lola / Mindless Child Of Motherhood / Polly / Big Black Smoke / Susannah's Still Alive / She's Got Everything / Days

The Great Lost Kinks Album

Til Death Do Us Part (mono) / There Is No Life Without Love (mono) / Lavender Hill (mono) / Groovy Movies / Rosemary Rose / Misty Water / Mister Songbird / When I Turn off the Living Room Light / The Way Love Used to Be / I'm Not Like Everybody Else / Plastic Man / This Man He Weeps Tonight / Pictures in the Sand / Where Did the Spring Go?

Picture Book box set

Disc one: Brian Matthew Introduces The Kinks / You Really Got Me / I'm A Hog For You Baby / I Believed You / Long Tall Sally / I Don't Need You Any More / Stop Your Sobbing / I Gotta Move / Don't Ever Let Me Go / All Day and All of the Night / Tired of Waiting for You / Come On Now / There's a New World Just Opening For Me / Ev'rybody's Gonna Be Happy / Who'll Be the Next in Line / Time Will Tell / Set Me Free / I Need You / See My Friends / Wait Till the Summer Comes Along / I Go To Sleep / A Little Bit Of Sunlight / This I Know / A Well Respected Man / This Strange Effect / Milk Cow Blues / Ring the Bells / I'm On An Island / Till the End of the Day / Where Have All the Good Times Gone / All Night Stand / And I Will Love You / Sitting On My Sofa

Disc two: Dedicated Follower of Fashion / She's Got Everything / Mr. Reporter / Sunny Afternoon / I'm Not Like Everybody Else / This Is Where I Belong / Rosy Won't You Please Come Home / Too Much On My Mind / Session Man / End of the Season / Dead End Street / Village Green / Two Sisters / David Watts / Mister Pleasant / Waterloo Sunset / Death of a Clown / Lavender Hill / Good Luck Charm / Autumn Almanac / Susannah's Still Alive / Animal Farm / Rosemary Rose / Berkeley Mews / Lincoln County / Picture Book / Days / Misty Water

Disc three: Love Me Till the Sun Shines / The Village Green Preservation Society / Big Sky / King Kong / Drivin' / Some Mother's Son / Victoria / Shangri-la / Arthur / Got To Be Free / Lola / Get Back In Line / The Moneygoround / Strangers / Apeman / God's Children / The Way Love Used To Be / Moments / Muswell Hillbilly / Oklahoma U.S.A. / 20th Century Man / Here Come the People In Grey

Disc four: Skin And Bone / Alcohol / Celluloid Heroes / Sitting In My Hotel / Supersonic Rocket Ship / You Don't Know My Name / One Of the Survivors / Sitting in the Midday Sun / Sweet Lady Genevieve / Daylight / Mirror Of Love / Artificial Man / Preservation / Slum Kids / Holiday Romance / (A) Face in the Crowd / No More Looking Back / Sleepwalker / The Poseur

Disc five: Sleepless Night / Father Christmas / Misfits / A Rock 'N' Roll Fantasy / Little Bit Of Emotion / Attitude / Hidden Quality / A Gallon Of Gas / Catch Me Now I'm Falling / Nuclear Love / Duke / Maybe I Love You / Stolen Away Your Heart / Low Budget / Better Things / Destroyer / Yo-Yo / Art Lover / Long Distance

Disc six: Heart Of Gold / Come Dancing / State Of Confusion / Do It Again / Living On A Thin Line / Summer's Gone / How Are You / The Road / The Million-Pound-Semi-Detached / Down All the Days (Till 1992) / The Informer / Phobia / Only A Dream / Drift Away / Scattered / Do You Remember Walter? / To the Bone

Dave Davies Solo Albums

Dave Davies (AFL1-3603) [1980]
Where Do You Come From / Doing The Best For You / Visionary Dreamer / Nothin' More To Lose / The World Is Changing Hands / Move Over / See The Beast / Imagination's Real / In You I Believe / Run

Glamour [1981]
Is This The Only Way / Glamour / Reveal Yourself / World Of Our Own / Body / Too Serious / Telepathy / 7th Channel / Eastern Eyes

Chosen People [1983]
Tapas / Charity / Mean Disposition / Love Gets You / Danger Zone / True Story / Take One More Chance / Freedom Lies / Matter Of Decision / Is It Any Wonder / Fire Burning / Chosen People / Cold Winter

Bug [2002]
Whose Foolin' Who / It Ain't Over, 'Till It's Done! / Lie! / Let Me Be / Displaced Person / Rock You, Rock Me / Flowers in the Rain / Fortis Green / Why?!! / True Phenomenon / Bug / De-Bug / Life After Life (Transformation)

Fractured Mindz [2007]
Free Me / All About Me / Come To The River / Giving / Remember Who You Are / The Waiting Hours / Rock Siva / The Blessing / Fractured Mindz

Ray Davies Solo Albums

Return to Waterloo [1985]
Intro / Return to Waterloo / Going Solo / Missing Persons / Sold Me Out / Lonely Hearts / Not Far Away / Expectations / Voices in the Dark (End Title)

The Storyteller [1998]
Storyteller / Introduction / Victoria / My Name / 20th Century Man / London Song / My Big Sister / That Old Black Magic / Tired of Waiting / Set Me Free / Dad and the Green / Set Me Free / Front Room / See My Friends / Autumn Almanac / Hunchback / X-Ray / Art School / Art School Babe / Back in the Front Room / Writing the Song / When Big Bill Speaks / The Man Who Knew A Man / It's Alright / It's Alright (Dialogue) / Julie Finkle / Ballad of Julie Finkle / Third Single / You Really Got Me / London Song

Other People's Lives [2006]
Things Are Gonna Change (The Morning After) / After The Fall / Next Door Neighbour / All She Wrote / Creatures of Little Faith / Run Away From Time / The Tourist / Is There Life After Breakfast? / The Getaway (Lonesome Train) / Other People's Lives / Stand Up Comic / Over My Head / Thanksgiving Day

Working Man's Café [2007]

Vietnam Cowboys / You're Asking Me / Working Man's Café / Morphine Song / In a Moment / Peace in Our Time / No One Listen / Imaginary Man / One More Time / The Voodoo Walk / Hymn for a New Age (Bonus track) / The Real World (Bonus track)

US version also included: Angola (Wrong Side of the Law) / I, The Victim / Vietnam Cowboys (Demo) / The Voodoo Walk (Demo)

The Kinks Choral Collection [2009]

Recorded with the Crouch End Festival Chorus.

Days / Waterloo Sunset / You Really Got Me / Victoria / See My Friends / Celluloid Heroes / Shangri-La / Working Man's Café / Village Green / Picture Book / Big Sky / Do You Remember Walter? / Johnny Thunder / Village Green Preservation Society / All Day and All of the Night / Postcard From London

See My Friends [2010]

With guest musicians and singers, listed beside each title.

Better Things [Bruce Springsteen] / Celluloid Heroes [Jon Bon Jovi and Richie Sambora] / Days - This Time Tomorrow medley [Mumford & Sons] / A Long Way from Home [Lucinda Williams and The 88] / You Really Got Me [Metallica] / Lola [Paloma Faith] / Waterloo Sunset [Jackson Browne] / Till the End of the Day [Alex Chilton and The 88] / Dead End Street [Amy MacDonald] / See My Friends [Spoon] / This Is Where I Belong [Black Francis] / David Watts [The 88] / Tired of Waiting for You [Gary Lightbody] / All Day and All of the Night/Destroyer [Billy Corgan]

Bonus tracks available as digital downloads:

Victoria [Mando Diao] / Moments [Arno Hintjens]

Index